Baseball Coaching

A Guide For the Youth Coach And Parent

Marty Schupak

1st Edition

Baseball Coaching

Youth Sports Club, Inc.

9 Florence Court

Valley Cottage, NY 10989

To order copies, call 845-536-4278.

Dedication

To Jeffrey, Michael and Lisa for being great kids and having confidence in me even after they became old enough to realize I wasn't as fast as Barry Sanders or could win Jeopardy every night of the week.

To my dad, who is missed more than he would ever know.

Acknowledgments

Special thanks to the Nyack-Valley Cottage Little League® who made it possible for me to share my coaching and practicing ideas throughout the years. And especially to all the field maintenance people who worked tirelessly to have one field available for the entire community each and every year.

I want to thank Hal Schweitzer and his whole family, including Maureen, James and Andrew. Whether it was for a baseball video, book, or putting together a baseball iPhone Application, I have never received a "no" from anyone in that family when I asked for help. Special thanks to Bobby Woods down in Egg Harbor Township, New Jersey, who is the best batting instructor I ever met. Traveling three hours each way just to see him teach kids and give me tips was and still is a thrill. Bobby's philosophy of always seeking new information on hitting and coaching is something I still try to do.

And thanks to the Albert family, Donna, Steve, and Dave. I was lucky to have known Jon. It was a thrill to coach with him. He would be proud of both boys, who have helped me a lot with their knowledge of baseball.

Special thanks to all the instructors and personnel at the Apple Store in West Nyack, New York, especially instructors, Hank, Jean Marie, and my good friend and fellow baseball coach, John. All of your patience and knowledge you shared with me was great! As untechnical as I am, I could have never overcome all the roadblocks put before my computer and myself without the three of you and your enthusiasm and interest in my work.

Thanks to the player participants: David Albert, Tim Coazzo, TJ Connery, Jordan Correra, Paul Giardano, Matt Lafemina, Dan Marcello, Taylor Schwarz, Andrew Schweitzer, James Schweitzer, PJ Spear, AJ Stellato, Martin Stellato, Matthew Stroud.

Thanks to Loretta Garney, who did a great job with the photographs throughout the book.

And thanks to my brothers, Howard and Paul, who were really patient with me when I first got involved in youth baseball. And my best friend Lenny Kaye who has been with me through thick and thin.

This book would not have been possible without Lennon Nersesian. Besides taking on the monumental task of editing, he has done an incredible job with formatting.

And thanks again to my wife, Elaine, who again has stood by me and encouraged me to do something I love.

Introduction

I have coached Little League® and youth baseball for over 20 years. In that time I have won championships, finished in last place, served on the board of directors, argued with umpires and parents, been threatened on the phone and in person, been called a cheater at our annual league meeting, been suspended, fought with my wife about time spent at the field, saw my son get 27 stitches in his head after being hit with a bat, tore my own rotator cuff pitching batting practice, had my windshield broken by a fly ball, and developed close friends.

Throughout the years, I have grown to enjoy, and even look forward to, the coming youth baseball season. I have developed as a coach and a person over the years and I approach the season now differently than I did when my kids played years ago. Even when I begin to doubt myself about the upcoming season and worry about things like my own energy level and the time sacrificed, once the season starts, however, I'm glad I'm still involved. I am definitely a different coach now than I was back at the time I began coaching. And I am still evolving.

Baseball is a great game, and although it has taken a pounding lately and has to compete with other sports, to me there is nothing like the baseball season at any level of play. I am located geographically in the Northeast US about 27 miles north of New York City in a town called Valley Cottage, New York. To me, the beginning of baseball means we made it through another tough winter.

I see coaches all year round either attending or speaking at coaches' clinics. I try to tell many of these parent/coaches that in our society today we are in need of heroes for our youth. We see things every day where the big league athlete, whom we admire and whose batting stance we copy and emulate, gets in trouble by an endless number of reasons. Yes, as a society we are indeed in need of heroes for people to look up to, and youth sports coaches are some of the prospects that kids ages 5-12 do look up to. Don't forget that this age group (5-12) is highly impressionable and the things we do as coaches in practices as well as games will have an ever lasting affect on some of the kids we coach. And if you do not agree with me then think of three people you have known personally who have affected and influenced your life. Chances are a teacher or athletic coach will come to mind for at least one of them.

Two of the most rewarding experiences I had because of coaching youth baseball did not occur on the field. In fact both did not even occur during the season. Being asked to write a reference for one of my players who was applying to a prep school in New England was one of the most flattering things that I had happen to me. Of course I said yes and with my lack of writing experience at the time, I struggled through giving this player a terrific reference. He ended up getting into this prep school and the addendum to the story is that he ended up graduating from Harvard University. As someone who hopes I touched some part of this player's life, it was a thrill to keep track of him all the way through college.

The second experience involved one of my favorite players. His father was my assistant coach one year and his older son was on my team. I was fortunate to later coach his youngest brother. The father was a great guy and very knowledgeable about baseball. He openly expressed how he wanted nothing more than to work and be able to attend both his sons' baseball games. Tragedy struck as he was one of the unfortunate people who was in the World Trade Center on September 11, 2001. This tightly knit family was crushed, just as were many other families of the people who perished on that day. A few years later, I received a call from the player's mother. She asked me if I would join her son to a family day at a college he was considering attending. Without hesitation, I told her I would be honored. We spent the day at the college, which he ended up going to, and I stayed somewhat close to the family ever since.

Stories like the above do not happen too often. Many times parents will go into youth coaching just to coach their own son or daughter and make sure they receive their share of playing time and are in line for the league championship, which is no great sin and probably the reason I began coaching.

I wrote this book for a number of reasons. I have been fortunate that as a result of my time coaching youth baseball, I produced a number of baseball instructional videos, as well as a book on baseball drills called, "Youth Baseball Drills." I remember making my first video, which is called "The 59 Minute Baseball Practice" with the intention of sharing a philosophy about running practices. Within these pages, I want to expand on my own philosophy, although a lot of the book will be dealing with practice organization and drills because this is where we get to teach young players the most about the game of baseball. The practices are a great time to go beyond stimulating the player, and is a chance to communicate with the team specific techniques, whether it is sliding to the back of the base furthest from the catcher when stealing or doing the pivot bunt rather than the square bunt. Some youth baseball coaches try to teach techniques and strategies during games. I cannot do it this way. I run practices with my players with a lot of repetitions so that the players will learn while also having fun.

Also covered in this book will be different issues that come up year in and year out. I'll cover tryouts and the player draft that is key to every season. I'll even express my own ideas regarding achieving parity in youth baseball leagues, which will make for a better season and improve the skills of the players during the season. I'll discuss why it is crucial to have a parents meeting. I'll discuss how I think a season should be run from the tee ball level through the twelve year-olds, which is what we call "The Majors" in our Little League®. I'll look at some of the best ways for leagues to improve at all levels of play. And I'll especially go into detail about running efficient practices where the players will improve as individuals, improve as a team, and have fun! I'll explain my own theories and philosophies about teaching kids 5-12 year-olds sports skills. In detail, I will go into my own "20/5 Teaching Theory" and why I maintain for the greater majority of youth baseball players that if you see the player doing 20 things wrong, it is better to concentrate on the 5 most important things and keep reaffirming the correct technique. By concentrating on correcting 5 techniques, the player will be less confused in the batter's box and on the pitcher's mound. Having the player's head clear in both of the above situations is a key to success. I will also explain why I believe a relaxed player, such as a relaxed hitter, is a dangerous player.

I will try to take you, the reader, from the beginning to the end of the season. I know seasons run at different times throughout the country, but give or take the start of opening day by a few weeks, most leagues are carbon copies of each other. Excluding weather issues and maybe field availability, the same situations that happen in Newton, Massachusetts also happen in Tempe, Arizona in Little Leagues as well as most youth sports. I will relate the timeline of our Little League® season as I experience it here in the Northeast. When I mention certain months of the year, you might have to adjust the month in your own mind to fit your geographical location.

While reading this book, please keep in mind that I have experienced many of the situations that you have, no matter how ridiculous the situation may sound. If you have a situation that sounds like a one in a million, I'm sure someone somewhere else in the country experienced the same thing. People like myself, who have been coaching for a long time, have been through a lot. I've had my best pitcher decide not to show up at the championship game, ball players tell me just before the season starts they didn't want to play baseball anymore, and players break fingers, wrists, arms, legs, some on and some off the ball field. I've had parents excuse their son or daughter from games for family functions, pool parties, schoolwork, and even for being punished (which punishes the teammates more than the player himself).

Hopefully this book will become a resource guide for you, the parent or coach. As your child moves up every year in your own league, starting with tee ball, you can refer to the drills and ideas in this book and use them at the appropriate age.

The goal of this book is to make the youth baseball or softball season not easier, but more efficient, as well as offer ideas that the parent/coach can use. I've always had the goal when producing my sports videos, which concentrate almost exclusively on drills, that parents/coaches should not just use my drills and ideas, but instead take these drills as a stepping stone to create their own drills and ideas.

A number of years ago I was fortunate to be an assistant coach to someone who later became a close friend of mine. Hal Schweitzer asked me to help him with his team after I took a two year hiatus from coaching. I remember the very first time he met the parents he explained his philosophy very simply as, "My goal is to have the players on this team like or enjoy baseball more at the end of the season than when the season started." This philosophy stuck with me and is now exactly how I approach each season. I try to have a baseball season where the players will not only enjoy the season but get an appreciation for the game of baseball. Relating stories of situations that have happened to me and my team over the years, talking about the Major League game that was on TV the night before, or just some historical baseball fact, can all add up to us all being ambassadors of the game of baseball.

There will be a lot of information in this book to digest. Sometimes you'll say, "I'm not going to do that," or, "That's too much work just to coach a youth baseball season." Maybe you'll think that the equipment involved in the drill section will fill up a house and be impossible to transport when in fact if you follow what I recommend, you'll have less equipment to lug around than the other coaches in your league. Dissect and filter out ideas you do not want to use or you just are not comfortable with. One of my goals in writing this book is to give the parent/coach an opportunity to do some minimal preparation to ensure a successful season. Just like you, I am a youth sports coach. I am not a former professional baseball player that can give you my expertise just because I played in the Majors. I don't have a million dollar PR firm that supports me or a huge practice facility with 8 or 10 manicured fields with a dozen batting machines at my disposal. I practice and coach in the same situations like most of you. We all scramble for field time. I've gone to practices only to find another team already there claiming to have the field. I run around during the baseball season just as you do with baseball equipment growing out of all parts of my car with any extra space being used as a lost and found with anything from clothes, water bottles, and gloves. I've come home at night after games with my answering machine full of messages from irate parents for one reason or another. I've raked and mowed our fields, pumped out water from our dugouts, and cleaned our snack bar and toilets. If you have been involved in youth baseball for a number of years, there is very little that you have done that I have not.

I have been fortunate, with all my ups and downs coaching baseball, that the ride has been incredible after all these years. I have met some of my best friends coaching baseball and have followed many of my players grow from 10, 11, and 12 year-old kids to become successful citizens in the communities that they have settled in to coach their own kids. In some cases I've had former players of mine coach against me or umpire one of my games. Whether you are coaching your son for the fifth season in a row or are a first year tee ball coach or an enthusiastic parent, I hope you enjoy your time involved with youth baseball.

Although I use the masculine pronoun in this book, I am by no means discriminating against or excluding parents who have daughters who play Little League or softball. All of the strategies and drills can easily be translated for parents who coach both sexes.

Readers should also consider the e-book version of this book. In addition to being a great supplement for coaches and parents, the e-book has an interactive section on the sample practices.

Chapter 1
Youth Baseball Overview

"People ask me what I do in winter when there's no baseball. I'll tell you what I do. I stare out the window and wait for spring."

--Rogers Hornsby

In the twenty-one years I have been coaching youth baseball, there have been numerous changes. Over the last five years, for example, I have seen the growth and strength of youth baseball travel teams. These travel teams are here to stay and are becoming more and more popular. Many times the organizer of a travel team can be an enthusiastic parent or a school assistant or head coach. Travel teams are made up from a group of talented players. These players are somewhat more talented than the typical recreational teams and sometimes tryouts are required as only a certain number of spots are available on the team. Travel teams can start for players as young as 8 year-olds. The teams usually play in one or more leagues and their games can conflict with the local recreational league. I coach in my community's Little League® for the age group of 10, 11, and 12 year-olds called the Majors. Almost every year I receive inquiries about coaching travel teams but pass on all of them. As you will see throughout the book, I thrive on baseball practices as the best way to teach kids the game. For me, the geographical locality of our Little League® makes it more appealing for me to schedule practices than traveling around the New York, New Jersey, Connecticut tri-state area to play games. I plan out my season in advance, and to spend the time it takes traveling to and from games does not make sense to me. There is a trade off. Without question, travel teams gather the more talented players and play a more competitive and longer schedule. A couple of years back I received a phone call asking if I would be interested in coaching a travel team. The season would start around the middle of June and go through August. There would be some perks such as reimbursement for travel and meal money. I then asked how many games the team would play. I was almost floored when the person on the other end of the phone told me 68 games. From the middle of June till the end of August is about 75 days. To play a schedule like that I thought was unconscionable for 12 year-old kids. I believe that balance is necessary for youngsters. I love youth baseball but the loaded schedule was a big turn off for me. Most travel leagues I see today are run well. I am getting closer to getting involved in travel leagues but only after my Little League® season is done. I have also noticed that most parents who have players in multiple leagues always let me know and I try to be respectful and keep track of pitchers who pitch in both leagues. I have spoken to players without the presence of their parents just to ask them their feelings about travel teams and most love them. With the increased competition and with the number of games, players have a great chance to improve. I also believe that players will play up to the competition, and this is especially true with travel teams. In other sports, like basketball, AAU travel teams are as important as a player's high school team in recruiting. This has changed completely since I went to high school where the high school team was the place players showed off their individual and team skills hoping to impress colleges. My problem with baseball travel teams is that some players are in multiple leagues. I am a huge believer in youngsters having diversity in other sports and to play in only one sport in multiple leagues can do more harm than good. You have probably heard the term Growth Plate. The Growth Plate is the area of developing tissue around the end of the bones in children. When the child reaches a certain age, the growth plates turn into solid bone. An injury to a growth plate can be caused by an acute event like a fall or a hard blow. It can also be caused by overuse, which is what scares me about players involved in too many leagues in the same sport. One season, one of my best players who eats, drinks, and sleeps baseball strained his growth plate at the most inopportune time. He was playing in our local league as well as a travel league. He showed up at one of our last games with his arm in a sling. His mother explained to me that he tore his growth plate. After a second opinion it turned out his growth plate was just strained and not torn. He still missed the playoffs and felt terrible about it. There is absolutely no proof of what caused the injury but overuse might have contributed to it.

I believe there is a place for travel teams for the talented players, however, parents and coaches must look at the whole situation (how many games will be played from April to October) and evaluate how much is too much. Players that pitch are a big concern. Consider a 12 year-old youth pitcher who is involved in two leagues. Suppose the pitch count slips away from an attentive coach or parent, or the coach sneaks in a few extra innings for a game that "the team needs." If this realistic scenario repeats itself enough, the perfect formula is created for serious arm injury. It is not difficult for parents to overlook this outcome when they are blinded by their personal motivations. Perhaps the parents are looking to vicariously relive their childhood.

Hopes of a college scholarship seven years down the road could also drive a parent down this dangerous path. So my advice to parents, players, and coaches is to play as much as you want, but proceed cautiously.

The second biggest change I've noticed to youth baseball while coaching has been the growth in popularity of lacrosse. For a number of years soccer league commitments would sometimes interfere with the youth baseball season. I remember I had a few players who played soccer every Memorial Day weekend in a tournament in Virginia Beach. The parents, for the most part, were very respectful telling me at the beginning of the season about this soccer tournament. I told them it was okay as long as when we approached our league playoffs they gave the baseball team the same commitment. Lacrosse is the fastest growing sport in the country and it is expanding by leaps and bounds. There are now youth lacrosse leagues that compete directly with youth baseball leagues during the spring season here in the Northeast. A few years ago when we picked our team, our top draft pick was a very talented 10 year-old. He ended up playing for us for only one season and then quit baseball and went to lacrosse. Another episode happened about five years ago when one of the best 12 year-old catchers I ever saw in our league just finished a great season. I remember approaching his father to speak to him about his son and how I thought if he continued playing catcher, he should be on the path to eventually becoming an excellent high school player. His father told me how this would be the last year he is playing baseball and will probably never pick up a baseball glove again because of his dedication to lacrosse. What is the reason for these two players changing sports? First of all, I have nothing against lacrosse or any other sport. In my mind if there is an empty field or a field with kids playing any sport, I'd rather have the field being used. What I see is that we are living in a much faster paced world. People who are on the internet hate to wait for pages to load and want instant results. Lacrosse is a much faster paced game than baseball. There is a lot more running around and very little standing around. In baseball, the typical game features the action based around only a few players at a time. What we baseball coaches have to do is figure out ways where there is less standing around by players both in games and in practices. In practices, if we are able to have drills that include every player and limit the standing around we are going in the right direction. The same thing can be true in games. If we teach fielders that they have to react on every pitch, know where and how to back up, know when the outfielders have to come to the infield on plays such as rundowns, then we have a chance of keeping some of these talented players we are losing to lacrosse and other sports involved in baseball past the age of twelve.

Coaching in my local Little League® I know there is going to be a real diverse group of kids talent-wise. On occasion there are some players who are in the league just for their parents' sake and have no interest in baseball. In our town, they still have a right to play, so as coaches I try to get them interested in baseball anyway I can. Coaching youth baseball for a long time rewards us in many ways when you have done it as long as me. On more than one occasion I have seen players who have limited baseball talent leave my team and become successful umpires. This is very rewarding to the league as well as myself. But how about we try to make youth baseball a little more interesting for young players both in practices and in games. Wouldn't it be something if a young lacrosse player went home and told his parents he decided to play baseball because a baseball team he saw practicing was having so much fun?

Chapter 2

Picking Teams

"You gotta be a man to play baseball for a living, but you gotta have a lot of little boy in you, too."

~Roy Campanella"

Just when it seemed like baseball season just ended with All Stars and some travel teams, a notice goes out about our local Little League® when school starts. In addition to registering for the league, if a player wants to participate in the major league or minor league division, he must go through an evaluation tryout. Tryouts in youth baseball used to be one of the most manipulative and corrupt things I've ever experienced. I've seen coaches have players purposely not try, such as wear the wrong glove or bat their opposite way. Most coaches are always looking for any type of advantage when in reality the league would be a better league if there was more parity in it. You might ask what proof I have of this? All I can say is if teams play more close games and learn to deal with playing under a little pressure and duress, players would improve more and leagues would do better in All Stars. I'll go into this more a little later.

Rule changes are an important part of each season and the managers and coaches need to be apprised of any rule changes put forth by the league under which it is chartered. An example of a rule change might be a pitch count limit going into effect for pitchers or a policy change in equipment. Whatever rules are changed or added must be reviewed. If it only takes the league president or commissioner putting it in writing, then that is fine, but if the league president or commissioner feels the new or changed rules are ambiguous, he should call a mandatory meeting to go over the rules in person.

The parents of players who want to play in the majors (in my league it is 10, 11, and 12 year-olds) are notified about tryout dates. In my area it is usually on two or three weekends in the month of October. There is no perfect system for tryouts. The system for each league is passed down from one generation to another. What usually occurs is the coaches will sit along the third base line in their folding chairs they brought and have some kind of system to rate each player. In my league, the tryouts usually consist of 4 or 5 players going out in the field at the same time. The person in charge will begin hitting grounders to each player, who will throw the ball to first base. Then the players will take turns in the outfield catching fly balls. Then comes the hitting, where each player will be given 5 or 6 swings, running the last one out. Sometimes the players will be given a chance to throw 4 or 5 pitches from the pitcher's mound. Coaches then rate each skill, fielding, throwing, hitting, running, and pitching. I've seen all kinds of rating systems. What I do, and have done for most of my twenty-one years of coaching youth baseball, is rate the player from 1-5 with one being the best number or highest rating. I do give halves such as 2.5. I have my own spreadsheet with columns for name, age, and for each skill on top. I leave one column on the far right and give my own comments like, "John had this kid in basketball and said he is a real athlete." As far as the actual tryout system, this works fairly well. One of the things coaches and leagues need to do is to try having the players who are trying out feel as relaxed as possible. Believe me, it can be quite intimidating trying to perform under the pressure of having between 6-12 grown ups line up along the third base line with clipboards knowing their attention will be on each player. A coach or board member should speak to each group with the sole intention of trying to get the players as relaxed as possible. One of the things the players trying out should be told is that they will only be judged on their successes and not from anything they do wrong. Isn't this true? If a player gets five swings and hits two over the fence but misses the other three, the coaches will usually judge and/or rate the player on the balls hit over the fence.

The system is far from fool proof. I've seen coaches bypass very obvious talented players when picking kids because they were friends with another player or with someone they carpool with in their kid's karate class. Players should be picked according to ability and talent. I'll go into how I would change this system. It is a system I call the "Schupak League Parity Plan." I had a coach come up to me during tryouts. He told me, almost as if he was berating my drafting style, "I know your trick Schupak for always having good teams. You always pick the fastest kids and then just work on baserunning." This was only partly true. Out of all the columns, the one that is most important to me is the one that has age. I know if I have a 10 year-old for three years, there is the potential I can develop him into a good ball player. The fundamentals I teach will carry over each year. So yes, I do always try to go for speed, but young speed. And most of the time I'll pick a younger player with a lesser track record in the league than a 12 year-old who may be more talented. I know that what I want to teach in youth baseball, from backing up to baserunning, etc., it takes me three years to get through to my players. Other coaches may be able to succeed in one year. I can't and I approach my coaching this way. What I really think needs to be done is for the major league coaches (10, 11 and 12 year-old players) to be required to umpire at least three minor league games (or the league below the Majors) during the season. For arguments sake, let's say there are six minor league games. If a major league manager and his coach umpire three games, they in essence get to see every player in their minor leagues play in real game conditions. Take this from someone who is not in love with umpiring. This works. When I umpire minor league games, I always keep an index card in my back pocket and take notes between each inning about any players who might have stood out. Nothing is really better than seeing players in this situation. I know I have picked my best players from seeing them in action in the minor leagues. I also always make it a point to attend the minor league playoff or All Star games. Here I get to see players play in a situation where they really have to perform at their best. I have found watching players play in two or three full games is a much more effective evaluation than just watching him in a 15 minute tryout.

When I am observing players, I try to look for a number of things that other coaches may not look at. If a particular player in the field catches my interest, I try to observe him on a play when the ball is not hit to him. For instance, if there is a third baseman who catches my interest, I watch to see what he does when a ball is hit to right field with runners. Is he setting up at third correctly? Is he giving his teammates instructions on what to do? Or does he just put his hands up and turn his back on the play and give up? These little things give me a chance to see a player's on the field awareness.

Observing a player batting, I love to see how he responds with two strikes. This might surprise you, but I could not care less if he strikes out in a pressure situation. If he is able to just make contact, and maybe foul one, two, or more balls off, this shows me a lot for a young ball player. If he is confident and knows the strike zone, being able to lengthen his at bat by two pitches is a great asset. In fact, taking this further, during the season I put a lot of value on players who are making contact with the ball, whether it is going fair of foul. This is especially true with the younger ball players, nine or ten years-old.

When evaluating young pitchers, I always go for the player who throws strikes. It doesn't matter to me if he is striking players out or getting shelled. As long as he gets the ball over the plate for strikes, this is the number one thing I'm looking for in young pitchers.

The last thing I look for in a young ball player is probably the most important: enthusiasm. I love kids who have a passion for the game and are enthusiastic on the field and cheer their teammates on. Years ago, I had a player named Andrew who overflowed with enthusiasm. Wherever I put him on the field, whether it would be shortstop or right field, you could always hear him cheering on his teammates in a very enthusiastic manner in a positive non obnoxious way. Players who rag on their own teammates are not my type of ball players. I had a great baseball player who was an outstanding pitcher. But this player would run on his own on the bases, not really follow my signs, and at times he would tell me that "I can't do it all alone." I finally had to read him the riot act about his position on the team. I said to him, "Look, you're playing baseball, which is a team game. If you are looking to succeed or fail alone then take up bowling or golf, which are both great sports."

Many coaches cannot and will not put in the extra time to observe younger players compete in their leagues and will instead rely 100% on tryouts or things that they may have heard about particular players. Tryouts are the beginning of the next season to me and really the igniter where the clock begins to tick toward the start of a new season.

Sample Page Of My Tryout Page

1-5 With 1 being the best grade-some leagues and coaches do it the opposite with 5 being best but I've done it this way forever and am more comfortable with this.

Name	Age	Fielding	Throwing	Hitting	Running	Pitching	Comments
Joe Smith	11	3.5	4.0	3.0	2.5	4.0	Good fielder. Needs work on throwing motion. Fast runner. Projected 3-4th rd.
Bill Jones	10	3.0	3.5	4.0	1.5	3.5	Played on All Stars in minors. Very fast runner. Weak hitter. Steps toward 3rd. Good upside. Projected 2nd or 3rd round.
Mark Davis	12	4.5	5.0	3.5	4.5	5.0	Limited ability. Did make Contact hitting on each pitch. Projected late round.
Steve Lewis	10	2.0	2.5	2.0	1.5	2.5	Was premier player. Father assisted in minors.

I have seen numerous types of evaluation forms over the years. Some are beautiful as far as organization. As of late, being in the new digital world, some coaches now bring down hand held devices and evaluate players on certain digital forms or applications that are made specifically for this. Coaches should have a comfort zone about the best way to do evaluations.

I feel most comfortable with the form you see on the previous page. A single page with a few columns and a space for comments. When I am evaluating a player, I want to limit the writing I need to do. And hopefully I am familiar with the player from seeing him play in a game during the regular season, or even better, in their team's playoffs.

When making your comments about players, make sure you do not put anything down that might be embarrassing or difficult to explain should somehow this page gets out. Rating players is a very sensitive issue to the player and especially to the player's parents. I have seen situations where ratings and/or comments about players are seen by other coaches or parents and it can get very uncomfortable.

One of the things I always like to ask each player when they are trying out is what school they attend. Other coaches used to laugh at me for asking this, but my motive was to establish if each player will have an opportunity to attend my practices. If a player goes to a private school over in another county, he may not get home until 6pm every night, and if I practice from 5-6pm, he will miss almost all my practices. He is better off with a coach who practices later.

At these evaluation tryouts, I always try to remember who the parent or parents are for each player. I have seen some parents never shut their mouths, continuously yelling out instructions to their son or daughter. For some, this might raise a red flag; these parents might be a pain. Many coaches will pick their players according to parents' behavior. I look at it differently, asking myself how much better this player might do if his parents are controlled. How would the player perform in a more relaxed atmosphere? One year, I was the manager in the minors. We were involved in a big playoff game. The pitcher's father would not shut up after every pitch. Finally, in the third inning I went out to the pitcher and just asked him one question. Do you think you would pitch better if your dad was not yelling instructions at you? Probably the only time this player was given the choice of not being yelled at every pitch. In almost tears, he said yes. I came off the mound and went right to the father and told him that both myself and your son knows he would pitch better if you did not yell out instructions. The father quickly jumped on my case, but I told him, "Let's see how he does one inning with you not saying a word. If you feel he is not pitching better, then go back to instructing him from the stands though I think you are 100% wrong." He refrained for one inning and his son pitched very well.

If you call managing too fine "micro managing", you can have some parents micro parenting. I used to look at this as a negative with over zealous parents. But I've learned that if you approach it correctly, have an effective parents meeting, and speak to parents in private, most will give you the respect, and tone down their sideline coaching.

Sometimes because of weather or the time of year, these evaluation tryouts end up indoors, such as inside the local high school gym. The practice can be done almost exactly the same way, adjusting the type of baseballs being used. Soft covered baseball or pickle balls are fine to use and will not scuff up the gym floor.

So in any given youth baseball tryout in different parts of the country, there is no exact science. I maintain coaches need to get out and observe players in the lower divisions either by umpiring or watching as spectators to get the most realistic evaluations with players participating in games.

The League Draft

One of the most fun times for me in Little League® has always been the league draft. It is usually in the commissioner's home or some neutral ground like the back room at the local batting cage or even a restaurant. It is a bunch of 30-50 year old General Manager wannabes that get a chance to evaluate the talent they observed the weeks or months before. It is usually attended by the league commissioner, the league president, and all the managers plus maybe one or two extra board members. The procedure in our league is the teams pick in the opposite order they finished in the year before. So the team that finished in last place will pick first, the team that finished second to last will pick second, and so on. Somewhat flawed, many have the theory, like they say about democracy, that it is a real bad system to have, but until someone comes along with a better system, it is the best. There might be some variables in particular leagues as to how many 9 and 10 year-olds can play, and if all the 12 year-olds have to be picked. This is a somewhat controversial topic, especially from someone like me who prefers picking younger kids and developing them. The issue with older 12 year-old kids who are not picked must be addressed. What is the league teaching these kids in the earlier divisions? Sometimes a league will protect a coach's child, which can also be controversial. And if a player who is picked has a brother in the league, he has to be picked in a designated round or in the next round in some leagues. If some of these things sound inconsistent with your league, you are probably right. The rules are constantly changing, plus there is always different interpretation of the rules. Sometimes the person in charge will just run the draft the way he wants. In fact, in the 21 years I've coached, I don't think there has been any two or three drafts that were exactly alike.

There are some leagues, such as ones with six teams, that will pick 1-6 in the first round. Then in the second round the order will be reversed so it goes 6-1. Our league has done this a few times. I'm not sure of which system is better or worse.

I consider the picking of teams as a way for setting the tone as to how the season will play out. To load or have an unbalanced league is doing not only the league but the players an injustice. Closer games with players having to perform under some duress will make for better players, a better league, and will pay dividends down the line. To have teams undefeated in a 20 game season or 0-20 does not say a lot for the way the league was set up. As much as I love draft night, I also understand that youth coaches may evaluate or pick teams in ways that might not be best for the player or the league. If it was up to me, I would impose a system to try to have the most balanced teams possible. Let's call this the "Schupak League Parity Plan." let me explain how and why I would implement this. My plan would have balanced teams arranged by all the coaches and then a supplemental draft to fill out the roster spots when needed. Suppose there were six teams in the league, made up of 12 players and each team lost players from the year before. This number is never exactly the same for each team so suppose it looked something like this:

Tigers-7 players returning (needs to have 5 players added)

Cubs-7 players returning (needs to have 5 players added)

Reds-6 players returning (needs to have 6 players added)

Blue Jays-6 players returning (needs to have 6 players added)

Giants-5 players returning (needs to have 7 players added)

Dodgers-4 players returning (needs to have 8 players added)

A couple of observations here before I go into the plan. First of all the Tigers and Cubs both with 7 returning players figure to be the strongest teams with all things being equal. This might not always be the case but you have to figure that these two teams have the most experienced players coming back. On the flip side, the Dodgers would seem to have the weakest team. The Dodgers might have won the league championship but would still pick last because they finished first. There is nothing wrong on the surface to pick teams this way and most leagues have been doing it like this forever. The "Schupak League Parity Plan" would take the number from the team that has to pick the least amount of players. In this case it would be the number 5 (the Tigers & Cubs need to have 5 players added), which would represent the number of players both the Tigers and Cubs have to pick. If there is a brother that has to be picked by a team then reduce the number of arranged players and draft an extra player. Then the managers would have a pre draft meeting and pick six balanced teams with five players each from the players that are in the draft pool. The key here is that the managers would rank players and discuss, argue, and finally provide six balanced teams. At this meeting in picking the teams, all managers must be in agreement. The motivation for making them balanced is that the managers will pick their team of five players right out of a hat. There is no picking a player because he lives next door or a coach needs a player because of car pooling. The picking of these six teams will provide some balance and parity in the league. After the team is picked on draft night, then the remaining teams who need players to fill their roster with twelve players will draft from the remaining pool. This will take courage for leagues to do but it will make for a better season and better baseball players. There has to be certain rules like absolutely no trading once the teams are picked out of the hat. Coaches will whine after they pick their team. "Now I don't have a catcher" or "I only have one pitcher." This can only be true if the managers did not sincerely pick balanced teams. It will motivate the coaches to do more skill teaching at the positions they need, such as pitching, which many managers use only 2 or 3 players who can pitch for the whole season. Leagues should try this for one or two years and if they feel it does not work, go back to the system they think is the most fair.

Another item that I see happen is many leagues pick teams around October, November, or December. The season doesn't start until April (at least here in the Northeast). Leagues have a policy that if a player who is eligible to play in the major leagues (10, 11 & 12 year-olds) and does not tryout, he cannot play in the majors. If a family moves into the area from another state in January and has one child who is an excellent 12 year-old, he will not be able to play. I don't know why leagues do this but it is unfair to the family, the player, and hurts the league by weakening your All Star team. Imagine having a 12 year-old right in your town who might be the best pitcher the league has seen in years not given a chance to participate in the league and All Stars? This would be a travesty. He would be forced to play in the minor leagues (if he decides to play) and will no doubt dominate that league while not even being given the chance for him to improve as a player. What I would do to resolve this is when the league picks teams for 12 slots, fill only 11 slots and have a supplemental tryout and a supplemental pick about 3 weeks before the season starts. This way we are giving kids who moved into the area a chance to play in the league. If this rule has something to do with the league charter or the individual league bylaws, then it will be tough to change. But it can be done. I've heard the argument that picking the 12th player in a supplemental draft is guaranteeing the player knows he was the last player picked on the team and will be very disappointed. I tend to disagree and think that the 12th player picked will jump for joy because he made it onto a major league team.

So now the teams are picked and the managers need to let their new players know they are on their team. If you are an experienced coach, like myself, already your mind is moving fast and you are picturing a baseball diamond and you are plugging in players at each of the nine positions; maybe even jotting down a tentative batting order once or twice. You are getting a feeling of excitement and anticipation. Just like the pros, usually everyone feels they picked a great team.

There is always the potential that parents or players might not want to play on a particular team. I used to be the commissioner of tee ball in my league. In tee ball, I was instructed to be more liberal with putting friends or car poolers on the same team. I disagreed because what we were doing was setting a bad precedent. I told my league president a story of how my oldest son was picked for a team in tee ball. It was my first experience in organized youth sports with my own kids. I, in fact, was one of those parents who made a phone call trying to change my son's team so he was with is friend. And the commissioner at the time wouldn't let me switch teams. I was upset and had a sour taste in my mouth. But what happened was interesting. My son was on a team without knowing a lot of the players. He met and made new friends. One of his newly discovered friends became one of my son's best friends. They maintained their friendship throughout high school, and in fact was recently invited to his wedding. There are always exceptions to everything, but I do think it is in the best interest of young kids to meet new friends and learn to be flexible.

After teams are picked, it is imperative that certain protocol are observed. No mention of the order of the players picked should be discussed outside of the draft room. No matter how committed coaches are with promises to keep everything on the "hush hush" sometimes more often than not, word leaks out and has the potential of being all over school the next day amongst the kids. I think this is wrong. It serves no real purpose for the kids to know who was the first pick of the draft, just as it does little for kids to know which players were picked in the last round.

After the draft, the league commissioner and/or president must insist that managers let the players know as soon as possible. It is best that each team is notified the same time or close to it.

The ideal situation is to call all the kids the night after the draft. But a lot of times this is a long night and players cannot be notified till the next day. As it always happens, there are some kids that know what team they are on and others who don't. Every effort should be made for kids to be notified around the same time.

Whenever the notifications go out, it should do so via phone call. If the players or parents who had their hearts set on playing in the majors were not called this could cause a problem The person giving out the bad news can be put in quite the uncomfortable situation. A suggestion for leagues is to do this procedure the following way. Suppose the draft is on a Monday evening. The players have to be notified by their coach within 24 hours. The league will then post the team rosters at their field on a bulletin board or an announcement chart or on the league website. This way the parents who still do not know either way can be told that the rosters will be posted in 24 hours. There is always disappointments, but this will help ease the burden of doing it with a phone call.

I always thought that the best way to do the league draft is a Saturday or Sunday afternoon. This way the coaches have the evening or the rest of the weekend to let the kids know and when they go to school that Monday, the teams for the upcoming season is usually the talk of the school day.

Another detail that may seem contrite, but I've seen it as an issue in the past, is for coaches to always keep their roster in alphabetical order, almost as soon as they leave the draft room. I remember one coach who always kept his roster list with the new players in the order that they were drafted. This can be a problem in a number of ways. I've seen a father upset after he found out another player was picked before his own son.

Even before teams step one foot on the field, there can be an issue. This parent found out from another coach. Keep in mind that parents have incredibly strong feelings about their own kid's ability and talent, and if the list ever gets out, there is potential for some uncomfortable situations. I've seen and been involved in numerous situations where people's sensitivities about their kids can actually ruin friendships unnecessarily for years. Trust me, if you are the manager, keep your roster in alphabetical order from day one, and hide your list of player evaluations and the draft in the back of a drawer at home.

As a manager you will also get phone calls from parents both before and after the draft. The reasons vary. I've received calls before the draft from parents who want their child to desperately play on my team with promises of offering to help me coach anytime. As a manager never make any promises to any parent or player about the upcoming draft. You are putting yourself in a possible horrible situation.

Some calls I have received after the draft went like this: "Marty, I am very disappointed you did not pick Andy for your team. I thought we had an understanding." I've also gotten call like, "Marty, anyway you can pry my son, Edward, off Mitch's team? My wife does not get along with his wife." These things happen more times than you could imagine, and I just tell them the truth. I never promise anyone, even my next door neighbor, I will pick his kid. I also tell them to teach our kids how to make the best out of a tough situation. Teaching our kids flexibility at an early age will not only toughen them up, they will also learn to handle certain tough situations better.

Sometimes during tryouts, I have my heart set on picking a certain player. I run through mock drafts and figure out how I can definitely make this player part of my team. And then, bang, the coach that picks right before me swoops him up with his pick. I'm disappointed, however, I make the most out of it. If we coaches don't have flexibility ourselves, how do we expect the families in the league to be flexible?

There is the manager who bullies his way to pick a certain kid. Many times the manager and the player's parent conspire to come up with something like, "If Allen doesn't play for me, then he won't play in the league." Usually Allen is a really talented player and the other managers usually adhere to his wishes. Not me. If I pick before this manager and he tells me this, I'll pick this kid. It happened once and I got yelled at from the manager and the parent. I didn't care. The parent told me his son is out of the league. I didn't say a word. The other manager wanted to trade for him and I wouldn't do it. I was told I wasn't a team player and the league will be weaker with Allen out of the league. It turns out he ended up playing for me and everything calmed down and worked out fine. Look I took a chance but I picked Allen because I owed it to my team to pick the best player available. And I think we would be setting a really bad precedent if we let these things go on.

When I first started coaching, I was as guilty as anyone trying to get an upper hand in picking my team. I learned that if everyone gets on the same page about picking fairly, it makes for a much better season with better baseball.

Now You've Got Your Team

After draft night or the night of picking the league teams, the manager should send out a letter to all the players and parents in the league as soon as possible. Some will just e mail the team. This is one of those times I like to send a hard copy letter to the whole team. Many parents and players will not know all the names of the players on the team and a letter to the team is a great way of introducing yourself as manager to the new members of the team as well as giving everyone a list of the players. Now what do we want to write? First of all, like almost everything in this book, the format of my letter is the suggested format, not required. You can do it entirely different and anyway you want or not do anything at all. All I can tell you is that I'm sharing every part of my 21 years coaching youth sports and trying to make things as smooth as possible for you. Do not make it a very long letter. Keep it as short and to the point. Of course you introduce yourself as manager even though you do have some returning players. Then you want to set the tone that the team will have fun while learning baseball skills. As we mentioned when talking about the draft, make sure you list the roster in alphabetical order. The other thing I do is mention the name of my assistant coach. This is very important. There might be a game or two you might miss and the assistant will need to take over for you.

I also touch on the point of volunteers. Depending on how your league is set up, volunteers might be needed for such things as the snack bar, field maintenance, umpiring, and more. I have found that if you are able to get a Team Parent to handle many of the administrative responsibilities, this is huge. If you have the right Team Parent, you'll see that you can devote more time to teaching kids baseball. I've been extremely lucky with the Team Parent over the years. If I didn't have one the last few years, I'm not sure I would have coached. He or she will be your bridge of communications to the other parents on the team. When a practice or game is cancelled because of rain or there is a day or time change, the team parent will be in charge of notifying all the team members. The team parent will also be involved in organizing other team volunteers to take care of necessary responsibilities the league has its teams do as well as help in the organization of your team cookout at the end of the season if you have one.

It is important right at the beginning in your first correspondence of the season to mention the need for volunteers. Parents vary from year to year. And as manager, you have to be cognizant that some parents work extremely hard and long hours, sometimes having more than one job and commuting long distances and find it hard to volunteer. Even though there are parents who will not volunteer for anything, I find that if you set the tone early just before the season at the parents meeting, you discuss that if everyone chips in a little at a time, the commitment is really very small. Most parents will help. I've never had too many volunteers in all my years of coaching youth baseball so you never want to refuse anyone who offers their help. And keep in mind that some parents want to help coach, if only a small amount, but really don't know how to express it. I am one who constantly picks parents out of the parking lot and asks them to help with simple tasks like supervising the pre-game ritual of hitting off the batting tee and making sure other players are not on top of each other.

In the letter I also touch on our goal, which is to improve as a team from the beginning of the season to the end. I've seen coaches, and I might have been guilty of this myself, state something like, "Our goal is to win the league championship." Now I don't want to sound like I'm not competitive, which I am, and you can and should be fierce competitors when playing your games. You should do everything in your coaching power to put your team in a chance to win every game as long as you do it fairly. I mentioned that I've changed as a coach from when I first started, and also changed my team goals. I adhere to my own mantra every year, which is: Improve as individuals, improve as a team, and have fun! You will have parents who are former high school and college players and want to win at all costs. You might feel the same way. I maintain you can be fair with your team while being competitive on the field. The point here is to set a tone where the majority of parents will feel comfortable with you as head coach.

I always address each letter I send to the team to both the parents and the player. This way you are almost certain that it will be read. Also, you are giving your players a feeling of importance, having their names on the same letter as their parents.

Dear Blue Hens Player & Parents,

Congratulations on being part of the 2017 Blue Hens Little League major league baseball team. We have a great group of players and we will be having fun while also improving our baseball skills. Even though the season is more than 3 months away, the time will go fast and before you know it we will be on the field.

Our team is comprised of many faces from last year as well as some new players added to our team. Here is a list of our roster:

John Andrews   Phil Martin

William Bass   Bob Newhouse

Ed Boykin   Richard Newman

Mike Caroll   Andrew Richards

Loyd Freedman   John Smith

Dave Jones   Robert Templeton

Our goal this season will be to see how much we improve as a team from the beginning of the season to the end of the season.

In addition to myself managing the team, we are fortunate to have Steve Bass helping out as coach. As you know, our league is a volunteer organization, and although coaches enjoy doing it, there are numerous things that we may need help and ask for requiring just a small part of your time during the season.

We will be in touch with you right after the New Year. Until that time, enjoy your winter sports and have a great holiday!

Sincerely,

Marty Schupak

9 Florence Court

Valley Cottage,New York 10989

(h) 555-5555

(c) 555-555-5555

e-mail:bluehens2011@____.com

Indoor Gym Practices and/or At The Batting Cage

A few weeks after the New Year many coaches will begin indoor practices. Remember that I am in the Northeast United States and the weather and outdoor field use will be different around the country. For years, our league would give each team access to an elementary school gym for about an hour per week. The other alternative would be going to the local batting cage and renting out space there. This is a luxury if you have a cage in your community. I'll address indoor practices first then practicing at the cage.

I always found indoor practices to be somewhat limited in what you can accomplish. In our area, if we started indoor practices in the last week of January, we can probably have between 8-12 before we go outside. It is important from the very first practice to make the new players of the team feel welcome, and coming from someone who has a life-long struggle with it, learn their names as quickly as possible. Just as sales people are taught to keep calling their prospect by their name, calling the new players by their name really is a positive step and will make the new players feel part of the team.

With the space limitation inside a small gym and sometimes even sharing the space with another team, there are still certain things to go over to set a good trend once you are able to go outside. As far as how to run these indoor practices with drills, etc., there are certain things you must do and must not do. One thing we can accomplish is to go over coaching signs. This is an interesting point because some of your new players coming up from the minor league will be very nervous about learning signs. I try to keep it as simple as possible. And what I do is usually teach only two new signs at each indoor practice and spend 5-10 minutes going over each sign.

As far as the type of drills to do and and equipment to use, coaches and leagues have to be aware of the limited space available. I have always found that recruiting parents to help out in your indoor practices will be quite beneficial. It is the perfect set up to do station drills. If you have three drills set up with four players in each drill, you can have one assistant coach or parent at each station. And you the coach can move around from station to station correcting anything you see that players might be doing wrong. What I like to do is go over each drill with the whole group and how to approach the skill. This way you are teaching both the players and the parent who is running that particular station. For instance, if one drill is "Fielding Ground Balls", point out to the team tips like catching the ground ball in front of you and not when the ball gets beyond the feet. You the coach can also put each drill on an index card and hand one to each parent or coach. Sometimes you will have a parent who knows nothing about baseball. You will have to spend more time paying attention to that particular drill.

On indoor practices, you want to make sure that the swinging of bats is limited. Remember that in a small space with bats swinging there is a greater possibility for an injury. This is the main reason you want as many volunteers as possible. And you tell them, and assistant coaches, no one is allowed to swing a bat unless the drill requires it.

Some communities have a local batting cage facility that might have anywhere from 4-10 batting cages. Some of these batting facilities will have an area like that of a gymnasium. Keep in mind that these batting facilities are in the business of making money. So you as a coach will have to end up paying for use of the cage(s) and/or other parts of the facility. This means you will end up collecting money from all the parents. Keep in mind not all parents can afford $5-10 each time your team goes to the cage. You ask for a suggested amount and most parents will pay it. From time to time you will be lucky enough to have one or two parents that will be in a position to provide extra money each time your team goes to the cage. Sometimes you'll be lucky enough to come away from the practice with more money. I keep this money in my house hidden in an envelope I mark "Team Funds." I also will let the Team Parent hold the extra money. With this extra money, you can offset future batting cage practice expenses as well as put anything extra toward a team picnic at the end of the year or a trophy.

Batting cages are run differently from one to another. The machines they now have are high tech with some being able to throw curve balls and change of speeds. I want cages that will pitch strikes. If I know I am going to use a batting facility, I will go down there and speak to the owner or manager. I want to get the best price I can at prime time. I know up here in the Northeast, weekends get booked very quickly. I am also concerned about the machines working correctly. One year we were at a cage and the machine had to be adjusted for almost every batter. It was like pulling teeth to get the people working there to show me and my coaching staff how to work the machines. For the consumers, as well as the batting cage owners, time is money, so we wasted time until we figured things out. I talked our way for a discount. The manager should have given my coaching staff and myself a 5-10 minute tutorial in adjusting the height of each machine. Remember that there is a wide variety of heights on a youth baseball team and you want to give each player the best chance to hit a hittable baseball. If you are going to use one of these facilities, make sure you go down in advance to find out the nuts and bolts of the whole system. In fact, watching another team for 10-15 minutes can only help your batting cage practice.

When it comes to the practice itself, I am somewhat particular in batting cage practices. Many coaches overrate the function of the batting cage. They are excellent change of pace in the middle of the season if your team is somewhat stale from practicing outside a lot. They are also good if you have a scheduled practice and it begins to rain during the day and if you coordinate it correctly with the team parent, you can easily change the location of the scheduled outdoor practice to indoors at the batting cage.

In my practices at the batting cage, I try to run it with the same philosophy as I do my regular outdoor practices. I want to give my players as many repetitions as possible. I usually ask the manager if we can rent two cages next to each other for 45 minutes rather than one cage for an hour and a half. I also ask the manager if there is one or two corners in the building near our cages that we can hit our rag balls or sock balls against a wall. Using a batting tee, we are able to hit our rag balls against the wall. We are also able to do the same thing with the soft toss drill. A rag ball or sock ball is a rag wrapped up or rolled up in a knot. It is then covered with two inch masking tape. If the batting cage manager is able to give two corners, then great. If we can only use one then that is okay also. So instead of using just one cage as just one station, I potentially have four stations set up. Two cages and two rag ball stations. We have at least four players working at one time. The one thing I detest is having players stand around doing nothing at any practice, whether it is indoors or outdoors.

I always give players numbers as they arrive at the batting cage and this is the number that they will bat. I usually have the players go from one cage to the other cage then to one of the other stations we have set up. Like I just mentioned for practices inside a gym, you will need help from parents. Most of the help is to prevent the kids from swinging bats outside the cage and around the rag ball stations.

My local batting cage, as well as many of the cages I have visited, have video games and other games that are available for use. It is almost impossible to keep the players away from these machines for a full hour. I try to set up these batting cage practices for 45 minutes and leave about 15 minutes for the players to have fun with the video machines and games.

You want to make sure the parents arrive on time at the end of practice, so if your indoor practice goes from 5-6pm, you want your parents arriving by 6pm at the latest. I have also rewarded players who arrive early by giving the first two or three to arrive one or two batting tokens or tokens for the games that are available. You'll find that after you do this once or twice at the batting cage, players will arrive on time.

Don't ever feel your team is falling behind because another team is using the batting cage two or three times a week four months before the season starts.

Chapter 3

The Parents Meeting

"Baseball was made for kids, and grown-ups only screw it up."

~Bob Lemon

The Parents Meeting

When I travel to different parts of the country doing my youth baseball coach's clinic, I spend a good 15-20 minutes out of two hours going over the importance of the parents meeting. I can't express how much lack of enthusiasm I receive from some of these coaches and parents whose main thoughts are "never mind that stuff, just get me to the Little League® World Series" or, "Give me some ways to increase my best pitcher's fastball 10 miles per hour." Then I hear from people who contact me during or after the season to tell me, "You were right on the money with that parents meeting." Others who wrote said, "I didn't take that parents meeting stuff seriously. Looking back, it would have helped to prevent certain problematic situations that occurred during the season." There is a saying in Real Estate "Caveat Emptor" meaning "Buyer Beware." There should be a saying for coaching all youth sports: "Do Not Have A Parents Meeting At Your Own Risk" or "A Parents Meeting Is Just As Important As A good Clean-Up Hitter." I am not in love with trying to get 12 sets of busy parents together to speak in front of them for 15-20 minutes. I learned early in my coaching experience that you can make the season run much easier if you approach this meeting correctly and touch on some of the main issues that come up year after year. For instance, one of my first years coaching I ended up always taking one or two kids home after practice. I couldn't run a taxi service, coach a youth baseball team, be a parent to three of my own kids, and work full time. I quickly put an end to this. When I coached the next year, I addressed this at the parents meeting noting that all parents must be at practice 5 minutes before it ends to pick up their kids. I then told parents that if they are late, not to worry, I would drop their kid off at the state trooper's office down the road. I have never really done this, but it shows the parents how serious I am about getting to the field on time at the end of practice. I explain how I have an extremely busy schedule. If it is constantly disrupted, I cannot carry out my coaching responsibility the best I can. With that said, you as a coach cannot leave a child alone at the field for any reason.

All these methods I learned during my coaching career, such as a parents meeting and having a team parent, will not cut out 100% of a coach's problems, but by instilling many of my ideas into my coaching practice, I'd say that all my coaching headaches, from parents complaining about playing time or positions, are reduced by at least 60%. You will never go through a season where 100% of complaints are eliminated. You really don't want them all removed just so you can tweak your own abilities for handling problematic situations, which will ultimately help you become a better coach. My goal in all these preparations is to try to give myself as much room and flexibility to be the best baseball coach I can for that particular season. I've seen coaches with the best intentions never get around to having a parents meeting. If you don't want to do it the way I recommend with letters, handouts, and a 15-20 minute meeting, that's up to you. But please, if only for 5-10 minutes before your first game, get the parents together and go over your goals. IT IS THE RIGHT THING TO DO!

If you end up coaching All-Stars, the parents meeting is even more important. You must have an All-Stars parents meeting mainly because the parents of All-Stars think their son will either be playing shortstop or pitching like they have done the whole year. Most of the All-Stars, if not all, were the number 1 or number 2 pitcher on their team, and now some will have to play the outfield. For a lot of players and parents this is hard to accept, but this is one of many issues that need to be addressed in the parents meeting for All-Stars. A coach in our league once asked me for advice on holding his first All-Stars parents meeting. I spent half an hour instructing him about the importance of a parents meeting. He took notes and kept agreeing with me, but never actually held the meeting. He ended up with a near mutiny from the parents that could have easily been avoided.

I try to make sure I have the regular season parents meeting before our first outdoor practice. Where I live, this is usually around the middle of March. You can also conduct the meeting before any of your indoor practices. I like to wait until we get closer to baseball season because even though we started indoor baseball practices, many parents' minds are still on their current basketball season or hockey season. I usually write a short note and send it to each set of parents anywhere from 7-10 days before the first outdoor practice. The letter reads something like this:

Dear 2018 Blue Hen Parents,

Our season is finally here! We will begin our outdoor practices next week with our first one being held on Monday March 19 at the Hurley Elementary School at 6pm sharp. Traditionally, I have a required short parents meeting with both parents before any player can practice. As someone who works more than one job I know how tough it is to get everyone together for one meeting. So with everyone's busy schedule, I will have two parent meetings so you can pick one that best fits your schedule and just show up. The first one will be held on Sunday March 18 at 4:30 pm sharp inside the Hurley Elementary School. If you cannot make this one, the other one will be right before our first practice at 5:30 sharp on Monday March 19 in the parking lot at Hurley. The meeting does not last more than 15-20 minutes and I find that going over certain team procedures will make for a much smoother season.

I look forward to seeing you at one of these two meetings!

Best Regards

Marty Schupak

555-5555

c-555-555-5555

e-mail: bluehens2011@____.com

PS If you find it impossible to attend one of these two meetings, please contact me as soon as possible.

Telling the parents the required meeting will last only 15-20 minutes and giving them two dates will ensure all parents' attendance at one of the scheduled meetings. I also overuse the word "sharp" when I mention the times for the practices and the meetings. I am setting the tone about being on time. Lateness is a real pet peeve of mine. I find that usually all the parents will show up at the first scheduled meeting. The ones who cannot make that one do in fact attend the second one. You always want both parents to attend but that does not always happen.

At the parents meeting I usually have a packet for each set of parents, which I have them sign so I know who received one and who didn't. If my team parent is returning, I have that person help me in the distribution of the packets. When the parents see the time I put into getting these packets printed and organized, they will realize the importance of this meeting. I set the tone early during the parents meeting so the parents know what type of coach I will be during the season. Efficiency, organization, and professionalism will also be three characteristics that show up during my practices and game day preparations. Again, do not be turned off by all of the written letters, meetings, etc. All this preparation will pay dividends as the season goes forward. If you are a returning coach, you will tweak the administrative details to suit your league, your team, and most of all ... you.

The meeting should be brief, just like you promised, and highlight the items that are in their packets.

2018 Blue Hens Parents Meeting

Welcome to the 2011 Blue Hens. Enclosed is our game schedule along with the team roster with addresses, phone numbers, and e-mails should you need to contact anyone from the team in case you need to arrange a ride for your child. I am happy to be coaching your child. I have coached youth baseball for 21 years and started back when I coached my own kids. I work in New York City, so the commute during baseball season is tough, but the reward makes it worthwhile. There are a few things I'd like to go over at the beginning of the season that will help make this season a positive experience for your sons or daughters while also increasing their baseball skills. I have had the most success coaching by practicing throughout the year as much as possible. I know everyone has busy schedules, but my practices are not just about learning baseball skills. We also have a lot of fun. If you make the effort having your son attend as many practices as he can I can almost guarantee he will become a better baseball player.

1) Arriving To Practice On Time

It is imperative to arrive to practice on time. My practices usually run from 1-1 ¼ hours. If your child is 10-15 minutes late, he will miss 25% of that day's practice. Also when arriving to practice I assign players numbers; first person to arrive is number one, and so on. During batting practice, the players will bat in the order they arrived to practice. Therefore, the first person to arrive to practice is #1 and gets to bat first during BP.

2) Practice Pickups

Please make sure after you drop off your child at practice that you are back 5-10 minutes before our practice ends. With everyone's busy schedule, this will ensure we are not waiting at the field too long after practice. Also, we sometimes offer individual help to players at the end of practice. We want to make sure we can devote our 100% attention to these players.

3) Opportunity Time

Even though our team practices are relatively short, we go at a spirited pace and cover a lot. However, we realize some players need or want extra practice in certain aspects of the game of baseball. After the first couple of weeks of the season, the coaching staff offers "Opportunity Time" whereby a couple of players at a time can come down 15-20 minutes early before practice and one or more of the coaching staff will work on any skill you and your son wants to work on. This can include batting, fielding, and pitching. Even though this is 100% optional we urge players to take advantage of these sessions.

4) Team Parent

We are fortunate to have Lori Freedman volunteer to be team parent. The team parent is extremely important in making this team functional during the season. If there are rain delays or cancellations, Lori will be the one to contact everyone. It is very important that we have as much contact information, such as work phone and cell phone, so we can contact you.

5) Playing Time

We will make every opportunity to be as fair as possible with regard to playing time. The rule book says we have to play every player at least two innings in the field and give each player one at bat. We go beyond this and try to play each player at least three innings each game during the regular season. We also do things a little differently than other teams. We try to have the player who bats 9th in the batting order play the whole game. Another thing I like to do is if a player is in a hitting slump, instead of moving him down in the order, sometimes we will move him up in the order, batting him leadoff to raise his confidence level as well as give him a chance to get a few extra at bats during the game.

6) Fan Behavior

Some games will be very competitive during the season. There is always a certain amount of tension. This is very natural. Please keep in mind that the umpires do the best job they can and sometimes they can miss a call at the most inopportune time. I ask all the parents on our team to maintain a good example for our kids and for the rest of the league.

7) Clothing

Please send an extra sweatshirt with your son or daughter for the first couple of weeks of the season. At our field, once the sun sets the temperatures could go down 10-15 degrees.

8) Water Bottle

Please have your sons or daughters bring a personal water bottle to each practice and game with their name written on it.

9) Equipment

Players must wear cups at every game and practice. If you are buying a bat for your child, our league adheres to a rule that the diameter of the barrel cannot exceed 2 $\frac{1}{4}$ inches. I do not endorse any one company, but recommend a lighter rather than heavy bat. You can contact me individually if you have specific questions about bats. The baseball glove should not exceed 12 inches in length. I recommend a smaller glove, which will yield better control for your son or daughter. If your child wants to use his own batting helmet, let me know and we'll make sure his wish is respected. If your child is a catcher and you want him to use his own equipment, this is fine as well. All we ask is that you be in charge of it and do not mix it up with our regular equipment bag and bring it home after each game. Cleats are not required in the league, but I recommend them. For games, we expect our players to come prepared, wearing their hats correctly and their shirts tucked in. There are also some clothes restrictions. Pitchers cannot wear a white long sleeve turtle neck.

10) If there is any medical condition or you need to speak to me privately about any personal issues involving your child, feel free to call me and I'll be happy to meet with you in private.

11) If you know you are going away during the season, please let our team parent or me know as soon as possible. We want to make sure we always are able to field a team for every game. We like to keep a general schedule of everyone during the season. If your child misses school because of a sickness, please let us know as well.

12) If your child is playing on any baseball travel teams or in any other sports please let me know. If your child pitches in both leagues, you also must let me know and inform me every time he pitches in his travel league and how many pitches he has thrown.

13) Please look at the handouts. Our league is a volunteer organization and we ask all parents to chip in a little. If you cannot do the snack bar or field duty on one particular assigned day, please try to switch days with someone and let our team parent know about it.

14) Please do not get nervous if your child is up in an important situation. It is very normal for you to want him to succeed. One thing we coaches can promise you is that no one will ever let your son feel bad about making the crucial out or error on this team. No one on this team is good enough to win or lose a game by themselves, and we tell the team this.

15) Our goal for the season is simply to: improve as individuals, improve as a team, and to have fun! We hope you can make as many games as possible and feel free to invite your relatives. Thanks for coming to this meeting.

Best Regards,

Marty

BLUE HENS SCHEDULE & DUTIES

Date	Day	Time	Visitor	Home	Concession Stand Duty*	Field Duty**
Sat, Mar 28	Saturday	3:00p -5:00p	Yankees	Blue Hens		Andrews, Bass
Tue, Mar 31	Tuesday	7:00p -9:00p	Blue Hens	White Sox	Boykin	
Thu, Apr 2	Thursday	7:00p -9:00p	Braves	Blue Hens		Caroll, Freedman
Sat, Apr 4	Saturday	5:15p -7:15p	Blue Hens	Braves	Jones	
Tue, Apr 7	Tuesday	7:00p -9:00p	Cubs	Blue Hens		Martin, Newhouse
Thu, Apr 16	Thursday	7:00p -9:00p	Blue Hens	A's	Newman	
Sat, Apr 18	Saturday	5:15p -7:15p	Blue Hens	Yankees	Richards	
Tue, Apr 21	Tuesday	7:00p -9:00p	White Sox	Blue Hens		Smith,Templeton
Sat, Apr 25	Saturday	5:15p -7:15p	Braves	Blue Hens		Boykin, Jones
Tue, Apr 28	Tuesday	7:30p -9:30p	A's	Blue Hens		Newman, Richards
Sat, May 2	Saturday	5:15p -7:15p	A's	Blue Hens		Andrews, Bass
Tue, May 5	Tuesday	7:00p -9:00p	Yankees	Blue Hens		Caroll, Freedman
Thu, May 7	Thursday	7:00p -9:00p	Blue Hens	White Sox	Andrews	
Sat, May 9	Saturday	5:15p -7:15p	Blue Hens	Braves	Bass	
Wed, May 13	Wed	7:00p -9:00p	Cubs	Blue Hens		Newman, Richards
Sat, May 16	Saturday	5:15p -7:15p	Blue Hens	A's	Newhouse	
Fri, May 22	Friday	7:30p -9:30p	Blue Hens	Yankees	Freedman	
Mon, May 25	Monday	7:00p -9:00p	White Sox	Blue Hens		Smith,Templeton
Fri, May 29	Friday	7:30p -9:30p	Blue Hens	Cubs	Martin	
Mon, Jun 1	Monday	5:30p -7:30p	Cardinals	Cubs	Templeton	

*Two people are expected in the concession stand. Please arrive 10 minutes before duty.
**Every family will have 3 nights of field duty.

BLUE HENS CONTACT INFORMATION

LAST	FIRST	HOME	PARENTS	CELL	E-MAIL
Andrews	John	555-555-5555	Julia & John	555-555-5555-Julia	@gmail.com
Bass	Bill	555-555-5555	William & Susan	555-555-5555-Susan	@verizon.net
Boykin	Ed	555-555-5555	Joe & JoAnn	555-555-5555-JoAnn	@optonline.net
Caroll	Mike	555-555-5555	Kevin & Cindy	555-555-5555-Cindy	@aol.com
Freedman	Loyd	555-555-5555	Joe & Jen	555-555-5555-Jen	@msn.com
Jones	Dave	555-555-5555	Cathy	555-555-5555-Cathy	@aol.com
Martin	Phil	555-555-5555	Denise	555-555-5555 -Denise	@aol.com
Newhouse	Bob	555-555-5555	George & Diane	555-555-5555 -Diane	@optonline.net
Newman	Rich	555-555-5555	Lou & Linda	555-555-5555-Linda	@optonline.net
Richards	Andrew	555-555-5555	Bob & Cathy	555-555-5555 -Cathy	@yahoo.com
Smith	John	555-555-5555	Dave & Marsha	555-555-5555-Marsha	@yahoo.com
Templeton	Robert	555-555-5555	Tracy & Kevin	555-555-5555 -Tracy	@optonline.net

				COACHES	
Schupak	Marty	555-555-5555		555-555-5555	@aol.com
Bass	William			555-555-5555	@aim.com
Newman	Lou			555-555-5555	@optonline.net
Freedman	Loyd			555-555-5555	@optonline.net
Marraccino	Joe			555-555-5555	@msn.com

That's about it. Preparing a 1-2 page agenda for 15-20 minutes of your time will make your life easier. Plus, the volunteer schedule for field maintenance and snack bar duty, which is usually done by the team parent, is a great way to avoid potential future conflict. Your season will not be problem free, but the 15-20 minutes you spend going over items will help immensely. You are much better off keeping the meeting shorter rather than longer. Make sure you preach whatever you put down in writing or else you will have your words thrown right back in your face. For example, the policy regarding playing the 9th batter the whole game, make sure you mention that you "will try" just so the parents know it is not a guarantee. This at least gives you, the coach, an "out" when there comes a time you have to sit the number 9 batter. In a game that became very competitive, I almost took out my 9th batter. At the last minute, I kept him in because of what I wrote down for the parents meeting. Since that episode, I changed the wording of the agenda. I always give myself a bit of flexibility. I learned that when parents see your intent for keeping it fair, they will let it slide once in a while if their son loses an at bat or an inning in the field, as long as it is made up.

As you coach for more years, you will guide the meeting to the problems that have come up during your tenure as coach. If you are only coaching for one or two years, go over the things that are important to you as a parent and what you would want to hear if you were attending your son or daughter's parents meeting. I always add things to each point while going over the list. I'm always trying to keep the parents at ease, especially the new parents, who might be nervous about their kids moving up to the Majors. Throughout the meeting, I always mention and reinforce how the team will work hard, but will also have loads of fun. I tell them not to be surprised if you find yourself scheduling your life around our practices and games during the season. This is not bravado. My own personal goal at every practice is to make sure every player who attended doesn't want to miss the next one. At the beginning of the year, I usually have parents who tell me about not being able to make practices because of karate or piano lessons. What ends up happening is the parents will ultimately reschedule those other responsibilities around my baseball practices.

I also introduce the team parent. Usually the team parent I choose works nearby home during the day. This makes things a lot easier, especially for someone like me who works about 27 miles away from my area. If the team parent is comfortable speaking at the parents meeting, I always give that person about five minutes to talk. Their talk is about the volunteer responsibilities, such as the snack bar and field duty that our league requires.

I tell the team parent to make sure they mention that if someone cannot make one of their dates, call the other parents to switch dates before letting us know. By doing this we are saving tons of time calling people for everyone else. This works very well, but there are times both the team parent and/or myself get a phone call with some extenuating circumstances. If you are stuck, but show that you are organized, usually other parents will step up and help share the responsibilities.

In the past, we have set up a phone chain that has had varying successes. The phone chain is a system where each person is listed on a predetermined page. The first person, who would be me, calls the team parent with team news, such as the cancellation of practice. The team parent then calls the next person, and so on. If a person is not home, they then have to leave a message as well as call the next person on the list. When this doesn't work right, it really fails. So in this day and age, I have found the quickest most efficient best way to communicate with your team is by e-mail. Include both parents' work and home e-mails. Texting has also become big.

The e-mail system saves a ton of time and it works really well. Either I or the team parent will send out an e-mail. If there is a family that does not have a computer, then you'll call that person. But in today's day and age, with everything moving at such a rapid pace, once you send out an email, either one or both parents will have read it probably within 30 minutes of the time you sent it.

At the end of the meeting, always give the parents an opportunity to ask questions. Sometimes you won't get any questions. Other times you'll get a slew of questions, such as, "How is playing time determined?" Another popular question is, "We are paying a registration fee so why do we have to work at the snack bar and do field duty?" These and other questions do come up. Be prepared to have some answers.

Throughout the meeting, you always want to come across as someone who knows something about baseball, and who is a responsible parent whereby other parents will feel comfortable entrusting their kids with. One of the reasons I got into coaching was because my wife and I were not 100% comfortable with my oldest son's coach.

You might be a one year coach who just wanted to make sure you had a chance to coach your son or daughter in the major leagues before you become a spectator again the following year. You may not think doing all this preseason organization is worth it. Again, not to sound redundant, the parents meeting will make your life incredibly easier during the season, although it is not an automatic cure for all complaints.

Commitment & Attendance

Players play youth sports for any number of reasons. They might love the game and cannot get enough of it. Like most of the readers of this book, I'm sure you were probably someone like me when you were young. You stayed out and played ball until your mom or dad came to get you. When coaching youth baseball, it usually doesn't take me very long to figure out why each player is there. Some do love the game. Others are there because their parents want them to play. Some of those parents look at youth baseball as a continuation of "Day Care"; a place to park their kids so they can do their own thing. But the players who really impress me are the ones who commit themselves to my team and really break their necks to attend every practice, convincing their parents not to miss any of Coach Marty's practices. These are the same players that take advantage of coming early for extra help. And you know, these players are not always the best athletes or ballplayers on the team. One year I had two of the nicest kids in the world come to every practice and ask to come for extra help. I worked extremely hard with both of them. One of the kids showed slight improvement. When it came to games, all things being equal, I tried to give these two kids more innings and more chances to succeed. And I may have sacrificed a few run scoring opportunities, but I felt in recreational baseball, our local Little League®, I had to go out of my way just a bit for both of these dedicated players. Even though as players both never really stood out or made the high school team, one eventually became a successful umpire for years. He really understands and appreciates the game of baseball.

I also have players who are excellent athletes. They live and breath baseball. Many of them end up making the Middle School baseball team their last year in the league. They end up having their parents take them from their school practice right down to mine. And they come in their school uniform, which is fine with me. These players are dedicated, however, sometimes I worry about them overdoing it.

The players that I, and coaches I meet, have issues with are the players that have very little interest in improving their game or being responsible. They miss a lot of practices and a good number of games. It's hard, but realistically we have to treat these baseball players the same as everyone else on the team. I'm not talking about the single mom who is running around town with her other kids while making the effort to contact you that her son will be late or might miss practice. When I see the effort or the burdens of a certain family situation, it is only human nature to take this into consideration.

I generally hate doing paperwork, however, in order to maintain a certain level of organization in our society we all must discipline ourselves to spend time organizing the things in our life. When I coach, I do it for the love of the game, being outdoors, etc. The administrative part is not my strong point, which is why it is important to have a very organized person as a Team Parent. With that said, I try to keep attendance for each and every activity during the season. I am not 100% diligent doing this, but I have found when I do it correctly, it really helps in the long run. Anytime we practice, have a game, or I meet a player for extra help, I have a clipboard to help me keep track of this. I take notes for a few reasons. First of all, I want to keep track of the really dedicated kids. I make a mental note of who shows up early to practice and mark down all the players who show up. If I get complaints from parents for any reason, I always refer back to the attendance sheet. Almost 100% of the time, the parents who complain the most are the ones whose child misses more practices and games then anyone else. I don't mind parents complaining, but there has to be some credibility backing up their complaint. If their son missed the most practice time out of everyone and has also never scheduled an opportunity session, I have ammunition documented in my attendance sheet if and when they start up with me. Remember, no matter what you do (parents meetings, rotate kids at positions, etc.) every parent will not like you the same by the end of the season. You do the best you can with what you have. And there is absolutely nothing wrong with giving a little edge to the players who shows their dedication to the team and the season.

The value of Opportunity Time is giving players a chance to catch up if they have certain obligations during the week and cannot attend most of the practices. The Sunday optional practices are also a way players are able to make up practice time. I keep track of who shows up and who doesn't. Again, I do it my own old fashioned way. If you are an expert in your hand held digital device and can take attendance this way, then go ahead.

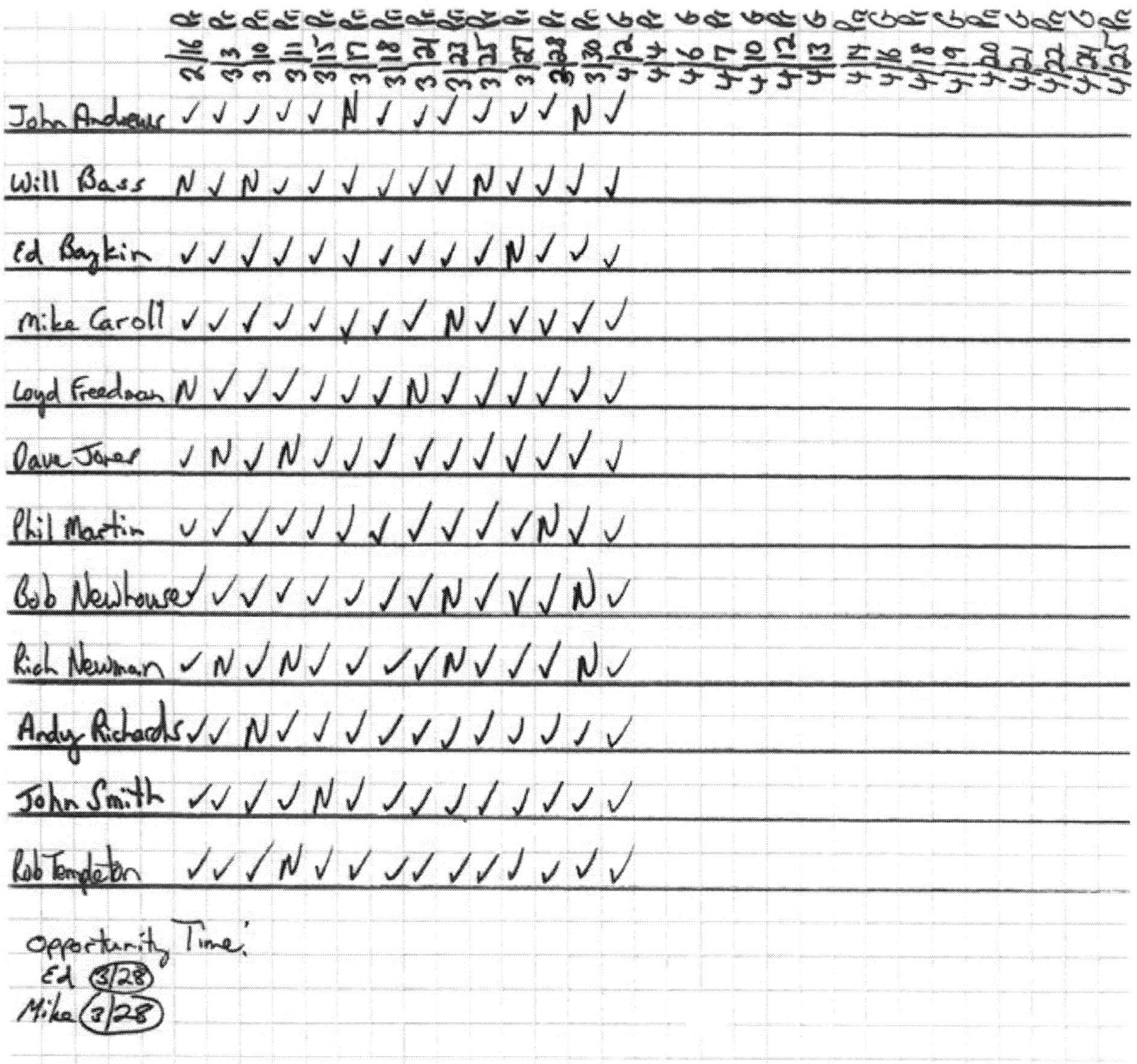

Attendance grid (handwritten). Column headers are handwritten dates.

Name														
John Andrews	√	√	√	√	√	N	√	√	√	√	√	√	N	√
Will Bass	N	√	N	√	√	√	√	√	√	N	√	√	√	√
Ed Baykin	√	√	√	√	√	√	√	√	√	√	N	√	√	√
Mike Caroll	√	√	√	√	√	√	√	√	N	√	√	√	√	√
Loyd Freedman	N	√	√	√	√	√	√	N	√	√	√	√	√	√
Dave Jones	√	N	√	N	√	√	√	√	√	√	√	√	√	√
Phil Martin	√	√	√	√	√	√	√	√	√	√	√	N	√	√
Bob Newhouse	√	√	√	√	√	√	√	N	√	√	√	N	√	
Rich Newman	√	N	√	N	√	√	√	√	N	√	√	√	N	√
Andy Richards	√	√	N	√	√	√	√	√	√	√	√	√	√	
John Smith	√	√	√	√	N	√	√	√	√	√	√	√	√	
Bob Templeton	√	√	√	N	√	√	√	√	√	√	√	√	√	

Opportunity Time:
Ed (3/28)
Mike (3/28)

This is how I keep track of attendance. I hand write a grid at the beginning of the season and put the names down for every player. I then make 4 or 5 copies and fill in the dates on top as the activity comes up. If it is a practice I might just put "P" or "Pr" or "Prc." If the activity is a game, I'll just write the letter "G." I usually have one page per month. I put a check mark if they attended and a "N" if they did not.

On the bottom, I keep tract of the Opportunity Time or the extra help I offer as it happens. A regular pattern usually takes place with most of the players. On certain days every week players will miss practice because of activities such as karate, piano lessons, etc. Many times if the kids are really into my practices, they will begin to try and reschedule their other activities around baseball practice.

This is a great back up should there be complaints about playing time and positions. It is always good to have as much ammunition as you can should there be irate parents. Typically most of the complaints come from the parents who really never make the effort to ask for extra help for their kids.

Team Newsletter

One year I decided to launch a team newsletter. I really did not know what was involved. I wrote it myself and made it a bi-weekly publication, covering the games that we had played and the results highlighting keys hits, pitching, and fielding plays. I found I was in way over my head as far as the time involved and the editing, which I really could have used a committee of editors. I kept it up for the year and struggled through it every two weeks. After the season, I was more exhausted from writing the six or seven newsletters than from my practices. When the season was over, I was thrilled I didn't have to do it anymore. My thoughts were in the right place but with all my other responsibilities coaching and planning practices, I took on more than I could handle. I remember telling my wife after the season that I was thankful I'll never do the newsletter idea again. The next year a funny thing happened. About a third of the way through the season, one of the parents came up to me and asked when the newsletter is coming out. He and the other parents looked forward to reading it. I was stunned. Not only did I find it a chore after the first few I put out, but I began to cut corners and knew the quality of the last few were inferior to the first couple I wrote. I told the parent I could not handle the responsibility with everything else. He asked if I would mind if he wrote the newsletter. He was into Desktop Publishing. I had no objection as long as he let me see the final version before it was sent out. We spoke about each issue before it went out to the other parents. He ended up putting out four issues for the remainder of the season. Because of this experience, I decided to ask at the Parents Meeting if anyone was interested in doing a team newsletter. If there was a volunteer then it would be done. Otherwise, if I could not get anyone to do it, we just would not have one for that season.

When I do get a volunteer, I try to make suggestions and have guidelines so the person doesn't have a hard time with the newsletter. In our three month season, it really is not necessary to come out with this newsletter more than three times. We usually play a twenty game season and I want about 6-7 games covered with each issue. I only want it one page long. I want each player mentioned at least once in every issue, whether it is about hitting a game winning home run or hustling down to second base making a slide to prevent the double play. We do not want to leave anyone out of any issue. I will give a basic summary of each game to the parent/publisher. Sometimes you will get a really creative parent who is into this and knows about all types of computer software to make it look as good as the Washington Post or New York Times. I've had parents who will take pictures and put them in the newsletter.

Now here is the one caveat the parent/publisher is required to do. In this age of computers, e-mails, etc., it would be easy just to send the newsletter over the computer to the team in the form of an e-mail. And with all the computer programs available, I'm sure someone creative can make a beautiful e-newsletter. But I want it printed into a hard copy and have at least 40 copies printed for distribution. I do this because I want to make sure that the newsletter is available to the kids' grandparents. The grandparents get the biggest kick out of seeing their grandchild's name in print. Most of them might not be computer savvy. I find that a hard copy is much more personal than a digital copy. Between the players, parents, and grandparents, the grandmas and grandpas love it more than anyone else. In fact, many of them save the newsletter or have asked me for some past issues, which I usually cannot accommodate. Kids have told me how they send copies of the newsletter to Florida and Arizona for their grandparents. It's amazing how some even send it to aunts and uncles around the country.

The interesting thing about this newsletter concept is that it works well if your team is winning a lot of games and even better if your team is losing a lot and having a rough season. On the losing end, kids will realize that there are some positives that can be achieved. The key is to have the right person as the editor so positive phrases are used to describe players' efforts even in a losing effort.

If you are able to delegate the responsibility of a team newsletter, then go for it. If you have to do it yourself, I would say skip it because of your other responsibilities as coach. And don't get crazy with this. For a 20 game season, 3-4 issues is more than enough to have the kids get excited. Some will even ask between issues, "Coach, is my name in the next newsletter?"

Here is a sample of what a newsletter might look like:

The Blue Hens Post

Blue Hens Win Opener 7-3

The Blue Hens opened the 2011 season with a victory over the Rockets 7-3. John Andrews who struckout 6 and gave up only 3 hits was the starting pitcher and Phil Martin came in to relieve him. Dave Jones had 3 hits including a home run. Mike Caroll chippped in with two hits along with Andrews.

Blue Hens Beat Mud Dogs 8-0

The Blue Hens put together their best game of the season shutting out the first place Mud Dogs 8-0. The Blue Hens used 3 pitchers to combine for the shutout. Bill Bass was the starter with Dick Newman and Johnny Smith coming out of the bull pen.Mike Caroll scored 3 runs with a hit and 2 walks.

Blue Hens Lose In Extra Innings!

The Blue Hens lost a hard fought battle against the Thunder 5-4 in 8 innings. Down by two runs 4-2 in the 6th inning, Andy Richards sparked a game tying rally with a lead off walk in the 6th inning. The Thunder capitalized on some fine defensive play in the 7th and 8th innings.

Blue Hens Fall To Thunder 10-4

The Blue Hens fell to the Thunder in a game where there was no giving up by tus. Being down 8-0, a modest 4th inning rally put the team back in the game. Phil Martin led the rally with a bases clearing doubles.The bats got a little quiet the rest of the game. The defensive highlight of the game was a stunning running one handed catch by Bob Templeton.

Blue Hens Win Again 5-1

The Blue Hens won their second game in as many nights beating the Knights 5-1. Ed Boykin made a fantastic play in the field in the first inning on an unassisted double play.
Loyd Freedman stole two bases in the second inning to ignite a 4 run rally for the Blue Hens. Bob Newhouse laid down a perfect bunt in the 5th inning.

Blue Hens Best The Thunder 3-1

The Blue Hens beat the Thunder 3-1 in one of the best games of the season. Dave Jones made a game saving play in the 6th inning in center field with the bases loaded. Mike Caroll pitched a complete game victory and Bill Bass got two hits.

Chapter 4

Equipment

"The other sports are just sports. Baseball is a love."

~Bryant Gumbel, 1981

Sports equipment is a multi billion dollar business. Like everything else in the business world, baseball equipment is constantly changing, improving, and getting more expensive. Every year new types of equipment and training aids come out. It has always surprised me to see kids show up at games or practices with the latest equipment advertised on television or on the internet. Some parents, who in my opinion send their kids outside with the wrong clothes, are sometimes the first people who go out and buy their son or daughter the latest $250.00 bat that just came out on the market. Compare bats and catcher's equipment today to what was out 25 years ago. The technology has changed the way youth athletes play the game.

When my kids first started playing Little League® baseball, I was one of the parents who did not really have the money to buy the latest state of the art equipment. Other parents were buying $150.00 hitting nets and setting them up in their backyard. I was creating my own props. I was able to invent something equivalent to a hitting net made up of a blue plastic 10'x12' tarp, four bicycle hooks, and four bungie cords wrapped around two trees. My invention was just as good and was made for under $20.00. When other parents were buying the most expensive bats, we poked around our garage and used bats that were, well, the best way to put it is "experienced."

Families are of different economic backgrounds and all have their own budget. Youth coaches need to be cognizant of this. Even in the toughest economies, parents try not to deny their kids anything while sacrificing other parts of their lives. This is incredible, but I see it year in and year out. I remember a parent complaining to me that he was behind in his mortgage. At the next practice his son shows up with a two hundred dollar bat. I was standing there with my mouth open and asked him why he bought the bat when he needed to catch up on his mortgage. His exact words to me were: "Marty, baseball and sports with my kids takes precedent over everything." This little episode really shed some light on how parents set their priorities.

Try to gauge the economic situation of each family on your team. Over the years, for one reason or another, I have accumulated a number of used baseball gloves. I always keep them in a bucket in my garage just in case I get a player on my team who really cannot afford a brand new glove. I also tell youth baseball parents that the best source for youth baseball equipment is right in your own neighborhood. Pick out a neighbor who has grown kids no longer playing baseball and out of the house for a number of years. Just ask them if they want to get rid of any of their kids' old baseball equipment. The parents, especially the mother, will jump at the opportunity and even roll out the red carpet to clean out these sporting good items that have been gathering dust for 5 or 10 years, or even longer. And for the beneficiary of the used glove, this equipment is just as good, and in some cases better, because they have been broken in already.

Just as you have to be aware of families who are strapped financially to buy equipment, I actually encourage those families who can afford it to buy as much as their own equipment as they can. For instance, lately parents have brought up the issue of purchasing a batting helmet for their son for hygienic reasons. I tell the parents of course they can, if they keep these helmets in their own equipment bag. We will color code them and make sure other players on the team do not use the helmet. This has been a popular request more and more over the last few years.

Parents who have kids that are catchers will also ask if they can use their own catching equipment. Of course they can. The equipment must meet league standards and must fit properly. Most parents whose son is serious about catching will purchase their own equipment. In conclusion, if you allow some of your players to use their own equipment, you have just cut down on the weight of the team's equipment bag, which you the coach will have to lug around.

As municipal budgets become more strapped and league expenses get higher, you will see more and more players having to provide their own equipment. Make sure your parents know that when it comes to the safety of kids, it is better to spend the extra money for the better equipment but always look for alternatives.

Bases For Youth Baseball

Bases have come a long way since my kids began playing. I've read some statistics that claim approximately 50% of all injuries related to baseball occur when players slide. It is highly recommended for leagues to use the breakaway bases. The base has a secured bottom piece and the top piece fits over it like a sleeve. When a player slides to the base, it gives, and in many cases the top breakaway part comes off. Putting it back on the bottom piece always seems to take time and sometimes can stall a game to annoyance, but for preventing injuries it is definitely worth it. When I coached my oldest son, I witnessed a player who slid into third base during an All-Star practice. The base was not a breakaway base and the player, who was very talented, broke his ankle. He missed the entire All-Stars schedule on a team that would have done a lot better if this player was healthy. Youth leagues have also begun to use the extended first base. This base has the white part in its regular place, but with a twin base colored orange that is nose to nose with the white base while sitting in foul territory. This was made for obvious reasons. Youth players tend not to play first base correctly. Many will plant their foot right in the middle of the base while waiting for a throw from an infielder. The baserunner is running full force down the first base line. He has a greater chance of tripping over the first baseman's leg if the fielder is not in the proper position. Both players can become seriously injured. The other concern would be when the first baseman fields the ball and must toss the ball to the pitcher or second baseman covering the bag for an out. This play has a high degree of collisions and injuries. The extended first base gives the fielder and the baserunner more of their own real estate to focus on to touch, although it does not eliminate the collision completely. Coaches should teach their first baseman the correct way to catch a ball from an infielder. And teams should practice other players covering first base and get use to the traffic there. My recommendation is for leagues to use the extended base. If a baseball purest cannot stand the site of it, then use it for the first half of the season and then progress to using just the regular first base. From tee ball up to the majors, leagues need to consider the progression method of coaching. Work your way up to where you want to end up. There is nothing wrong with using the youth baseball game itself as a training ground to get players to play better and learn the game. Of course, like any other suggestions, age and skill level should always be taken into consideration.

For practice bases, I have used almost anything from cardboard to paper plates to chalk. This is because I practice in some of the most obscure areas in my town, and I have to become creative. As of late, I now like the rubber throw down bases. I keep a set of these throw down bases in my car. I go through one or two sets each season. These are great for practice, fairly cheap to buy, easy to handle, and take up a minimal amount of space. And one thing I do with these bases, as well as most of my equipment, is to label them with my last name and phone number with a huge black non erasable magic marker. Let me state right here that you should spend time labeling all of the equipment you buy along with the equipment given to you by the league as long it does not violate any policy of defacement.

A few years ago, I started to color code half of the rubber throw down bases so the base runners can have a target to touch. If we are practicing on a regular field, I'll throw these rubber bases over the regular ones. What I also like about these rubber bases is that if I run a parking lot practice, they do not slide or move like regular bases do if you use them on concrete or blacktop. If you end up practicing in the outfield, or any place with just grass, these throw down bases are also very good.

I have also accumulated a few regular bases I keep in my garage. When we practice sliding, I take these out and we practice our sliding drills in a grassy area in the outfield. When the players slide into these bases, the bases go sliding away from the player, which is fine for these drills. Some coaches will wet down the outfield grass a bit so the players get an exaggerated feel to sliding.

Baseballs

I have always found the make-up and composition of a baseball interesting. Most baseballs feature a rubber or cork center, wrapped in yarn and covered in leather. It is 9 to 9.25 inches in circumference (2 7/8 inches to 3 inches in diameter). The yarn or string used to wrap the baseball inside the leather can be very long and some insist it can be up to one mile in length. I remember when I was younger, me and some of my friends unwound a ball and couldn't believe the amount of guts inside. In the Major Leagues, teams can use between up to 60-70 baseballs in a regular game. Like baseball bats, gloves, and other equipment, manufacturers of baseballs have grown over the years. Your league should supply baseballs. Usually they provide two types of baseballs. One type is practice baseballs and the other type is game baseballs. Except for maybe a different type of label, there is not much of a difference the way the ball comes off the bat or how it bounces on the ground. At least I can't detect the difference. I meet baseball coaches and managers who are able to detect the difference just by the sound of a baseball being hit. The quality of the cover between baseballs makes the biggest difference.

Some managers I have met will lecture me on the benefits of one brand of baseballs compared to another. In all honesty, unless I am using practice baseballs at the end of the season that are water logged, I can't really see a huge difference in the different brand of baseballs. Managers should have more baseballs than what the league supplies. I'm not into coaches having to dig into their own pockets each year, but if you spend your own money for any one item, make it baseballs. The more baseballs coaches have will ensure smoother and more efficient run drills with more repetitions, especially batting practice. Don't think for a second that just because I have a few extra dozen baseballs I'm not careful with them. I have become frugal when it comes to baseballs and I will stay after practice walking and scouring the field going to the base of the fence, over the fence, and looking behind bushes, searching for and usually coming up with extra baseballs at each practice. It is even good for your players to see you value the baseballs. With this being said, if you are going to run a lot of practices, stock up on the baseballs. Any extra money your team may have, I would put toward baseballs. The more baseballs you have available to you during practice, the more repetitions you players will have doing drills, and your players will ultimately become better baseball players.

The league also should have baseballs with a rubber or cloth outside coating that they usually reserve for tee ball and the leagues below the majors. Make sure you get a hold of a couple dozen of these type of baseballs. The last few years, I have been using these safety baseballs more and more on fielding drills in practice. In most of my drills, I use more than one baseball, and a lot of times the balls are flying back and forth with players moving from one station to the next. For safety, I have become a big believer in using these safety baseballs. For batting practice, I still use regular practice baseballs. I will say this more than once: You can never have enough baseballs.

If you perform the soft toss drill, it really should not be done against a screen with a regular hardball. Years ago, I went down to the field with my son and his friend for extra batting practice. I decided to warm them up with the toss drill. Using regular hard baseballs against the fence, one happened to hit the support bar and bounced right back at my son's friend and hit him squarely in the eye. We ended up spending three hours at the local hospital. He ended up being okay, but it was an awakening for me. Since that incident, I never use hard balls for the toss drills against the fence. Leagues should not even allow it. Besides the safety factor, it is not good for the fence itself. I don't even think the soft covered or rubber covered baseballs should be used for soft toss against the screen, but it is better than the hardballs. I recommend what I call rag or sock balls or a plastic type pickle ball or wiffle ball. Stick to rag balls when doing the toss drill against a wall.

Besides the normal baseballs your leagues will furnish, I will also use any type of ball for any number of drills. I've used ping pong balls as well as kick balls for hitting drills and many sizes in between. I've used golf-sized plastic balls. I have also used empty plastic soda containers to hit. I've also used a rolled up newspaper to simulate a baseball. With any type of hitting drills, just be safety-conscious when using different size balls for the various drills. Accidents will happen in the course of the season, but as coaches, we always want to bring down the odds as much as we could for young players getting hurt.

Bats

The baseball bat industry is actually an entity all to itself in the sporting goods world. The research, time, and money spent developing bats is incredible. It is a boom to these baseball bat companies when a star or future superstar succeeds with a particular company's bat. On the youth level, bats can be made of wood or aluminum or other material if it is approved by the league. Most youth players, even up to high school and college, will use aluminum bats.

Picking a bat is always an issue. The first thing you should do is know the league requirements as far as the circumference of the bat allowed. Many parents will buy the most expensive bats for their child with the thought that the bat will somehow do magic once it is in their child's grip. Sometimes as coaches we have to convince parents that the only real formula for becoming a good hitter is natural ability plus a good practice regimen with good coaching. Parents tend to buy bigger and heavier bats than they should for their kids. I am very adamant about players using a bat that is light enough that they can handle.

Many coaches will tell you that the bat should not be too light. From my experience, two of the biggest changes I've seen in my 20 years of coaching youth baseball for improving a player's batting besides natural ability, drills, and technique is improving a player's vision with glasses (or contacts) and changing bats to a lighter bat. If you change players' bats to lighter bats and make sure they have adequate vision, it is not a guarantee their batting will improve. A lot goes into turning youth players into successful batters. Let's give young players who play baseball or softball a fighting chance to be successful. Having a comfortable manageable bat that they can handle is one of the prerequisites to making contact with the baseball.

The University of Arizona, along with the bat manufacturer, Worth, put out a recommended bat chart for baseball players from the youth level and up. One of the things I like about their chart is that they take the size of the player into account. Many batting charts will just list the age, even though at 11 or 12 years-old there can be a 6" difference plus a 30 pound weight difference between the biggest and smallest kid on the team. The players size must be taken into consideration.

When shopping for a bat, you will find two numbers on the end. The top number is the length and the lower number is the weight. If a 32 is the top number and 28 the lower number it means a 32 inch bat weights 28 ounces. Baseball bats are measured using their length to weight ratio, a negative number represents how many ounces a bat weighs compared to its length in inches. For example, a 32 inch bat that weighs 28 ounces is a - 4.

Little League® put out a list of bats that were banned in their games. These bats are called composite bats and are bats that are made of substances such as titanium or carbon fiber with certain items called resins added in. These are all put into aluminum and are lighter than many of the metal bats that are on the market. Little League® states that in a study by the University of Massachusetts these bats actually become more lively with use. This is going to be a real conundrum each and every year to keep track of all the banned bats. Bats will be added and taken off this list. I predict eventually most leagues will go back to all wood bats.

A system I started a few years ago has really helped as far as organizing and recognizing team bats. I take a piece of hard cardboard, about 20" x 20." I then take all my team bats. I plug a small hole in the cardboard just so the knob of the bat squeezes through. I then take a can of spray paint, usually I use red. I then spray paint the bottom of the knob (only) for each of my team bats that were assigned to me with my equipment. I lay them out and let it dry. When done correctly, the red paint should be only on the bottom of the knob and never up on the handle. This little technique has helped me over the years keep control of my team bats and makes it easy to recognize. It has solved a lot of potential arguments about which team owns what bat. I also open this color coding system to the player's personal bats. Some want it done and others do not. Make sure you get the okay from the parents before you apply anything to any player's personal property. I proposed to my league that each team do this with an assigned color. The suggestion went in one ear and out the other with members of my league. I continue to do this for my own team. This is one small technique that will make any coach's life a little easier. It takes no longer than 15 minutes to do and costs about $5.00 for the spray paint. Colored electrical tape can also be used to help identify bats.

Baseball Gloves

The baseball glove is also called a mitt. When baseball first began it was played barehanded. Toward the end of the 19th century, players began to use gloves to prevent getting hurt. The glove has developed over the years, getting bigger in size while at the same time fitting more snug at the fingers for better control.

Anyone who has followed baseball will tell you there is almost a romantic relationship between a baseball player and his glove. At all levels of play you'll see players doing funny stuff with their gloves treating them almost like a "being." Players have been known to talk to their gloves on good plays and bad. Before the 1950's, in professional baseball, players used to leave their gloves on the field. If you have ever seen old films of baseball, you'd see some players flip their gloves in the air after the last out, which would be a real joy to watch. Like everything else though, things change.

The baseball glove becomes almost part of the ball player's body, an extension of the hand. The technology for gloves has also evolved. When purchasing a glove, depending on the manufacturer, some of the recommendations for breaking in a glove might be: putting it under water, rubbing shaving cream into it, or using neatsfoot oil. Then the instructions might say something like, put two baseballs in the pocket and tie a rope and leave it for a few weeks, or put it under your bed. Whichever glove you get, follow the specific instructions for that brand. Do not use a technique from another manufacturer unless it is recommended for the glove you bought. My experience is that it can take up to one year to break in a new baseball glove. As far as the size of the glove you purchase, make sure, like with bats, you know your league's qualifications. Some leagues do not allow a glove that is more than 12 inches wide. I was one parent who always thought it was better to buy bigger gloves. I have since changed. The glove should be smaller rather than bigger. A young ball player can control a smaller glove better. A number of years ago,

I was at a major league game and it was probably the only time I sat in seats close enough to see which player shaved the night before and who didn't. The party I was with knew the second baseman and he came over to us before the game to talk to my friend. When he came over, I paid particular attention to his glove and was amazed at how small it was. The glove was not really much bigger than his hand. Seeing this helped change my philosophy about glove size, although the position the player plays can vary with the size of the glove. I have noticed over the last few years on my team that some players who play first base come to practices and games with two gloves. This is fine as long as we coaches don't start demanding each player carry two gloves. People now buy gloves online, which is fine. I have always recommended buying them in person if possible, or at least try them on in person before purchasing.

As far as catcher's gloves, it is extremely important that you try to locate one that is used. Hand me down catcher's gloves are the best. Try to avoid buying a new glove at the beginning of the season. I've never seen a catcher's glove in youth baseball become broken-in the same year it was purchased new. I've had catchers use new gloves. It is frustrating for them not being able to close the glove, dealing with the stiffness of the leather. On these new stiff catcher's gloves, the catcher is lucky if 25% of the pitches don't end up on the ground in front of him. Besides retrieving each pitch thrown by the pitcher, it is problematic on plays to the plate where catching the baseball and tagging a runner in one motion is extremely important. It has always amazed me that leagues hand out brand new catcher's gloves at the beginning of the season and this is the glove they expect the team to use. Each team should be supplied with a used and new catcher's glove. The used glove should be used during the year for games. The new glove should be used sporadically at practices so it is broken in for teams the following year. And leagues should let the coaches know this is how we break in new catcher's gloves. If this is done each year, leagues will never have a problem with their catchers using stiff new gloves that are hard to handle. Again, I strongly recommend for catcher's gloves to consider purchasing them used or getting hand me downs. I am left handed and the best gloves I ever had growing up were from my brother's friend who lived up the street from me. He was lefty and a really good baseball player. When he got a new glove, his mom or dad always called up my house to let us know. And before my parents even hung up the phone, I was out of the house running up the street to get my new used glove.

Baseball Batting Helmets & Protective Cups

The one piece of equipment that probably prevents more injuries than any other piece of equipment is the helmet. Personally, I pay special attention to protecting the head. A number of years ago I was jogging in Boston and had a collision with someone on a bike. As it turned out, I ended up with a concussion and had short term amnesia. To make a long story short, it was not a fun experience. In the pros, batting helmets were not mandatory until 1971. Youth leagues began using them well before then. Usually two or three times each season, one player is hit by the pitcher squarely on the helmet. When you hear the loud thud, there usually is a chorus of "Oh God" as the player goes down. Usually one parent will always say out loud, "Well if you are going to get hit with the baseball, that's the place to get hit." The parent is probably correct. Other parts of the batter's body are exposed but the head is protected with the helmet. The helmet should have double ear flaps. It is especially important for players to wear their helmets on the bases. Getting hit with a thrown baseball can occur especially on a run down or with a play at the plate. Some players wear helmets that are too loose. Coaches need to have players wear helmets in practice and have them run around the bases at full speed. What happens a lot that drives me crazy is when a player is running around the bases for an extra base hit, and because the helmet is loose, he begins to run while holding the helmet with both hands so it does not fall off his head. Players need to pick out helmets that fit comfortably, but are snug enough so they will not fall off when running at full speed. Chin straps will help keep the helmet from falling off.

Some leagues try to institute helmets with masks. This is somewhat a controversial topic, but if it prevents injuries, then leagues should seriously look into making the masks mandatory. I think if a league is going to make the masks mandatory, they should decide when to start the policy, such as right after T-Ball. The players who are used to the masks will always think it is a natural part of the helmet. It will be tough to get 11 and 12 year-old kids to switch over to helmets with masks when they have been using only one type of helmet since they began playing youth baseball.

Leagues should consider making coaches wear helmets in the coach's box. A 40 or 50 year-old coach might not react quick enough to a hard hit line drive that is foul. Youth leagues always require youth base coaches to wear helmets, but not adults. When adult baseball coaches are base coaches, they are not provided helmets, even for optional use. Coaches should consider purchasing helmets at their own expense. Probably because they all think their manhood is being questioned, coaches in youth baseball and high school baseball do not wear helmets. The same thing goes for college baseball coaches. It can be somewhat of an inconvenience and tough getting used to, but without a doubt, this will prevent injuries. At the same time, we are showing our players how concerned we are for safety.

On July 22, 2007 a tragedy happened in the minor leagues. The team was the Tulsa Drillers and first-base coach Mike Coolbaugh, a former Major League player, died after being hit in the head by a line drive during a game. To their credit, Major League Baseball put in a rule that base coaches have to wear helmets in the majors and minors. But no amateur league, including youth, high school, and college, put this rule into effect. This is a mistake, and coaches should consider the downside by not wearing a helmet. From my own experiences, my reflexes are not what they used to be. Sometimes when a big kid or a strong hitter is up, I always move back in the coach's box and up the line a bit. Numerous times it has been a close call with some baseballs whizzing past me.

I just began wearing a helmet while coaching third base, and though I'm not crazy about it, once I'm involved in the game I don't even know it is there. Players should always wear a snug fitting helmet because it prevents head injuries. While leagues supply these helmets, it is okay to encourage parents to purchase helmets just for their own kids. Coaches should do the same.

As far as cups, the protection for the player's testicles, I see no reason why all male players on the field should not be wearing a cup. Many leagues require only the catcher to wear a cup. With the ball coming off the bat quicker and quicker the last few years, leagues need to make more safeguards for the kids. Many coaches, including myself, teach their players to slide almost all the time, even if it is not a close play. The comfort or discomfort of wearing a cup will become a matter of habit. Parents, make sure the jock or strap the cup sits in is not too tight or too loose.

Catching Gear

When it comes to equipment fitting correctly, it is most important with the catcher. He must be fitted so he is protected from being hurt, while at the same time, he cannot be encumbered from moving as quickly as possible to block balls. The development of catching equipment started toward the end of the 19th century. When the rules of baseball changed so that the final strike, including foul tips, had to be caught on the fly for an out, catchers began to physically move closer to home plate. Because of the the possibility of getting hurt by the ball from being closer to home plate and the batter, catchers began wearing equipment, such as the mask and chest protector. It was the opening game in the Polo Grounds in 1907 when the catcher, Roger Bresnahan of the New York Giants, first introduced shin guards. This was the final piece of the catcher's armor. The evolution and the perfection of catching equipment continues today.

In youth baseball, I see many catchers that are not fitted correctly. I always ask for and receive two sets of catching equipment, and I make sure they are different sizes. Before the season starts, I ask my players who would be interested in catching and those who would fill in during an emergency situation. Whoever steps forward, and it is usually 3-5 kids, I take the time to outfit each one (they must have a cup) and throw 5-10 pitches to them. This takes time, but it is so worth it, especially if you get down to one of the emergency catchers.

When fitting the shin guards, they should come over the player's cleats up to the knee and fit comfortably when the player is squatting in the correct catcher's stance. The straps that go behind the leg should be criss-crossed to hold them on. One of the biggest things that delay games is when the straps come off. Coaches have to remember that the clip faces out. Many shin guards now have "knee pads" that go behind the knee. They are also known as "knee savers." These are supposed to combine comfort as well as saving the wear and tear on a player's knees. I've had players that love these and others that don't. Like everything else, if they fit properly, they are useful. I know that when I have catchers that buy their own equipment, these pads are usually included.

The chest protector must fit comfortably and cover the area below the neck down to the waist. It should have a snug fit. If a different catcher uses the same chest protector, he sometimes neglects to adjust the size of the chest protector with the strap in the back, and the player will not only look uncomfortable but will be constricted in his movements, especially when throwing. It is a pain in the neck to do, but coaches must take the lead here and learn about the catcher's equipment, especially how to adjust the size for each piece.

Unlike when I played youth baseball, the helmet is now usually attached to the mask. Many times, the helmet is too small, but kids will wear it anyway because of the way it is attached. What can happen here is a large gap between the face mask and the helmet. If the gap is too large, part of the catcher's head is exposed and therefore he can get injured.

Also attached to the mask is the throat guard. This piece snaps around the bottom of the mask and hangs loosely to protect the player's throat on a pitched ball or a foul ball. I always try to carry at least one or two extra throat guards with my equipment. They attach fairly easily and are a valuable piece of equipment. In fact, most youth leagues will now refuse to let catchers play without the throat guard. This makes perfect sense, especially with hard foul tips.

I already addressed the catcher's glove, however, I will readdress it here because it is so important. Coaches should do everything in their power to make sure that the catchers on their team are not using a brand new glove. There are options available to the league with used sporting goods stores that carry broken in gloves. Some coaches are under the opinion that youth players should never buy brand new gloves. Instead they should only purchase used ones. I like the idea of a player breaking in his non-catcher's glove before and during the season. I feel that when bought new, if the player is given the responsibility of breaking it in, he will take great care of it. The catcher's glove is a completely different animal.

When parents purchase catcher's equipment for their own kids, I urge them not to make it a holiday gift in December. Our league starts our games in April. The kids in this age group can grow at alarming rates and catching equipment that fit well in December might be too small in April. There is no perfect way to purchase equipment. I have seen players grow out of their equipment during the season.

Baseball Uniforms and Cleats

Uniforms and handing them out is a big deal in most leagues. In our league, and probably most leagues, players love the day they get their uniform. This is true in all divisions. Even in Tee Ball where teams are just using tee shirts. The players love getting them. Asking for the sizes and giving them to the league well in advance will save tons of time and money. There are always problems about fitting correctly. For the most part, if you are organized and parents fill in the correct sizes when asked (knowing there are children's sizes and adult sizes), then many problems will be avoided. The way I usually work the whole uniform process is to have my team parent, usually a mom, handle this. The team parent will collect the sizes for each player. Many leagues will now ask for the uniform size for the kids right on the registration application. This is fine as long as someone from your team confirms over the phone the size.

When the uniforms are ordered, some leagues will now ask what numbers the kids want and ask for three choices. At first I thought this would open up a huge can of worms and be more trouble then it is worth. However, since my league has been doing it, it has gone very smoothly with the kids accepting any of their three choices. It is interesting to see what numbers are most popular in certain geographical areas of the country. In my area (New York) the number 7 has always been the most popular number, with many of the parents being brought up with Mickey Mantle as their hero. In Massachusetts, the number 8 for Carl Yastrzemski has been the most popular over the years. Each city with a Major League team has specific numbers popular with their youth players.

The day uniforms are ready for handing out are exciting for the team. The way I usually handle it is to have my team parent get two or three volunteer moms to help. I give the uniforms to the team parent who will put each player's uniform in a separate box or plastic bag. I coincide handing out the uniforms with one of my practices. I send over two players at a time to get their bag. The players will take their uniform into the restrooms at the field and try them on and show the "moms" how they look. If there is a problem, the team parent will take notes and we will contact the person in our league in charge of the uniforms. Any league will correct size issues. Many times, there are special circumstances when players ask if they can purchase their own pants. I've seen this done because a player will favor a certain fabric, whether it is just the feel or he has allergies. Also, some big sized kids prefer their mom to fit them with their pants. This should be fine as long as the league okays everything.

Players should also get stirrups that go over their socks. Leagues are lackadaisical about this. Some players wear them and some don't. I like to either have the whole team wear them or not wear them just so the team looks consistent.

Cleats are a huge issue. I try to give my twenty plus years of coaching experience to help parents not overspend while at the same time making sure their kids are fitted properly from head to foot. When it comes to cleats, there are a few issues I address. Like catching equipment, parents should not buy them for holiday gifts 3-4 months before the baseball season starts because of players growing out of them. What I tell parents is to try to see if their kids can use last year's cleats for the first two or three weeks of practice, only if they still fit comfortably. I recommend this because in our area in the Northeast, once the snow melts, we coaches all begin to practice. The ground is still very soft with a lot of muddy spots. If players wear brand new cleats, they will get dirty fast. If last year's don't fit, and most don't, I tell parents to have players wear olds sneakers to the first couple of practices. I'm really trying to forewarn parents that the first couple of weeks of practice their kids will be coming home quite muddy some days.

Some parents will insist on dressing their kids with their new game pants for our practices. This is something that needs to be addressed at the parents meeting or when the uniforms are handed out. I like my team to get practice pants on their own. Some will wear last year's game pants or sweat pants, which is fine, but make sure parents understand that long pants must be worn in practices.

Something that happens all the time, especially the first really warm day, is that some kids will show up in shorts. Players have to learn that baseball is a long pants game. And not just for sliding purposes. I've seen players get hit with baseballs wearing shorts and they end up having a nice baseball-sized tattoo for a few weeks.

Training Aids And Other Equipment

Wouldn't it be great if you could take the best medical surgical tools in the whole world, have the average educated citizen handle and get used to them and practice on say a watermelon, then put that person in the operating room to perform some surgery? I don't think you or I would be that trustworthy on the operating table. Just knowing a person has access to the best medical equipment in the world doesn't give him the training to perform surgery. If life were that easy we would put all our resources toward equipment taking away the crucial necessary training.

Every year I go to a number of baseball clinics and conventions. Within these conventions, there are exhibiters who show the latest in baseball equipment. The spectrum runs from the largest of the sporting goods companies to the smallest entrepreneurs, who in many cases have put in a lifetime of savings to come out with the next "baseball wheel." When you walk into the exhibit areas, the big companies, whose names we hear everyday, have the most beautiful exhibit booths with the best locations. When you go to the back area, that is where you will find these individuals who have spent a lot of time, sweat, and money on their own invention. What I have found is that almost half of the new products that come on the market every year are a waste. Generally, I am from the old school of "activity specificity" for improvement. This means that to improve at hitting, practice the actual specific skill of hitting by having someone pitch to you. With that said, I have been wrong on some of the baseball products I have seen, thinking they never had a chance to make it. The next thing I see is everyone using it. I happen to enjoy speaking to the individual entrepreneurs to hear their explanations of how and why they invented what they did. Some of them are incredibly creative and focused on getting their product to as many people as they can.

Historically, when I was coaching my own kids, I could not afford some of the products other people had set up in their backyard. My son had friends who had a regular batting cage set up in their backyard with a pitching machine along with not one, not two, but four or five $200.00 bats at their disposal. My kids and I began to be inventive with whatever we had around the house at our disposal.

I remember my brother tying a heavy string through a Wiffle ball. He hung it down from a tree so my nephews could swing at the ball on a string. Thanks to him, I did the same thing with my kids at my house, but lacking a good tree for this, we used our deck, dropping the ball from one of the corner wood supports.

I remember making a batting tee with a coffee can filled in with cement. We put a 2-3 foot piece of PVC pipe into the cement. We made sure it dried and was straight. Then we purchased a piece of rubber tubing from an auto parts store and was able to squeeze it over the PVC pipe. The ball would rest on the rubber tubing and my kids would hit it off this home made batting tee.

When I did purchase my first batting tee, my middle son was just starting Tee-Ball. I thought a baseball was tough for a 5 or 6 year old to hit. How can I build up his confidence while at the same time giving him quality repetitions? I went out and bought a new bathroom plunger. I turned it upside down inside the batting tee and placed a kick ball on it. I had my son hit the kick ball off the tee for a couple of days. And guess what, he hit them all because I made it achievable for a youngster. We then progressed to a small rubber ball, a little bigger than a softball. Then finally a tee ball.

There is something to be said for being creative and making equipment out of household items. Projects that a parent and child work on together have ever lasting effects. And not just for the item, but also the bonding between the parent and child.

Engineering is not my strength and I am not an expert by any means but I like to use items before I give an opinion on them. I also like to see what the results are from these training aids and what it takes to put some of them together. If a manufacturer claims a pitching machine takes only 15 minutes to put together, and it takes me 3 hours, then something is wrong. Either the instructions are inferior or the machine requires special tools that were not mentioned until you bought it. I call the manufacturer and let them know.

It would be impossible to review just a fraction of the baseball equipment that is on the market. I will review three pieces of equipment that I truly like. Believe me, there are tons of great baseball equipment on the market. Remember that everything has a price. Don't let equipment interfere with teaching true fundamentals.

Batting Tees

Of all the pieces of baseball equipment on the market, the batting tee is by far my favorite. With the limited amount of space you need and the variety of hitting drills you can do, the baseball batting tee is terrific! There have been a few theories on the history of the batting tee. During my research, by the time I came across the third person who wanted to be credited with inventing it, I gave up. It does date back to the 1950's.

Batting tees have been used by major leaguers since the 1960's, but it was in the 1980's when batting tees gained enormous popularity. Though it cannot be substantiated, Don Mattingly of the New York Yankees has been given a lot of credit for the popularity of the batting tee in the majors. He would takes hundreds of swings every day. His success as a hitter, who worked very hard, spread quickly amongst other major leaguers. Other hitters and batting coaches became huge believers in its benefits. This trickled down to colleges, high schools, and most other amateur leagues.

The old fashioned type that has a heavy rubber base with a stationary outer neck and an adjustable inner neck for height is excellent. Although this type of tee is somewhat clumsy and heavy, I really love it. Today you have an incredible array of choices when it come to batting tees. There are some that have movable slots in the base. The more modern ones fold up for easy transport. As of late, I have been using one called the Advanced Skills Tee, which actually has an "L" attached to the main holder to reinforce a batter's compact swing. I encourage all coaches to have players begin on the batting tee early and often. During our batting practices, we set up a batting tee outside the fence so players can warm up.

Pickle Balls

I came across Pickle Balls from a coaching friend of mine in Texas a number of years ago. The game of pickle ball apparently was invented in the North West United States and the name is actually named after one of the owner's dogs. I'm not sure of the actual game itself, though I know it is played with a couple of paddles. As of late it has become popular with retired senior citizens in Florida and in Arizona. The ball is the key item. It looks very similar to a wiffle ball. The difference is the durability. I've tried using other plastic balls with my drills, but they crack fairly easily. The pickle ball is made out of thicker plastic. It is very durable and very rarely do they crack. However, if you use them below 45 degrees, they can crack. I swear by these balls and do tons of drills with them. Hitting off the batting tee or doing the toss drill into a fence works great with these balls. But make no mistake, if you get hit in the face with a hard hit pickle ball, you will feel it. So make sure if you are playing some fun games with your team using pickle balls, have your players wear their gloves.

Instant Screen or Portable Nets

As stubborn and frugal as I am on spending money for special equipment, the Instant Screen is a really good item. One year, one of my parents would bring his down to my practices at a field where there was no fence or wall. This was a welcome addition for the season as we were able to provide the right situation for our kids to get their repetitions with different drills. The brilliance of these portable screens is the portability as well as the ease of setting up and taking down. Someone with two left thumbs, as myself, is even able to do it.

"L" Screen

One year I was pitching batting practice and a line drive was hit with incredible speed right back to me. Not being able to get my glove up on time, the baseball hit me inside my left ribs, about 4-5" below my heart. I'm not sure if anything serious would have resulted if it had hit closer to my heart, but I had a black and blue mark for about 10 days like one you've never seen in your life. If I was using an "L Screen" it would not have touched me. This is a great item for leagues who are big on batting practice and might have a separate batting cage. The "L Screen" has protected me from numerous balls since that incident. You have to do a little trial and error when using the screen to know where you should start and end your pitching delivery. Most "L screen" are reversible, so both lefties and righties can use the same screen. Remember, on some of my batting practice drills, I move up on the mound to pitch closer to home plate. I never do this unless there is one of these screens. Even for the regular field, I encourage leagues to purchase an "L Screen." Some even have wheels to make them easy to move. Some taller coaches like to sit on a chair and throw from behind the "L Screen" because they believe the ball will travel back at them on the same plane as the height of a 11 or 12 year-old batter. Personally, I prefer to stand.

Chapter 5

Throwing & Fielding Techniques

"There have been only two geniuses in the world. Willie Mays and Willie Shakespeare."

~Tallulah Bankhead

Throwing Techniques

Coaches in youth baseball are guilty of a number of things. Players that cannot throw correctly is a constant problem year after year. It has always amazed me how many players get to the 10, 11, 12 year-old major league division in our Little League and cannot throw properly. Not only are children throwing improperly, they are also establishing bad habits, and by the time they are 12 years-old, trying to correct their throwing becomes very difficult. Leagues must teach players proper throwing techniques at the Tee Ball level.

Different stages of a child's throwing development have been identified by many doctors and psychologists. Youth baseball leagues, coaches, and parents should pay attention to these stages. The first stage that young kids go through is tossing a large ball, such as a kick ball, underhand with both hands. Youngsters will then progress to doing the same motion underhand, but this time with only one-hand. This stage usually occurs at ages 2-3 years-old. The children use their arms without moving the rest of their body, including the feet, which remain stationary. The third stage of throwing develops at the ages of 3-5. The children will fling the ball, usually not straight. The feet will either be stationary or will include a step of the foot on the same side as the throwing arm, which is wrong but absolutely normal in the development process. The fourth stage occurs around age 6 and showcases more of an overhand throw rather than an uncontrollable sidearm fling. There is more movement with the children's hips. In this stage, the children will still usually step with the foot on the same side as their throwing arm. It isn't until the next stage, around 6-7 years-old, the children will step with the opposite foot as their throwing arm, which is the correct motion. Stepping with the opposite foot will develop maximum body torque, which is movement or rotation.

Many Physical Education teachers will use the phrase "Step, turn and throw." Here are some tips teaching young kids how to throw. Make sure you break down the activity to a single action. If you are teaching throwing, do not combine this with catching, especially at your first Tee-Ball practice. In fact, it is probably best to divide the team in half, the six year-olds with one coach and the five year-olds with another coach. The basics should be practiced with the first year players, the skills reinforced a few practices in a row. A coach can also use different items to throw, not necessarily just a baseball. Don't be embarrassed or self-conscious as a coach to use items, such as bean bags, yarn balls, and even sticks. You are giving your kids a terrific teaching lesson that might eventually make a difference in throwing a ball correctly 5 or 6 years down the line when they are in a championship game. Remember, you are only working on throwing. It is best to throw the object against a wall or fence as long as it is not a hard object. Make sure the kids are spread out. Really spread out.

Whatever object the kids are throwing will wander in all directions. This is the age where you really have to recruit parents to help out. The more parents involved means the more bodies you'll have to help retrieve the thrown objects. This will translate into more repetitions for the kids. Encourage first time throwers to throw for distance and velocity. If they try to throw for accuracy at age 5, most kids (and their parents) will get frustrated. What generally happens is many of the basic fundamentals are overlooked and the coaches and/or the parents are intent on their kids hitting and fielding like future Hall of Famers, even at age five or six.**1**

When kids get to the majors (10, 11 & 12 year-olds), and if they are throwing wrong, they are usually throwing with a stiff arm, which means they are not bringing their arm all the way back and not leading with their elbow near the point of release. I try expressing to players who do not throw correctly to think of their arms like a rubber band, or like the old cartoon character, Gumbee, with a lot of elongation. I try to correct a lot of problematic throwing motions using only a few techniques.

I will bring in a football or even a basketball to practice. Some young players seem to master the motion of throwing a bigger object a little easier. With the bigger object, they realize they must bring their arm all the way back to make an effective throw and follow through.

After fielding the ball, the player must plant his back foot and step toward his target with the front foot. The follow through is just as important as the throw itself.

Notice both players here are doing the same drill. Look at their back legs upon release of the ball. Both follow throughs are correct because they use their whole body. Many young players will throw incorrectly by only using their arms exclusively, not including the lower body or legs.

Coaches should practice throwing without any balls so the players can just focus on their movements.

Using the basketball has worked with some players who do not bring their arm all the way back. The tendency to throw just from one's ear seems to be automatically corrected when using a larger ball. Stepping toward the target is also naturally corrected with the bigger object.

Fielding Techniques

Fielding is a skill that can be improved with a lot of repetition. At the early stage, I want to urge coaches to make catching a ball a progression, using practice balls and other props leading up to the hardball. Coaches should start with the most basics and work their way up depending on how individuals on the team respond. Remember, you will have kids on your team of the same age group at different levels in their development. The different levels of development in catching and fielding happen for a number of reasons. Part of it has to do with a natural athletic ability. Also, if the parents spend time playing catch with their child this can help further the development. The biggest advantage I see kids have is if they have an older brother or sister who is athletic and spend endless hours playing ball at home. Many times a combination of the younger sibling observing as well as participating will help that child progress faster than other kids in the league.

Like throwing, there are different stages in the development of youth players being capable of catching a ball. In the early stages of children's development, they will catch large balls, such as kick balls or large plastic balls, by cradling the ball against their body when the ball comes to them. The stage where a child is comfortable catching a ball with their hands can come as late as 8 or 9 years-old. Remember, kids develop at different paces. I've had kids in Tee-Ball that looked like they would never excel on the ball field, but with a spurt in the development in their motor skills, coupled with practicing, they went on to excel in baseball. Youth coaches should explain to frustrated parents the development process of their child's catching and throwing skills. I've seen parents visibly upset when other players excel at early ages and their son or daughter appears to remain behind. This is especially true of parents who are ex-ball players and have very high hopes for their kids. This is a great topic to bring up at the "parents meeting." I remember my oldest son was well ahead of his peers at 9 or 10 years-old. This is probably because all we did was practice baseball together for hours. Probably too much.

He was noticeably better, but by the time he was 13 or 14, the other players had quickly caught up in skill level. I see this happen over and over again.

In order to have youth players develop confidence, we must put them in the best position to be successful at a very young age. I've seen Tee-Ball coaches line up their kids during their first practice and begin throwing fly balls with a regular hard ball. The easiest way to turn youngsters off from an activity is to get them hurt. From that point forward, they will have tremendous fear whenever participating in the same activity in the future. I suggest parents try to eliminate as much fear for the youth athletes as they possibly can with simple drills that encourage success and fun. Use soft covered balls and even larger-sized balls. Make their initial objectives to make contact with the ball (or object) and not necessarily catch it before progressing to activities that stress learning fundamentals and techniques.

A perfect example of this is when teaching young players how to catch fly balls. One of the best techniques I've found is to take one of those Scatch sets made with velcro. If you have never seen one, the set is comprised of two paddles about 10" in diameter with a velcro face. There is a strap on the back going from one side to the other so participants can squeeze their hand in it and control where the direction of the paddle goes. The ball itself also has velcro covering the whole ball and will almost automatically stick to the surface of the paddle upon contact. Most young kids are familiar with this and love using it when learning to catch fly balls. I use Scatch sets to introduce catching fly balls to players coming from our minor division who are not used to catching deep fly balls. I highly recommend this to other coaches and parents. I hit the Scatch ball high in the air with a tennis racquet. The player has to secure it on the Scatch (or velcro) paddle. This works and has been successful for me, especially when I get players coming up from the minor leagues (8 or 9 years-old) and find they have not been drilled or are nervous about getting under a fly ball on our major league field. The one thing about using this technique to catch fly balls is that it will never be easier for these young players. But isn't that our goal? Progression teaching is breaking a skill down to its most basic component and practicing it with easier to handle props at a slower pace before working up to the natural skill progression.

In any fielding drill or technique, coaches and parents should put their creative hats on to give kids the best chance to feel confident fielding a hardball. Whether it is throwing a ball and fielding it against a wall or catching a ball rolling off a roof, be creative!

Ready Position

Coaches need to teach their youth fielders the correct 'ready' position as the pitch is being delivered to home plate. This "ready position" is the foundation to sound fielding fundamentals. Players who are in the proper fielding position will have the best chance for recording an out. In the proper ready position, the fielders' feet should be a little more than shoulder length apart as they bend at the knees, not the waist. Players don't want to bend too low and become off balance. The players' hands should be in front of their body, between their knees, and relaxed with the palms up or facing one another. One common mistake is for the fielders to have the glove almost on the ground. This position will cause tension. On the youth level one of the biggest mistakes I see is players getting into the ready position too soon. It is imperative that youth players are relaxed as they can be both in fielding and in hitting. Asking a 10, 11, or 12 year-old youth player to stay in the ready position for up to 15 seconds in 85 degree heat with a lot of humidity is difficult. Players can and should relax and get into the ready position when the pitcher goes into the wind-up. This is extremely important on the youth level because it is somewhat difficult for a young player to stay in one position for an extended period of time without becoming unfocused and off balance. When in the ready position, fielders should place their weight on the inside balls of the feet so they could push off and move in either direction. Make sure players do not rest their elbows or forearms on their thighs.

As the pitcher gets into the wind-up, the player here is getting into the ready position.

The player has the best chance of making the play because from the ready position he is already in a position to easily transition into fielding a ball. When players get older, their coaches will tweak the ready position.

High school coaches will teach that the pivot foot should be slightly behind the striding foot (the pivot foot is the glove-hand foot). On the youth level, don't worry too much about being this precise. Get the players to go from being relaxed to a position where he is ready to field the baseball, which is the main goal.

Ground Balls

Players should be taught at the earliest possible age that they must move to where the ball is and try to field the baseball in the middle of their body. Young players have a tendency to reach for the ground ball rather than moving their feet to where the ball is. Some might look at this as laziness, but it is only natural to reach for the baseball without using the feet. Another mistake young players make (and even professional major league players) is they lift their head up before the ball is in the glove. The players need to follow the baseball into their glove. In order to field ground balls properly, they should begin by getting into the "ready position." I teach infielders (and outfielders) to relax and get into the ready position only when the pitcher begins his windup. Whether a young player is batting or in the field, it is hard to hold a sustained period of concentration.

Another concept I preach at my coaching clinics as well as to my team is that a young player's measurement of success should not necessarily be catching the ground ball, but instead just stopping it and keeping it in front of the body. Too many young athletes are intent on making the catch. Getting them to understand that stopping the ball and keeping it in front of them can still yield a very good chance of making the play. I intertwine this in some drills you will see later on. The concept of keeping the ball in front of you and not necessarily catching it cleanly becomes even more important when players begin playing on the big field (90' bases) where they have more time to make the play. Coaches should begin teaching this positive habit at an early age.

When actually fielding of ground balls, fielders start in the ready position. If a ground ball is hit to them, they move to where the ball is so that they are square to the ball. They follow the ball into the glove (with two hands) keeping their head down the whole time. Upon securing the baseball, the fielders should then bring their glove up with both hands toward their chest. When starting the throw, the fielders will step with the opposite foot of their throwing hand and release the ball at the correct point and follow through.

There is an endless amount of ground ball fielding drills. I try to invent new ones every season. The repetition will provide muscle memory where the youth player will start to almost be automatic with the fundamentals. Keep in mind the player will do the same bad techniques over and over again unless we coaches can correct them. And the younger we are able to correct the techniques, the better chance we will be putting the player in a position to be successful.

There are many issues when fielding ground balls. Coaches and parents should only concentrate on a few. First of all, players must get into the habit of bending their knees when in the "ready position." Another big mistake youth player make is not catching the ground ball in front of them. They end up catching it under their body between their legs and way too deep. This is wrong. By doing this, the player is making it harder to watch the baseball go into the glove. Also the player must make sure the glove is open all the way. This gives the player the most surface area to catch the baseball. If you look at all the pictures, with the glove in front of the body, there is an imaginary triangle going from both feet to the glove. Practicing both stationary drills and drills that get the fielder moving laterally to each side is important.

Fly Balls

It is extremely difficult for youth players to catch a fly ball the first time they play the outfield. At the very young level, I would again encourage coaches and parents to use a progression method and work the young player's way up to catching a hardball. You want your player to feel comfortable catching a fly ball and not putting his glove in front of his face as a means of protection rather than the skill of catching. There are many creative techniques I've used over the years to have players develop confidence and even be aggressive when a fly ball is hit in their direction. I mentioned using a Scatch, and this technique works well. I also will hit a tennis ball, soft-covered ball, or sponge ball, with a racquet high in the air. You want to show the ball to your players before running any drills to alleviate any fears they might have of getting hurt if they don't catch the ball with the glove. Here is a great teaching tip. Make the goal of catching the pop-up attainable for youngsters. Tell them just to make contact with the ball with their gloves. They do not necessarily have to catch it. This will take pressure off them. We want to build on their successes. The more they succeed at a basic skill the quicker we can challenge them with a tougher one.

Like fielding ground balls, players should also begin in the ready position before catching a fly ball. As I mentioned with ground balls, young players have a very limited attention span. We do not want them standing like a statue concentrating for an extended period of time. Have them get into the ready position when the pitcher begins the wind-up. When a fly ball is hit in their direction, the correct first step should be back until they have judged the ball and know where it is going. If a ball is hit over the center fielder's head, the fielder should turn his shoulder toward where he thinks the baseball is going and run in that direction. Many times a youth player will back peddle with his shoulders square toward home plate. I don't like this technique because the outfielder is not moving fast enough. More often than not, the baseball will go over his head. It is not the end of the world if players are comfortable only with the backpedal at first as long as the player catches the baseball. Catching a fly ball takes concentration and practice. Players should keep their eye on the baseball and follow the ball into their glove about chin high. Encourage the players to catch with two hands, especially if they are stationary and camping under the ball. Do not insist on catching a fly ball with two hands. I differ from other coaches in that I think we overdo the expression, "catch it with two hands." The players should catch the baseball anyway they can. For example, if a player is running full speed to catch a baseball with both arms extended, the arms will not be equidistant to the ball while on the move. As a coach, I want my player to make the catch anyway necessary. I don't want my players thinking on a tough running catch that they have to make the play with two hands. I really think the "two hand" catch is overrated, but teach your player what you think is the best way they will make the catch.

When catching a fly ball, players should do so the most comfortable way. It is important for coaches to have their players practice catching the baseball with two hands and with one hand.

Chapter 6

Position Play

"This is a game to be savored, not gulped. There's time to discuss everything between pitches or between innings."

~Bill Veeck

Position Play - First Base

When showing each of the nine positions and how to play them, nine whole books can be written. The first baseman's importance to the infield cannot be overlooked just for the fact that he is responsible for the majority of the putouts on ground balls hit in the infield. Most players who play first use the specific first baseman's glove. Lately I've noticed many players have more than one glove if they play first or catcher and other positions. I have my first baseman play four to six feet off the base. You can adjust this depending on the particular situation, such as defending against a lefty hitter or a hard throwing pitcher. When a ball is hit to one of the infielders, the first baseman should square his shoulders to the position where the throw is coming from. If the first baseman throws with his right hand, then his right foot should remain on the inside of the bag as he stretches out with the opposite foot and arm to meet the ball. It is the opposite for lefties. When teaching young players, I do not overemphasize having the foot on the inside of first base. I try to teach the first baseman to keep his foot on the front half of the base, at the very least. I don't like to over-complicate the footwork with youth players by trying to explain the exact location of where the foot should be. Besides, if the league is using the extended first base, the location of the foot is not much of an issue.

Many first baseman stretch for the ball before the ball is thrown to them, which might not be the best way to act as a receiver because they will be off-balance if and when they have to readjust their stretch to compensate for a not so accurate throw. First baseman must be comfortable stretching to catch low balls, high balls, and even scooping balls out of the dirt. An important fundamental to playing first base is knowing when to come off the bag to catch an errant throw. This can be hard to teach to some players because many think their foot is cemented to the base. Coaches have to teach players that the number one goal is to catch the baseball. Leaving the bag may result in the batter reaching safely, however, it could also prevent the runner from taking an extra base on a wild throw. If the throw takes the first baseman down the first base line, he could apply the tag to the runner before he reaches the bag. This play is extremely important, especially in youth baseball, and should be practiced.

First baseman also must know when to leave their position to field ground balls between first base and the second baseman. Communication is key, as it is for every other position. Practicing repetitions, such as a ground balls to the right side of the infield, will help first baseman get comfortable and proficient leaving their position near the bag.

Another responsibility for the first baseman that my team practices has to do with a rundown between third base and home plate. The first baseman must come down the line to cover home during these rundowns if the catcher is already engaged in the play. On multiple throws, the catcher may be out of position as he chases the baserunner back to third, leaving home plate uncovered. The same occurs when the baserunner takes a very aggressive lead between pitches. If the catcher runs up the line to move the baserunner back to third base, the first baseman again must cover home. Some coaches will have the pitcher cover home if the catcher begins to move up the 3rd base line. I prefer the first baseman covering home. This is another one of those things that you need to go over with your first baseman during practice and reinforce during the games.

On occasion, I have the first baseman become the cut off man on a throw from the outfield. I pick and choose how I will use the first baseman for cutoffs depending on the skill level of my team. I have used first baseman take the cut-off at the top edge of the pitcher's mound on a ball hit to the outfield with runners on base.

Another skill I began practicing with first baseman is tracking down and going after foul balls just outside the foul line. It sounds a lot easier than it is, but when going after a foul ball the first baseman may incur a number of obstacles. During practice I like to put out obstacles like bats, bags, and gloves in foul territory for the first baseman to navigate around while tracking the ball. I only use props the player won't get hurt with. If there is a fence nearby, it is especially important to have the first baseman, and everyone else on the team for that matter, practice running up against the fence to catch a fly ball. I've seen players go after pop ups in foul territory then give up on them only to have them fall within two feet of the fence. This can drive a coach crazy.

The first baseman has the correct foot on the bag. In this case, for a right handed throwing player, his right foot is on the bag. He also stretches toward the position where the ball is coming from.

The first baseman must be coached that his main goal is to catch or stop the baseball. If this requires him to come off the base, then he must do so. Coaches should give each player a chance to practice at first base. Each player should practice catching accurate throws as well as throws that are not accurate, such as wide of the bag or even in the dirt. As with teaching ground balls, emphasize to first baseman that stopping errant throws any way possible is the main priority and not being overly hung up on making the out at all costs. Again, the concept of the fielder acting like a hockey goalie and making stops is important for young players to recognize.

When there is a baserunner, the first baseman can play either behind or in front of the runner. Coaches should have their first baseman practice both, taking ground balls in both positions. Some players will be distracted while trying to field a ground ball if a baserunner is running in front of the play. Playing in front of the runner limits the area to cover. A player's reaction time must also be ultra quick. Playing in front of the runner helps take away the bunt to first base. I usually prefer my first baseman play behind the baserunner because I know my team would have practiced balls hit to the right side on the infield.

Position Play - 2nd Base

The second baseman has numerous responsibilities, such as covering the base and backing up. Many times in youth baseball, you don't need a player there who has a really strong arm. I prefer my middle infielders (second & shortstop) to be average or above average in size. This is hard to do if your team has limited talent, but let me explain my reasoning. With runners on base, I love to give my smaller and quicker players a lot of steal signs because they are harder to tag (or find) by the defensive team when sliding. Conversely, when coaching defense, I like my middle infielders (shortstop and second baseman) to have good size so the catcher has a nice target to throw to when runners are trying to stealing second.

On my teams I have the shortstop cover second on the steal. The second baseman must back him up on the throw. Some coaches will have the second baseman cover the steal when a right handed batter is up and the shortstop when a left handed batter is up. The reason for this is the vision of the catcher is less obstructed. I prefer to simplify as much as I can with young players, so designate one fielder, the shortstop, to cover second on 90% of the steals. Part of the responsibility of any coach on any youth sports team is too keep it as simple as possible for kids to follow as far as instructions go. I do have one specific defensive play where the second baseman takes the throw on a steal of second when there are runners on 1st and 3rd and we have a play to throw the ball through to get the out.

The key in all youth baseball is not avoiding mistakes, which all teams do every game, but it is backing up and covering up for those mistakes. I teach communication to my team. When a player on the opposing team reaches first base, it is the responsibility of my shortstop and second baseman to communicate with each other before the next pitch. The dialogue goes something like this:

Shortstop to the second baseman: "Johnny, I got the steal."

Second baseman response to shortstop: "Danny, I'll back you up."

These players have to communicate exactly this way. Do they have to say the other's name? Absolutely. Everyone on my team will practice both positions and repeat this dialogue. You may ask why. Saying the teammate's name ensures everybody knows who everybody is talking to. Saying the name exaggerates the communication and stresses the importance of it.

The second baseman also must be ready to cover first base on a ball hit to his side (right side) of the infield that is fielded by the first baseman. This can be tough because sometimes the second baseman and first baseman either will both go for the ball or both will start to go and stop, figuring the other is fielding it. This takes practice and drilling.

When there are players on base, the second baseman must run to back up the catcher's toss back to the pitcher after every pitch. This takes a lot of work and hustle, but the players must realize this is part of being a team. When I coach baserunning, I teach my players to follow the ball back to the pitcher and get ready to run on a bad throw back to the pitcher. Teams must try to take advantage of every single opportunity that occurs from the first pitch of the game to the last.

Surprisingly, one of the first things I tell my second baseman, and my other infielders, is to not get overly concerned with getting the double play on a ground ball with a player on first base. Our immediate goal is to get the lead runner. This is not to say that my team never makes double plays. We do on occasion. But in youth baseball, as well as all levels, I've seen fielding plays blown because the defensive team is trying to hurry to "turn two " but ends up getting no one out. Like everything else I teach in youth baseball, there is a progression, and the immediate goal of the second baseman with a runner on first should be to get the runner out at second.

Another responsibility I teach to the second baseman when there are runners on second and third or the bases are loaded and there is a wild pitch or a passed ball is to have the second baseman come to the base of the mound to stop a potential overthrow while the pitcher covers home to tag the runner trying to score from third base. Many times when the pitcher runs in to cover home to receive a toss from the catcher, who had to run to the backstop to get the wild pitch or passed ball, the pitcher will misplay the ball or the catcher will throw it wildly to him, and more than one run will score. I teach my second baseman to go to the base of the pitcher's mound to back up the catcher's toss to the pitcher covering home in case that toss is an errant one. Having the second baseman do this has saved me runs every year I have coached. You have to go over this in practice and reinforce this during the game when it comes up. I consider this one of the most important responsibilities of the second baseman.

There are many issues when fielding ground balls. When a ball is hit on the ground to right field, the second baseman must line himself up with the base and retrieve the throw or relay. He should always turn to his glove-side ready to throw the ball in case the runner tries to stretch his hit into a double. On a ball hit into the outfield to left field, the shortstop will go out to retrieve the relay and the second baseman will cover the base. Coaches must emphasize to the second baseman, as well as all infielders, that the further a ball is hit, the further the player must go into the outfield to retrieve the relay throw. Too many times I've noticed the infielder will overplay his position, staying closer to the infield on deep balls that necessary. The infielder should instead be closer to the outfielder because the first goal is to reach the infielder on a clean throw.

On a steal I always have the shortstop covering the base. The second baseman's responsibility is to back up the throw. And on an overthrow, the second baseman should not necessarily catch the baseball but instead keep the baseball in front of him. The second baseman should not be too close to the shortstop as a backup because an errant throw will go past both players. I like my backups not to play exactly behind the fielder they are backing up, but instead to remain on the side so they can follow the throw and get into a position to field the ball without being screened.

One of the most frustrating parts of coaching is on overthrows that are not backed up. When this happens, the team is literally giving up extra bases. The second baseman's backup at the base of the mound on a wild pitch or passed ball is extremely important. I always pick my second baseman as the player to back up the throw coming to the base of the pitcher's mound while the pitcher is covering home. We practice this with different players at second and it is important to reinforce this during games.

Position Play - Shortstop

Many times the shortstop is one of the best athlete on the team. In youth baseball, the shortstop is also probably a pitcher on the team. The shortstop is the captain of the infield. I expect my shortstop to be a team leader, which is a challenge in youth baseball. The shortstop will almost always cover second base on a steal. It is important for the shortstop and every infielder to understand that on a steal, I instruct my catcher to throw the ball to the base and not the fielder. This is challenging the shortstop to get to the base quickly. In practice, I condition the shortstop to hustle to the base by having him play deep and closer to third than normal. He must still get to the base as the throw gets to the bag. If you practice this a few times, the catcher will get used to throwing the ball to the base and the fielder will learn to move quickly to the base to cover the throw.

When the shortstop covers second on the steal, it is important to teach him not to leave his position too soon. You don't want to have too big a hole between second and third because the shortstop is covering second on the steal. Many times I've seen players on the youth level anticipate too quickly even though the runner can't leave until the baseball crosses home.

I also like to have my shortstop be of the most vocal players on the field. The shortstop should shout out the number of outs when a new batter is up, once to the rest of the infield and once to the outfield.

With a baserunner on first base and the ball hit to the shortstop, the player must learn to either run over and step on the base himself or toss it to the second baseman covering the bag. This is an underrated skill that can be taught only through practice and experience. It is always better in youth baseball to limit the number of throws, whether it is a rundown or a simple force play. Always encourage both your shortstop and second baseman to make the play themselves, only if they are sure they can beat the baserunner. Players know their own speed, but should practice an unassisted force play with baserunners of all speeds just so they get a feel for the situation.

If there is a baserunner on first and a ball is hit to the shortstop, he must know whether to throw the ball overhand to the second baseman or toss it underhand. Too many times when there is a force out and the player throws the ball overhand, it is very tough for the person receiving the throw to handle it. This is one of the reasons why I believe coaches must have all their infielders practice tossing the baseball underhand at close range to the fielder covering the base.

If the ball is hit to the third baseman, the shortstop should get over there to back up the play. This is harder than it sounds but teaching the shortstop as well as the rest of the team to react to balls hit to the fielder near him is good basic baseball fundamentals.

A pop fly behind the third baseman, as well as ones in foul territory along the third base line, can be the shortstop's ball, although whoever calls for it is the one who should catch it. Because the player at this position is usually one of the most talented, I like to have my shortstop call for a lot of pop flies in the third base, shortstop, pitching, and second base area.

The shortstop must know when to go into the outfield as the relay man on a base hit. If the ball gets into the left field, he should sprint out onto the grass, line himself up with second base at a reachable distance from the outfielder, and be ready to receive the throw.

Bunting is a big part of youth baseball. When there are players on base, the shortstop must communicate to the third baseman and the second baseman what is the plan of action on a bunted ball. The options must be practiced. For instance, with a baserunner on second and less than two outs, if the batter bunts, does the shortstop rotate to third while the third baseman is fielding the bunt or does the third baseman stay at his position with the intention of having the pitcher field the bunted ball?

On the youth level, many coaches refuse to play left handed throwers at any infield position besides first base. I try to urge coaches to let lefties play all positions as long as they are skilled enough to make plays. When these ball players get older, these left handed players probably will not be given the chance to play other infield positions. So give them the chance on the youth level.

The shortstop can be the key to the success of any baseball team. Even on the youth level, sometimes I am amazed at the talented plays some shortstops make.

Many coaches will have different fielders covering second base on a steal depending on if the batter is a lefty or righty. I am trying to keep things as simple as possible, giving young players the least amount of things to think about. I have decided that my shortstop will cover the steal at second base at all times. The catcher is instructed to throw to the base itself and not the fielder.

Communication and reinforcing the number of outs cannot be over emphasized. I have my shortstop yelling the number of outs to the infielders and then turning around to tell the outfielders.

I know some coaches are reluctant to play a left hander at any infield position but first base. I cannot disagree more. At the youth level, this is where you want to give all players a chance to play positions they wouldn't normally play when they get to high school.

Position Play - Third Base

When I was ten years-old at summer camp, I played third base for our bunk softball team. I was a lefty with no real speed, but better than average reflexes for my age. My counselor taught me, as a third baseman, to be a moving vacuum cleaner. He taught me to go for everything, such as trying to cut off all balls, even ones going toward the shortstop. And on the ones I couldn't get that the shortstop could, after making the attempt, I was taught to stay low so the shortstop doesn't hit me with the ball on the throw. He would drill me and I would come out of every practice and game with my uniform dirty. What this counselor taught me stuck with me through the years. I teach third base the same way in youth baseball. I always play the shortstop a little deeper than the third baseman and instruct the third baseman to go for any balls he can. Remember, his momentum is moving toward the first base side of the infield, so in some instances, he has a better chance of making the play than the shortstop.

Third base, or what many people call the "hot corner," can possibly be the position with the most amount of responsibility. People describe third base as a reaction position where fielders don't even have time to think but can only react when the ball comes off the bat. Some players will naturally play third base better than they might play other positions because of it being based on a combination of reflexes and skill.

The theory I preach to all my position players, which involves keeping the ball in front of them either by catching it or knocking it down has never been more important than at third base. The ball gets to the third baseman (and the pitcher) quicker than any other infield position. He has the benefit of throwing the baserunner out if he knocks the ball down and keeps it in front of him. Coaches must coach youth players not to give up on a play just because they don't catch the ball cleanly. And if they do knock the ball down, they should hurry but not over hurry their throws. If they do hurry their throw too much, a wild throw can turn a single into an error with the player ending up at third base or even scoring.

Since the ball can get to the third baseman quickly, it's important for him to get a little lower to the ground than the shortstop or second baseman when getting into the ready position. He must keep his glove lower as well. The third baseman must be ready for a hot shot hit right at his feet. It is easier and quicker for a player to bring the glove up than it is to drop it down. And with the hands coming up, the fielder still has his body to block the ball.

Fielding bunts is one of the biggest responsibilities for third baseman. As soon as the third baseman recognizes the batter getting into the bunting position, he should be charging toward home plate. Think of it. A batter lays a bunt down toward third base. On a good bunt, the ball moves slower the closer it gets to the fielder. He charges the ball with his momentum going toward home plate. He fields the ball and must be able to control it cleanly. One small bobble will usually result in the runner being safe. Once having control of the ball, he must stop his momentum, plant his foot, and make an accurate throw to first base. Even if the third baseman does all this correctly, there is still a good chance the batter will arrive safely at first. Coaches must practice bunting on the offensive and defensive side. Many coaches in All Stars will put their best fielder at third base. This is done because of the high frequency of bunting in competitive youth baseball. I like to drill my team and see their reaction when the batter squares to bunt. The quicker the third baseman reacts running in when he recognizes a bunt, the better chance he has to make the play. The third baseman must also be aware of the batter pulling his bat back to swing away. If this happens, he should quickly stop where he is and get in the proper ready position.

One of the tactics I use at practice early in the season is for the third baseman to concentrate on throwing accurately to first base and not necessarily reaching on a fly. Some players will not be able to reach first early in the season. The ball getting there on one or two bounces is fine. This is especially true with the younger and smaller players.

The third baseman should go after every foul ball to the right side of the foul line. This is something that is never really practiced by many coaches, but should be with everyone on the team. Dealing with obstacles like a fence, dugout, and bats on the ground is tough to deal with without practicing first.

Because third base is the closest position to the batter, coaches should realize that unless the person playing third has some natural skills, there is some danger with the fielder getting hurt. There is always a chance any skilled fielder may not have fast enough reflexes on a hard hit ball by a kid who is big, but coaches need to use their common sense when choosing a third baseman.

The third baseman must react quickly when the batter gets into the bunting position. When the batter does get in the bunting position, the third baseman must rush toward home plate all the while getting ready to field the bunted ball. If there are runners on base, it must be determined beforehand how to play the bunt.

One of the most challenging aspect of any infield position, including third, is being able to ready yourself to field the baseball before covering the base on a steal.

The throw to third base on a steal can be tough for some young players because of the different skills involved. The third baseman must wait for the throw while also knowing the baserunner is coming in hard and probably will slide. Too many times, a young third baseman will anxiously take his eye off the ball too quickly, resulting in dropping the ball while trying to make the tag. Coaches need to practice this situation with the third baseman, as well as other infield positions. Coaches need to constantly reinforce and practice drills with baserunners so their team knows how to cover each and every base. Defensive drills involving baserunners include force play, wild pitch, steal, and tagging up. And coaches should rotate players at different positions.

Position Play - Outfield

In today's day and age, everyone, including kids, like things faster, whether it is the speed of the internet or the speed of a sport. Baseball has been losing kids for a number of years because it has become known as a slow moving game. Coaches must share some of the blame for this dilemma. Coaches in youth baseball have a chance to make every position as exciting as possible. In youth baseball, many times players think it a punishment if they are asked to play the outfield. Coaches need to instill the concept that every position on the fielding team is important to the overall success of the team. And as coaches, we need to teach players to move when the ball is hit. In addition, coaches should always try to involve the outfielders in as many plays as possible. Young players can very easily go into a trance standing alone in the outfield. I am also constantly telling my players that the outfield is more important than the infield just for the fact that if a ball gets by an infielder, it is a single but if it gets by an outfielder, it can be anything from a double to a four base hit. The concept that I repeat over and over again is that whether the player is in the infield or outfield, stopping the baseball and keeping it in front of one's body, and not necessarily catching the ball cleanly, is effective and should be reinforced to youth players over and over again. Please keep in mind that when practicing position play, it is important to practice the mistakes that occur in games. Always practice the correct methods, but coaches should also go through game-like situations practicing overthrows, errors, and wrong base coverage.

Left Field

I teach my left fielders to back up every force play at second base with the throw coming from the second baseman to the shortstop covering the base. The left fielder must learn to hustle, not only in toward the infield, but also learn to place himself at the correct angle to anticipate an overthrow. The left fielder is also very important when there is a runner on second base. On a steal attempt to third, the outfielder must back up the throw. I am particular about how I teach this. I do not want my left fielder to take an angle right toward third base. I coach my left fielder to go to the foul line and run up along the foul line to backup the throw from the catcher without being too close to the infield. I also usually have my left fielder back up the center fielder on balls hit that the center fielder comes in on and might dive for.

Center Field

I have always instructed my center fielder to play the position like he is the only fielder in the outfield. The center fielder should be on the move on any ball hit to the outfield. If there is a fly ball between two outfielders I want my center fielder calling for the ball because he is usually the better athlete. Backing up the throw to second on a steal is an important responsibility. Again, the player should not come in too close so the thrown ball from the catcher will go past both the infielder and center fielder backing up the throw.

Right Field

Of the nine positions on a baseball field, right field has always been treated like a joke, when instead the coach should actually convince the team of its importance. The right fielder backs up the throw to second base on a force from the shortstop. The right fielder must hustle to get into position and be at the correct angle should an overthrow occur. Another responsibility of the right fielder happens when the batter bunts. The right fielder must quickly go to back up the area behind the first baseman. Depending on who fields the bunt (catcher, third baseman, or pitcher) the right fielder should take the appropriate angle. Backing up on this play has helped my team, at least once a year, keep a bunt single from becoming a three base hit because of an overthrow. I always teach my outfielders not to be a spectator and help out whenever and wherever they can. This includes rundowns. On rundowns, I want all my outfielders closing in on the infield to anticipate an overthrow. We will practice this on rundowns. I will tell one of my infielders (in secret) before the drill to overthrow the ball on purpose. Outfielders should definitely move closer to the infield on rundowns to protect against a possible overthrow that might end up in the outfield. Knocking the ball down or cutting it off in the gap by taking the correct angle should be reinforced by drills and by reminding them verbally. I will also make my team aware of how grass that hasn't been cut or is wet will affect a moving ball in the outfield.

With no one on base and if the batter squares to bunt, I always have my right fielder get in the position to back up first base in case of an overthrow. Of course the right fielder must adjust his angle depending on who throws the ball and where it is thrown from. The left fielder must likewise back up the third baseman when a player steals third base.

One of the hardest things to do with youth players is to teach them to communicate in the field. This is the case in both the infield and the outfield. I prefer the center fielder call for most catches that he is able to make.

One of the most important responsibilities of the center fielder is to back up the throw to second on a steal. Practicing to back up an overthrow is the best way to teach it. Most coaches wait until game situations before telling the backup player what to do. Players must be taught not to back up the play too close. As mentioned a few times already, reinforce to all players on backups and ground balls that stopping the baseball in most cases is just as good as catching the baseball.

Position Play-Pitcher

No baseball coach would take the field with only eight fielders. Not having pitchers practice fielding may sometimes make it seem like the defense is playing shorthanded. I see multiple mistakes every year by pitchers not making plays in the field that could have been avoided with just a little bit of practice. I've seen balls hit right back to the pitcher, who fields the ball off balance. A sure out becomes a hit or even a two base error. I've also seen balls bunted back to the pitcher, who either cannot make the fielding play or throws the ball away. The pitcher also tends to automatically throw a fielded ball to first base instead of trying to get the lead runner out. I see pitchers making plays and throwing the ball away when their body momentum would make it easier for them to just run and tag the base themselves. These and other situations are more common than uncommon for many youth baseball teams and can be avoided by practicing situations where the pitcher fields as well. But for some reason, baseball coaches at all levels do not practice pitchers fielding.

It is extremely important that the pitcher realizes he has another responsibility besides pitching; field baseballs hit near him. Many youth players who pitch are focused on their pitching and not on the fielding part of the game. After the delivery, the pitcher should be in a position to field the ball. Proper pitching mechanics should force a pitcher to be squared to home plate in a ready balanced fielding position. Being ready to field a hit baseball will put pitchers in a position to catch either a ground ball or a line drive hit right back to them.

As a basic fielding drill, coaches should have their pitchers throw to the catcher. As the ball crosses home plate, the coach hits a ground ball back to the pitcher to field and throw to first base. Not only will this improve a pitcher's fielding techniques, it will also promote good pitching mechanics, forcing the pitcher to follow through so he is ready to field the ball. Many times, with runners on base, a ball is hit back to the pitcher, and he will automatically throw to first base when he could have thrown out the lead runner. If there is a runner on second base, and a ball is hit back to the pitcher, the pitcher should check the runner to see if he has a play. If the base runner has taken off for third base, the pitcher can throw the ball to the third baseman or run and tag him out on his way to third. The pitcher can also run the baserunner back to the base he came from. Another play I've seen occurs when the bases are loaded and there are two outs. Most coaches will tell their infield the play is automatically to first. I do the same thing but tell my pitcher that if it is a slow grounder hit back to him, go home with it. We practice this play. When the bases are loaded, no matter how many outs, if it is a slow grounder to the pitcher and his momentum is going toward home, that is where he should make the play, usually with an underhand toss. Many times the pitcher can easily outrun the baserunner at third base and touch home himself. These are very common plays in games but are rarely practiced.

Another important, yet overlooked aspect of the pitcher's position is to cover first base on any ball hit to the right side of the infield, particularly to first base. Sometimes the first baseman has to come off the line to field a ball. If he doesn't have time to beat the runner to the base, the pitcher must be taught to explode off the mound and run directly toward a spot about 5-8 feet before first base on the baseline then change direction and run up the baseline at first base to beat out the runner and receive a toss from the first baseman. The pitcher should step on the inside of the bag. Coaches should encourage pitchers to cover first base on all balls hit to the right side, even if the first baseman can call him off and take the out himself. This is a very tough task for young players, but I find if you practice "right side" situations enough, you will get more outs than if you did not practice it. You also want to encourage communication amongst all the infielders on a play when 2 or 3 can converge on the ball.

Covering home after a wild pitch or passed ball is another fielding skill that youth pitchers need to practice. I always make sure every pitcher and catcher on my team practices this play. Having the pitcher cover home and receive a toss from the catcher and apply the tag to the base runner is a lot tougher than it looks. It amazes me how many players never see this play until it happens in a game. What usually happens is the pitcher is looking back and forth at the catcher and the baserunner. Upon converging at home plate, the pitcher will miss the ball because he is looking at the baserunner just as the ball is coming from the catcher. In these, and other fielding situations for the pitcher, minimal practice will reap benefits just with the exposure of the play.

In this shot, the pitcher just released the baseball. He makes sure he is ready to field the baseball. Notice how the legs are square to home plate just a little more than shoulder width apart. Many times a pitcher who is off balance is not ready to make the play on a ball hit back to him. In addition, on a bunt in front of home plate the pitcher's chances of making a play on the ball are diminished because he must reestablish his balance before running off the mound to retrieve the ball. This extra step will hinder him from making the play most of the time. Practice having pitchers knock the ball down, pick it up, and make the play.

A mistake that comes up a lot occurs when there are players on base and the ball is hit back to the pitcher. He automatically throws it to first base. I was in a game where there was a runner on second with one out and the ball was hit back to the pitcher toward the right side of the mound. Even though the baserunner took off to third on contact, the pitcher did not even look at the baserunner going to third and threw the batter out at first. When there are players on base, all fielders must ask themselves, "What I am I going to do if the ball is hit to me?" In this photo, the pitcher fields the baseball and correctly gets the lead runner.

When the bases are loaded with two outs, normally you think the third out must be made at first base on any ball hit to the pitcher. On a slow roller to the pitcher with his momentum moving toward home plate, I have him toss the ball underhand to the catcher who steps on home for the force. This makes more sense than having the pitcher stop short, turn, and make a longer throw. I also have the pitcher field the ball and step on home plate himself.

Position Play-The Catching Position

I find that youth players who play catcher either love it or hate it. Very few are in the middle. When you do get your catcher, I feel there are some basic things to go over. I have a special section in the drills section of this book specifically designed for catchers. I already addressed the equipment and urge coaches and parents to buy used catchers' gloves. I would like to go over some techniques I always work on throughout the season with my catchers.

Catching Stance

There are numerous tips to go over for the youth catching stance. First of all, the catcher should be comfortable in his squatting position. A good target should be given with the catcher's glove directly over the center of home plate. This will give youth pitchers ages 9-12 the best chance of throwing strikes. As players get older, even the location of the glove for a target becomes more strategic. But on this level, the youth level, we are looking for the pitcher to have as much success as possible throwing strikes. The catcher's throwing hand should not be exposed as the pitch is coming in. Youth catchers should have their throwing arm behind their backs, out of harm's way to protect from a wild pitch or foul tip. He should relax his wrist right before the pitch is thrown.

Squatting Distance Behind the Batter

Many catchers in youth baseball set up either too far or too close from home plate. Setting up too close or reaching for the ball with their glove can cause catcher's interference when the bat makes glove contact, which will award the batter first base. The best way for the catcher to set up an appropriate distance is to work with the batter's shoulder or elbow. Once the hitter is in the batter's box ready to hit, the catcher can reach out with his glove toward the batter's shoulder or elbow and set up at that distance, a foot or two further back. Conversely, coaches want to make sure the catcher is not too far back for a number of reasons. First, he will be at a longer distance from the pitcher. Second, this can impede the umpire from calling a strike because he is too far to judge the ball as it crosses home plate. Remember, the umpire will set up behind the catcher. I've even seen umpires move a good foot or two from beyond where the catcher is set up.

Guard Against The Steal

Many times, especially on the youth level, an aggressive coach will have his baserunners take an exaggerated lead after the pitch. I do this. There are certain things the catcher should and should not do when guarding against this aggressive lead. For instance, let's say the runner on first base is a fast runner and takes an extra big lead after the pitch. The catcher might throw the ball behind the runner to first, which gives the baserunner a green light to go to second. Coaches on the youth level need to practice and school their catcher, as well as their whole team the correct way to defend this running play that prevents errant throws and extra runs. When the baserunner at first takes an over aggressive lead, the catcher should run right at the baserunner. Make sure the catcher is actually running at an angle that takes him ahead of the baserunner. If the runner commits to the next base, the catcher should then stop, plant his foot, and throw the baseball to that base. Otherwise, he should run him back to the original base. It doesn't matter if the runner is leading too much off first, second, or third base. The catcher should always run at the runner, throwing over being a last resort option. If the catcher runs at the baserunner off of third, I have the first baseman come down the line to cover home.

Throwing From The Knees

Catchers, especially on the youth level, have a tendency to get lazy. Sometimes the throw back to the pitcher will be executed from their knees. This must be addressed because opposing coaches will look for indicators, such as throwing the ball back to the pitcher from the knees, to take advantage of for generating steal opportunities. The catcher should never throw from his knees when there are runners on base. Coaches should teach young catchers the position requires two types of focus, one without baserunners and one with baserunners.

When catchers set up in the crouching position, it is important they are not too close or too far away from home plate. When the batter gets into the batter's box, the catcher should reach out toward the hitter's shoulder with the glove hand. This arm's length distance from the hitter's elbow should be how far the catcher sets up behind home plate. Many times in youth baseball the catcher will set up too far away. This creates a disadvantage for the pitcher because he is now throwing at a longer distance. The umpire is also not getting a true picture of the ball crossing home. Catchers also need to be taught not to reach for the ball when receiving a pitch. If he does, he may hit the bat on the swing, which is catcher's interference whereby the batter is awarded first base. When catchers are taught correctly, they will develop their own routine for setting up as they get more experienced.

In youth baseball we must teach catchers that their job is not only to catch pitches but also to try throwing out runners. He is responsible for runners not moving to the next base on anything that is not a hit. We must reinforce to catchers not to throw baseballs around unnecessarily. Time and again I see baserunners taking a lead, enticing the catcher to throw the baseball. The catcher throws behind the runner, who then takes off for second base. More times than not he is safe. I teach all my catchers to first learn how to run at the baserunner. It does not matter whether the baserunner is leading off of first, second, or third base. He must run at the runner. If the runner suddenly sprints towards the next base, then the catcher can throw in front of the runner. You don't want to have too many unnecessary throws. The team that throws the ball around the field more is usually the losing team. Remember, if the catcher runs toward a runner at third base, the first baseman must come down the line to cover home. There are times I do have the catcher throw behind the runner to try for the out, but this depends on the personnel we have on the field.

Blocking

Youth catchers must realize they will not catch every pitch, especially balls in the dirt. Blocking is a technique used to keep the ball in front of the catcher with runners on base. The purpose of blocking is not to necessarily catch the ball with the glove. The glove is used to block the ball from going between the legs of the catcher while the body acts as a backstop. When the catcher recognizes a pitch is going into the dirt, he should move in front of the ball, drop to his knees, and put his open glove on the ground in-between his knees. This makeshift human shield prevents the ball from going behind the catcher. This takes work and practice to master.

Catcher Turning Head

Young catchers have a tendency to flinch or turn their head or body on short hop pitches. Coaches need to teach and reinforce to the youth catcher that he is safest from injury when his body is square to the pitcher. When he turns his head to the side, his body will follow. This will leave the side of his body vulnerable to get hit because the player's side, from the neck down to the waist, is not protected well. If by chance the catcher does turn his body on a short hop pitch, he can get injured in the rib area.

Wild Pitch or Passed Ball Throw Back To The Pitcher

On a wild pitch, catchers will sometimes throw the ball back to the pitcher from the spot where they pick up the ball after the baserunner advanced to the next base. This should never be done. This long throw is a potential disaster and a recipe for a throwing error because the base runner will take an extra base on the throw back to the pitcher. There is a chance one or more extra bases can be taken by the opposing team. The correct way is for the catcher to pick up the ball and walk back to home plate, or even in front of home, and then throw the ball back to the pitcher. Catchers should get in the habit of throwing the ball back fairly hard to the pitcher with players on base. Opposing coaches will always recognize how the opposing catcher throws the ball back to the pitcher. A soft throw, or high arc throw, is a green light for opposing coaches to try something on the base paths during the game.

Covering Home Plate

One of the most exciting plays in baseball is a close play at a base, especially at home. Sometimes these plays at home separate good catchers from great catchers. Whenever the catcher fields the ball, he must always be aware of where he is, as well as the baserunner, in relation to home plate. When there is a play at home, the catcher should make sure that once he has the ball he is in the base path between home plate and the baserunner. If the ball is caught off line, the catcher should instinctively turn to the base path, move the ball to a low position and expect contact. It is of the utmost importance the catcher protects the ball as best he could to prevent the ball from coming loose. Practicing will help make these techniques habitual. Practice some of these techniques at different fields as no two base paths or home plate areas are exactly the same. The sweep tag is when the catcher catches the ball in front of the base path, doesn't have time to set himself perfectly in front of home plate, and instead sweeps the glove in one motion right where he expects the baserunner to end up with his slide.

Framing A Pitch

When a pitch looks like a borderline strike, experienced catchers will move their glove with a subtle flick of the wrist to frame the glove and the ball in the strike zone. Framing would be considered an advanced technique on the youth level. Many youth players who try to frame a pitch will exaggerate it too much, especially when the pitch is well out of the strike zone. If you do teach framing, make sure the catcher understands that the pitches to frame are a borderline strike. A catcher, who can frame well, can be extremely helpful to a pitcher working the corners of the plate. If you try to teach a young catcher how to frame, make sure it is practiced before games. The framing motion is smooth and should not be done in a jerking motion.

In a normal steal, the baserunner goes when the pitch reaches the strike zone or crosses home plate. In the delayed steal, the baserunner goes when the ball leaves the catcher's hand on the throw back to the pitcher. Sometimes the catcher will throw the ball back to the pitcher from the knees. This must be addressed because catchers who throw from the knees will not generate enough power in their throw. Opposing coaches will take advantage of this by attempting the delayed steal. I always look for two or three indicators that tell me there is a chance to attempt the delayed steal. Knowing what I look for on the offensive side, I teach my team how to stay out of putting us in a position where the other team will attempt the delayed steal. Coaches should teach young catchers that the position requires two types of focus, one without baserunners and one with baserunners.

Catchers should never throw from their knees when there are players on base. They must stand up and check the lead runner before they throw the ball back to the pitcher. Catchers must also never throw the ball back to the pitcher with a rainbow-type loop throw instead of a hard line drive.

I want my pitcher to move up to the base of the pitcher's mound before my catcher even throws the ball back to the pitcher. If the pitcher is standing on top of the mound on the rubber looking to retrieve the baseball, I teach my catchers not to throw the ball back.

Players who want to play the catching position don't realize that it is a lot of work. Even on the youth level, the position is a thinking person's position that requires a lot of grit and toughness. Many players will try the catching position and decide it is not for them.

Chapter 7

Hitting Techniques

"Baseball is the only field of endeavor where a man can succeed three times out of ten and be considered a good performer."

~Ted Williams

Hitting Techniques and Coach Marty's 5/20 Theory

When it comes to hitting, volumes of books have been written about this great skill. I'm sure you've heard the old axiom that hitting a baseball is one of the hardest things to do in sports. Getting a hit only 3 out of 10 times spells success. I've been to many baseball clinics and have attended numerous workshops on hitting. Of all the clinics and lectures I've been to on hitting, no two have ever been exactly the same. I've attended clinics on hitting by high school, college, and even Major League baseball managers and hitting coaches. In fact, sometimes I come out of these clinics more confused than when I went in.

There are many ways coaches approach teaching hitting. In youth baseball I approach the skill a bit differently than other coaches. I find that in teaching youth baseball skills to players 7-12 years-old, there is a tendency to over coach and under teach. Coaches tend to give the youth player endless suggestions that we either have read or heard other coaches tell their players, and expect the player to become the perfect contact hitter. I have established a 5/20 theory when teaching hitting (and pitching for that matter). Work on three-five things to correct, even if there are twenty things wrong, and make those three-five corrections habits.

New managers and coaches should not feel intimidated by their knowledge or lack of knowledge on hitting. On the youth level, sometimes it is beneficial if you do not know too much so you cannot fill a 10, 11, or 12 year-old player with too much information. If you have studied hitting, attended seminars, read books, bought videos, and feel somewhat of an expert on teaching hitting, you might come up with 20 things you feel need correcting with one hitter. My advice here, and I can back it up with over 20 years of coaching youth baseball experience, is to just concentrate on the three-five most important flaws you may find. Let me explain why I am adamant about this. We are working with youth players 7-12 years-old. The best chance the youth player has in being a successful hitter is to be relaxed. If we fill the young player with too many instructions, he will go into the batter's box thinking about everything he has to do. Many times when we correct the most important and most obvious mistakes, some of the others with correct themselves.

There are a few exceptions to my 5/20 rule. If a player has six or seven things you see obviously wrong with a swing, do not go over five problems just because of Coach Marty Schupak's 5/20 rule. You may have some fathers of very talented players who are enthusiastic about getting hitting lessons from a former minor league player who works part time at the local batting cage. Don't stop these parents from doing this, but make sure you are in concert with the batting instructor and the father about trying to reinforce the techniques the hired expert is imparting to the player. You may also want to be in direct contact with the local high school coach. Many high school coaches are very knowledgeable on hitting and pitching while some are not. The local youth league should always work with this coach and have him and his staff run one or more clinics. Some of the players will eventually play for this coach, so he might end up changing the players' batting stance, etc., five years later.

Sometimes the simplest way to improve a youth player's hitting never takes place in the batter's box. For instance, I've had players who needed glasses and did not know it. And once they were fitted for glasses or contact lenses, these players increased their chances of hitting the baseball. This has happened to me twice, and probably would have been more if I had known better earlier in my coaching tenure. One time, I had a player with a great swing, but just missed the baseball. I told his parents to get him an eye test. He just so happened to need glasses. Another player could not hit during night games. We found out he had some kind of stigmatism after I suggested to his parents to take him to opthamologist. He also was fitted for glasses and instantly became a different ballplayer.

Many players use bats that are way too heavy. Players must be able to control the bat during the swing and not the bat controlling the swing. Like other pieces of equipment, remember that if you make it a holiday gift in December, your son or daughter might not use it until 4-5 months later. You don't want the bat too light. I always recommend parents buy bats and other equipment 3-4 weeks before the season starts.

I have spoken to many high school coaches about my 5/20 theory on hitting and most understand the concept, not just from an athletic perspective, but also from an educational one because it helps young players listen and absorb. With this being said, I am going to go over a few of the most common mistakes I see in hitting that come up over and over again in youth baseball.

Hitters Are Too Tense

A relaxed hitter is a dangerous hitter. In a crucial hitting situation give me a youth player of lesser skill who is relaxed and confident once he steps into the batting box over a highly skilled player who is in the batter's box and over-thinking. Is the player going over in his head, right up through the pitch being delivered, hitting techniques like, small step, swing high to low, and rotate hips? I try to teach my players to be as relaxed as possible once they are in the batter's box. By being relaxed, I'm not saying they should not be a little nervous, however, at certain levels of tension, the player is diminishing his chances for success. I tell all my parents and my assistant coaches that once the player is in the batter's box, no instruction should be given to him. No yelling things out like, "Elbow up or elbow down," or, "Step closer to home plate," and "Move to the back of the batter's box." Between coaches yelling out instructions and the player's parents doing the same from the stands, the batter usually will become more confused. Instructions should be given in practice not during the games. If a player tends to stand too far from home plate, one of the coaches should remind the player while he is on deck. There is always a parent who will yell out instructions and you'll speak to them after the game and you'll get the line, "What, I can't give advice to my own son?" This is an issue that you should really address in the parents meeting. As a parent, I don't ever want to be censored from being able to advise or speak to my own kids. When dealing with parents you have to be diplomatic, explaining, as a coach, that in your experience you believe it is best for their child not to receive too much instruction once in the batter's box and that they have a much better chance of being successful.

One thing I see over and over again is batters getting into the batter's box and immediately getting into their stance, not moving an inch while waiting for the pitch The batter stands like a statue concentrating on the pitcher even when the pitcher is not even close to beginning the wind-up. I've even seen the batter get into the hitting stance while the home umpire is turned around with his back to home plate retrieving more baseballs. Even a major league hitter cannot hold a stance for an extended period of time and be successful. How do we go about correcting this? I teach my players to move the bat around while in the batter's box to relieve tension. Whether it is just rotating the bat or doing elephant trunks (swinging the bat back and forth underhand) as the pitcher prepares to step on the rubber. Once the pitcher winds up, I instruct the hitters to then, and only then, get into a ready stance with the bat off their shoulders. Most young players will not yet have any real relaxation habits so what I tell them is to keep the bat rested on their shoulder, and only when the pitcher begins the wind-up, should they lift the bat off their shoulders and get ready to hit.

I also notice that when players foul off a pitch, their feet move, but they never reset themselves correctly in the batter's box before the next pitch. They set up in a different spot without even looking at their feet. I like to teach players to be consistent on every pitch.

Here we see the pitcher tying his shoe. The picture on the left shows the batter ready to hit when the pitcher is not even close to his wind-up. The batter should relax with his bat resting on his shoulder until the pitcher begins his wind-up.

Batter Not Completing The Swing

Youth players love to make contact with the baseball. But many youth players do not necessarily finish their swing. I'm not sure why this is so prevalent in youth baseball and why players who end up on my team tend have an incomplete swing after they have been in league 3-4 years before I even see them. The hitter will take a really healthy cut, but once contact is made with the ball, the batter slows down the swing, almost to a complete stop. There is no real follow through with the bat. When hitters do this they are diminishing their chances of getting a hit. To correct this, I work with players individually on the batting tee. On every swing, I tell them to make sure to swing through the ball. I carry this over into batting practice. I also have the player take up to 15-20 practice swings without hitting a ball. Having one of your better hitters demonstrate a swing is also a good idea.

Here we see the batter swinging. He is slowing his swing down upon contact. If you look closely, you can see his whole body relaxing too much when instead he should be forcing the bat through the ball.

I find the batting tee to be one of the best creations for solving numerous hitting problems. When the player does not finish his swing, I stand near him while he is on the tee and reinforce for him to "swing through the baseball." In this sequence, he is concentrating so much on finishing his swing that he knocked the tee over, which is fine.

Having the player work on the skill himself is important for a couple of reasons. First we are encouraging the player to practice on his own. We are also teaching young kids they have the ability to figure out how to fix problems on their own.

Hitters Step Toward 3rd Base

Out of all the hitting mistakes youth players make, the one that is the easiest to recognize, but probably the hardest to correct, is when hitters (right-handed hitters) take a step with their front foot toward third base instead of toward the pitcher. Lefty hitters incorrectly steps with their front foot toward first base. When hitters step "into the bucket," they are lessening their chances of being successful. A combination of balance and power are affected when hitters step to 3rd. The hitter's head will tend to move too much as well. In many sports skills, if the performer does one thing wrong, usually one or more other skills will be affected in a negative way. If hitters step incorrectly toward third and is lucky enough to actually hit the baseball, it is usually hit toward first base or second base. I correct this in practice. I take two 2x4 pieces of wood about 36-40" long, (or two baseball bats). I Put the piece of wood on each side of the player's feet while in the batter's box. Make sure the wood is not too tight and the player does not feel restricted with his feet. What we are doing here by having the two pieces of wood is conditioning the hitter to step toward the pitcher. Players also tend to over-stride when they step the incorrect way. It is important that the front foot step is about 6-10 inches long, and in some cases even shorter. I have heard hitting instructors not endorse placing objects at the player's feet while he is hitting. Just remember as youth baseball coaches that some techniques will work with some players and some won't. I'm giving you ideas, and as coaches you should have a library of baseball instruction to use for a particular player. As of late, many batting instructors frown upon a step with the front foot and instead teach having the batter just lift up the foot and put it back down in the same position, which is fine if this achieves weight transfer.

Here we see the player's front foot moving toward third base. The importance of stepping with the front foot is the transfer of body weight and also the rotation of the batter's hips, which is where he gets his power. Coaches can experiment with different techniques with hitters who are having a tough time stepping toward the pitcher.

Putting two 2X4's or baseball bats on each side of the batter's feet can help solve the problem of the batter stepping to third base.

Back Foot Moving

Hitting a baseball is a combination of motion, stepping, hip rotation, follow through, and surprisingly stillness. The stillness I'm referring to is the right foot (for a righty). The batter steps with his left foot during the pitcher's wind-up. The step will either be a short step forward or just lifting the left foot up then putting it down. During the movement of the front foot, the right foot must remain in the same location, but will rotate so that the toe is pointed toward the pitcher. Many young players will move their back foot, shifting the actual location of the foot, as if they are dancing with both feet. When swinging and making contact, the back foot will move but not actually lift up off the ground. Some hitting coaches will preach the "squishing the bug" technique when the back foot twists. I like the natural twist movement. But the movement we are concerned about as youth coaches is the back foot actually being lifted off the ground and being put back in a different spot. So what we want to correct is the initial part of the swing where the player must move with his front foot but must keep his back in the same general location. How do we correct this back foot from moving excessively? We take two bricks, putting one on each side of the back foot during batting practice. This will prevent him from moving his foot too much. It is important to remember that the rotation of the batter's hips starts with the back foot. This is where he gets his power. The rotation basically does all the work and the swing is the finish. This is why it is essential youth players learn to keep the back foot still, except when swinging when the back foot twists, but never really lifts off the ground.

Putting the bricks on each side of the player's back foot will help keep the batter from making any unnecessary movements because the batter is cognizant of the bricks on either side of the foot. The importance of keeping the foot in the same location when twisting forward will result in the all important hip rotation.

Excessive Movement of The Head

Another very common mistake with youth baseball hitters is that they move their head prematurely before the ball is hit. This common occurrence happens not only on the youth level but for batters of all ages. Human nature makes it so players are anxious after they make contact to see where the ball is going. Even when youth players don't make contact, they are turning their head too soon to see where or how far the ball has been hit in the field. Players must keep their eye on the ball at all times, and that is especially true for hitting. They must watch the barrel of the bat make contact with the ball.

One technique I use is with the batting tee. When the player hits the ball off the tee, I instruct him to yell "hit" when the bat makes contact with the baseball. This forces the batter to focus on the baseball by following the bat make contact with the ball. This technique is very effective and can also be applied when using the soft toss. When the coach tosses the ball, the player will again yell "hit" when the bat makes contact with the baseball.

Another drill I use to help correct this is to have a pitcher pitch a baseball with the batter standing in the batter's box. We color code the baseballs. Some baseballs will have blue painter's tape on it and some will have yellow tape. The pitcher then pitches the baseball. The batter must follow the ball into the catcher's glove and recognize the color. Once the batter recognizes the color of the pitched ball he will yell out white, blue, or yellow, depending on the color of the ball. The batter never swings, but instead must focus on the ball. This forces the hitter to follow the ball all the way into the catcher's glove. This technique reinforces not to move the head during the swing to look at the field. This is what is called tracking the baseball. Setting this up without having the batter swing is segregating the hitting skills. The batter does not have to worry about the hit. The only goal here is following the baseball. Separating multiple skills into single individual skills is an excellent technique to do, not only with young athletes, but with all athletes in all sports.

Here the hitter turns and lifts his head prematurely, therefore missing the ball completely.

Having the player focus on the ball and yell "hit" when he makes contact is forcing the batter to track the pitch all the way.

Hitters Will Uppercut with their Swing

Many youth players tend to uppercut on their swing. Like other bad batting habits, this is a tough one to correct, but it can be done through repetition. Uppercuts are exaggerated swings, where the bat starts low and ends high. I believe a good swing should go in a high to low motion and then have a slight upward movement toward the end of the swing during the follow-through. There can be numerous reasons why a youth batter uppercuts. One theory says hitters drop their hands too much. The hands should be somewhere around the hitters' chest in a comfortable position. Once the hands drop too much, hitters are almost forced to uppercut if the ball is pitched below the location of the hands. Another reason for having an uppercut could be if hitters drop their elbow once they start their swing. A third theory centers around batters overstriding, which collapses the back leg to compensate. This puts the batters' shoulder low. An uppercut is almost inevitable. There are many more theories. I tend to think if you explain these or other theories on the uppercut to a young player, it might be counter productive. I prefer to drill the player the correct way, develop good habits through repetition. I use the "chair drill" in practice with players who uppercut. Placing an old chair in front of the batting tee with the back furthest from the tee will force the batter to swing high to low and thereby avoid uppercutting on the baseball. Make sure when you do this you take a chair you won't want to use again because it will take a beating. Coaches can also use two batting tees. Set up one behind the other at different heights with the back tee higher. Just like using the chair, the batter has to avoid hitting the back tee without the ball on it. This is not a 100% fool proof solution, but I have had success.

Here we see the batter uppercutting. The second picture shows the batter's hands dropping too low, which will also cause the batter to uppercut.

With the chair drill, the player swings high to low. If the batter doesn't hit the chair, his swing is correct.

I want to address a few general theories of mine when approaching hitting on the youth level. Teaching youth players about hitting encompasses some philosophy that coaches and parents should not be shy communicating with players 7-12 years-old. Making hitting goals achievable is important. I always tell players that hitting success does not mean getting hits every three out of ten at bats. Making contact with the ball should be the foremost goal of every hitter. Giving the players confidence that they don't have to hit a line drive in the gap every at bat will take pressure off the batter. On the youth level, as I mention continuously, coaches have to do everything in their power to keep kids relaxed.

Here are some of the basics I try to teach young players without getting too technical. On the youth level, I really believe both hitting and pitching must be approached quite differently than when the players become school ball players. For some hitting situations, I used to teach players to wait for a strike before they begin to swing at pitches. I have moved away from this philosophy about ten years ago and noticed my players have hit better. In my youth baseball league we have either volunteer umpires or paid ones that can range in age from 13 and older. Not to knock any of these wonderful people for giving their time, but we have to remember the level of play and the skill level of the participants. When I had players wait for a strike, my goal was for them to see at least one pitch. But if you analyze it, suppose you have your batter take a pitch, and the first one is called a strike, then the second pitch is fouled off. Now the batter has two quick strikes on him. At this point, we are putting the at bat in the hands of a 13 year-old umpire to call the next pitches correctly. This is a tough situation, and I changed my philosophy because of some questionable calls over the years. I now want my players to control their at-bats as much as they can. I want them ready to hit the first pitch if it is in the hitting zone. I want my batters to be aggressive and set the trend for the game. I'm not interested in stretching out a pitcher's pitch count if it will affect the chances of my batters' success. I have found that when taking this approach, my batters have hit better as team. I mentioned the pitch count. I believe we coaches are doing our batters more harm than good by trying to strategically stretch out a pitcher's pitch count just to put the team in a potentially better position to win the game. Aren't we there to teach hitting and give our players the best possible chance of being successful? Well then, let's have our players swing the bat.

On the technical part of hitting, using the correct bat is a must. Also being ready in the batter's box is extremely important, and in a lot of cases overlooked. Pitchers at all levels pitch differently from one another. Some work faster than others. I notice on the youth level that players do not adjust to pitchers who are quick to throw the baseball. If coaches see this, they must tell the whole team that when in the batter's box, they must get ready much quicker than normal. I've seen batters get in the hole with one strike because they are finishing their practice swings and the pitcher is already in his wind-up. Batters must realize that they have to be ready in case the pitcher is a quick worker.

On the youth level it amazes me how many players will set up differently on each pitch. I've seen players swing and miss or foul off pitches and they set themselves up from the last point of their swing instead of starting all over. After their swing, they will set themselves up from that point. I want my batters to be comfortable on each pitch. They can determine the flow of the game by calling time out if they have to so they are set up the correct way in the batter's box.

The last few years I have had my players practice picking up the baseball at the pitcher's release point. It is amazing that players just look at the pitcher and not where the actual ball is coming from. Players need to step toward the pitcher or move their front foot on each pitch. In some cases I've seen players just lift their front foot and put it down with very little front movement. This is fine and helps produce weight transfer. A smaller front step is better than a longer one. Less movement of the head is better than more movement.

Forget the old expression "keep the elbow up." I don't think this is correct. I also love the expression on the swing, "high to low," which means the swing starts high and goes low. I like to teach my players that their hands should not drop too low, and after the swing, their back knee is pointed toward the pitcher. Teaching batters to recognize this is a must and will show youth players the importance of rotating the hips. This is where they gets their power.

There are tons of pieces to the puzzle when teaching hitting and I only touched upon a few, which I do on purpose. If a youth player hits well but his stance looks odd, leave him alone.

Chapter 8

Pitching Techniques

"Good pitching will beat good hitting any time, and vice versa."

~Bob Veale, 1966

Pitching

Pitching can also encompass volumes of material, just as hitting can. Just as there are certain philosophies I follow in hitting, I also follow specific techniques and drills for pitching. When it comes to pitching, I usually see two extremes. The first is a coach who says nothing to instruct the player during practice. The other end of the spectrum includes coaches who don't stop instructing. There is the expression, "if it ain't broke, don't fix it," meaning sometimes you will get a natural pitcher who throws very well and looks to have great form. With a player like this, don't try to improve upon what already works. The worst thing coaches can do is break the habits of very skilled pitchers by filling their heads with an encyclopedia of instruction.

Over-coaching can be counter productive for youth players. As coaches and parents, you want to fill your pitchers with overflowing confidence. Strikes are more important than speed. This is especially true if you have a younger pitcher, say 10 year-olds, who might be accurate but lack velocity. The velocity will come as they get older and bigger. Even on the youth level, I've seen accurate 10 year-old pitchers become really good pitchers at twelve because the velocity of their pitches improved and they already laid the groundwork for throwing strikes. When that happens, the pitcher is able to get away with throwing pitches outside the strike zone for two reasons. First, because his velocity has increased, the batter now has less time to make up his mind about swinging at the pitch. Second, because he has a history of being accurate, batters will tend to swing at more pitches out of the strike zone.

I make sure I gather my whole team at the beginning of the season and give them a simple short lecture on pitching, espousing my own philosophy. Even if kids do not want to pitch, it is important for all of them to listen. I tell them when they are pitching, the game or at-bat does not start until you throw the baseball. Young players have a tendency to rush. I want them to know they are in the best possible position on the field to take their time. Before they throw the first pitch of an inning, I want my pitchers to turn around on the pitcher's mound and scan the field to make sure every fielder is ready to play baseball. Too many times I see an inning start when the outfield is not even finished doing their warm ups. In my opinion, this is not even the umpires' fault. It is the pitcher's. This also happens after a play, particularly on a foul ball, when a player had to run a long distance to retrieve the ball then walk nonchalantly back to his position. I've seen pitchers start to throw another pitch when one or more fielders are not even at their position, which can drive a coach crazy.

Make sure your pitchers have cleats and not sneakers. Most youth baseball players will naturally have cleats, but once in a while you will have parents, for whatever reason, who don't provide cleats for their kids if they pitch. Pitching with sneakers will not work for a number of reasons and can actually be dangerous if the pitcher slips after the pitch and is way out of position to field a hard hit line drive right back to him.

One thing I am adamant about is pitching a ball outside of the strike zone on an 0-2 count. When a pitcher is ahead of a batter 0-2 and there are no baserunners on, I instruct my pitchers to throw the ball out of the strike zone on purpose. I cannot stand it when a player gets a hit when the count is 0-2. My own preference is for my pitcher to miss the strike zone short, almost reaching home on one bounce with a slow moving pitch. Many times you will get an anxious batter swing at the ball and you'll get to steal a strikeout. But remember this must be done with no runners on base and you must have all your pitchers practice this. So you might be asking; Does Marty Schupak endorse pitchers throwing balls out of the strike zone? The answer is 100% yes. And why not? Aren't there situations in other sports, like basketball, where a player must miss the back end of two foul shots and hit it off the rim to get a chance to get an offensive rebound to win? Shouldn't these players practice missing? You don't have to practice this every week, but once or twice during the season is sufficient.

Pitching in youth baseball is highly skilled. Just as with hitting, I maintain you are better off as a coach to limit the number of corrections you intend to or want to make. A lot of pitchers will take private lessons and you as the coach should find out who does and respect what the pitching instructor is trying to teach. After all, the parents can be spending a small fortune on these lessons. If you do make corrections, don't try them all at once. Correcting one mistake, then reinforcing the correct method before moving onto the next correction is the way to go. Coaches and parents should not feed their players with too much information at once. To give a 10, 11, or 12 year-old numerous things to think about is a mistake. I maintain my 5/20 theory of coaching applies to pitching as well.

Pitchers Balance

Balance can be a major problem for some young pitchers. Sometimes the problem isn't even their fault. I've seen many youth baseball fields around the country. For many I find the area right in front of the pitching rubber, where the pitcher is supposed to pivot, not manicured correctly. There is a deep hole where the pitcher's foot is supposed to land. This will easily throw the pitcher way off balance. In defense of all the board members in charge of field maintenance, many fields get so much use with games going on one after the other especially on weekends. It is hard to keep the pitcher's mound area in perfect shape. In addition, athletic fields can also be affected by towns and municipalities always under pressure with budget cuts. Many leagues do not have the luxury of multiple fields at their disposal, consisting of a couple of game fields plus a practice field. I go around the country to different leagues and different facilities. I am amazed at how beautiful some are. But for every stunning multiple field facility I see there are many that are in need of major landscaping work. The best way for youth pitchers to be assured of being balanced is to start their pitching motion from the stretch position. The stretch position is used in advanced leagues when the pitcher needs to hold a runner close to the base. The stretch position will yield a loss in the velocity of a pitch, but on the youth level, I find this a great technique for pitchers to remain balanced. And on the youth level, the amount of velocity lost is minimal. Some youth players are quite comfortable with the full wind-up. As youth coaches, if the field is in good shape, I still suggest to start pitchers from the stretch position and then integrate the full wind-up, maybe having him do it one inning then increasing from there. The Yankee pitcher Ron Guidry turned his career around by pitching from the stretch position. Don Larson, who pitched a perfect World Series games, also liked to pitch from the stretch.

Taking An Improper First Step

Young pitchers should start on the pitching rubber with both feet about shoulder length apart. For a righty, he should start the wind-up by bringing the left foot back so that the left toe is even with the heel of the other foot. This first step is important and is key to establishing correct balance, rhythm, and focus. Many coaches teach pitchers to start with their heels on the pitching rubber. Coaches should not obsess over this with young pitchers. One mistake I see from youth pitchers is they step to the side rather than back. Pitchers can still be good if they step to the side. I've seen pitchers who are very talented take this first step to the side rather than behind and still be quite effective. If a player does step to the side and pitches effectively, I would leave him alone. However, all things being equal, I like to teach the pitcher to take his step back because when he goes forward he will gain momentum exactly toward the area where he will be throwing the baseball. Some coaches teach pitchers who are righties to move to the right side of the rubber and lefties to the left side. The theory being you never want the batter to see the ball coming in on a straight line. It is also always best to keep the head over the the pivot foot. This will help with the weight transfer. The way a pitcher starts his wind-up or pitch can help determine his effectiveness.

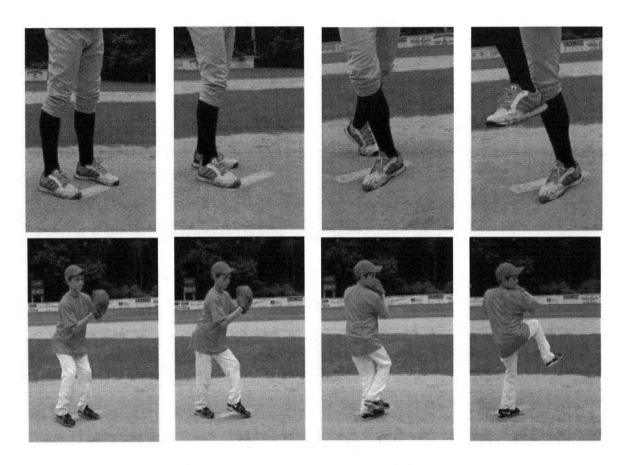

The top row of pictures shows the pitcher's feet. He does not have his heels on the rubber like the bottom pictures. Many pitching coaches prefer pitchers to start with their heels on the rubber. Coaches need not make this a huge issue on the youth level. Coaches also need to teach players they have to bend their knees. Too many times in pitching, as well as hitting, a player is standing straight up and is thus diminishing his power. A good term to use with kids may not be bending the knees but having soft knees. The player is never really standing straight up.

Elbow Too Low & Landing Foot Wrong

Another big problem I see with young pitchers is they drop the elbow of their throwing arm too low. The correct form is for the elbow to be about equal to the height of their shoulder. Many experts feel when the elbow drops too low or below the shoulder, this could bring about injuries to the elbow or shoulder area. When the young pitcher does a lot of throwing with a flaw in his motion, potential injuries to the muscles, ligaments, and tendons supporting the elbow can be at risk. For young pitchers, what the medical profession calls the growth plates can be affected. There is a ligament attached to the inner side of the elbow. This begins to pull one of the growth plates away from the rest of the bone. Because the bones are still growing, the growth plates are weak and susceptible to injury. This is not intended to scare potential coaches or parents. Just be aware of where the elbow is during a pitcher's wind-up. Coaches also need to be aware of the shoulder dropping during the course of a game. This can indicate that fatigue has set in. Many new coaches do not feel comfortable recognizing the location of the elbow and other mechanics. This is something that comes with experience and watching different pitchers. Remember, we are also improving as coaches by trying to recognize basic flaws in technique. I recommend for coaches, even on the youth level, to pay attention to the location of the pitcher's elbow when they watch a baseball game.

The front foot upon landing should also be facing where the pitcher wants the baseball to go. Some youth players land with their foot going in all types of directions.

In these pictures, the first two shows the elbow about the same height of the shoulder. The last two pictures show how the elbow is dropping below the shoulder.

The first two pictures are correct with the feet pointing to where we want the pitcher to throw the baseball. The last two pictures show the front foot all over the place, diminishing his chances of throwing a strike and being ready to field the ball if it is hit back to him.

Chapter 9

Baserunning & Bunting

"Ninety feet between home plate and first base may be the closest man has ever come to perfection."

~Red Smith

Baserunning

Great news for all youth baseball coaches who might feel they have a weak team and want to still be competitive. Here it is: Baserunning. Hardly anyone practices this underrated skill. Your offensive coaching philosophy should be to make your opponent defend the entire field, from the front of home plate to the outfield fences and everything in between. To accomplish this task, time needs to be allotted for learning all the skills needed while on base. I got into the baserunning aspect of youth baseball after the first few years of coaching. Another rival coach in the minor division was using some strategies that really threw my team off. Staying with my own personal philosophy, I went to the next few games just to watch the way this parent coached his team. I started to use some of the techniques this coach used against his opponents and developed my own strategies over the years. I learned and created numerous baserunning drills that have become a regular part of my practices. And I saw something happen that I found to be quite amazing. I saw that if I practiced baserunning, there was a residual effect. Players as young as 9 or 10 were much more focused on the base paths. Even between pitches their heads seemed to wander less than my earlier teams before we practiced baserunning. What I observe in youth baseball is coaches explaining to young players from the coaching box what to do in different baserunning scenarios. Instructions would be relayed to a player on second base, such as, "Johnny, if the ball is hit to the right side of the infield, run to third right away. If the ball is hit to the left side of the infield, don't run until the fielder throws the ball to first base." Most of the time these explanations are correct, but these are the situations that can very easily be reviewed in practice. I tell coaches all the time that having young players experience the situation is much better than just explaining it to them at the time it occurs on the field. The one baserunning technique I urge all youth coaches to teach their players is to slide almost all of the time at the bases, except for first base. Even when there is a close play and the player knows he is going to be out, teach him to slide. The sliding might disrupt the fielders or help break up a double play that is not too frequent on the youth level but is fundamentally sound baseball. Teams that have a reputation of sliding almost all the time will also force the opposing team to rush the play and can cause mistakes that would not have been made. And trust me, no matter how much you practice this and try to reinforce it, players on the youth level will forget to slide. I used to get incredibly frustrated when this would happen. I learned it is something we coaches have to accept. It is just human nature for 9, 10, 11, and 12 year-old kids to forget to slide.

Coaches also need to remember that their fastest baserunner is not necessarily the best base runner. Some young players will just gravitate to being aggressive instinctive baserunners. I see this all the time. A player with average speed will just excel at baserunning. Explain and encourage to your players when they go to see a professional team play (or high school and college) to take a little time to observe baserunners and not the pitcher or batter on some pitches. It is eye-opening to see how they approach baserunning and how they react after each pitch. This is an important point for families that watch a lot of baseball on television. The TV is usually always focused on the pitcher and hitter. When you are at a live game, you get to see the whole field and the players on base go from their initial lead to their secondary lead. It is especially critical to see when there is more than one player on base.

Most of the baserunning techniques and drills will be addressed in the drill section, but I highly recommend for youth coaches to spend 5-10 minutes at every practice going over different aspects of baserunning.

1) Coaches should put aside 5-10 minute of every practice to go over a different aspect of baserunning.

2) Make it a habit for every base runner to aggressively bounce off the base on each pitch.

3) Allow even the slowest player on the team the opportunity to steal a base in a game.

4) Teach players to read the pitch or follow it on its flight home when on base to anticipate possible wild throws or past balls to advance a base and to follow the path of the baseball when the catcher throws it back to the pitcher.

5) Players should always slide into the base on a steal, force play, close play, or a play at home because it is sound fundamental baseball and sliding may help create defensive blunders.

6) Encourage your players to watch the base runners carefully when at higher level baseball games. Point out how players touch the base and make turns on extra base hits or go from first to third or second to home. Show them the difference between a base runner's primary lead and secondary lead.

Going Home to Second

I like to practice these three scenarios at least once before the season starts. Going from first to third we put a cone in foul territory for the baserunners to make a little loop in their trajectory towards the base. I will also throw down a rubber base on top of the regular base with the inside half darkened as a target for the baserunners. It is always best to round the base in foul territory this way because it puts the baserunner in the best position to head to the next base. He should always step on the inside of the bag, where the colored portion of the base would be.

Going From First to Third

Going from first to third requires the runner to know when to slow up as he approaches second and to touch the inside of the base. Don't over-coach players to touch the inside corner of the base. The inside half is fine.

Going From Second to Home

When running from second to home, not making an exaggerated wide turn at third is incredibly important. The turn can determine if a player will be safe or out on a play at home.

Bunting

Just as baserunning plays a big role on my team, bunting is also a huge part of youth baseball and I really enjoy teaching the skill. I tell parents at the parents meeting and my players at the beginning of the year that I am partial toward players who bunt. With this said, I give every player on my team tons of opportunities to improve or perfect their bunting skills. There are different drills where I reward players for bunting successfully. I will go over this in my batting practice section. Bunting is a very interesting baseball technique that goes back to almost the beginning of baseball's history. The act of holding back or selling your opponent that you are going to swing away as in a regular at bat and then shortening up on the bat in a way where some havoc is created for the fielders is a challenge for every batter. When performing the actual bunt, make sure the ball deadens and slows to a stop where whoever picks it up, whether it is the third baseman, pitcher, or catcher, is in a location that gives the baserunner an excellent chance of being awarded a single. Just think of it! A player who gets a bunt single in the real major leagues on a ball hit about 15-20 feet on the ground gets more credit in his statistics than a player who hits a baseball 400 feet in the air and is robbed of a home run for an out. Just incredible! This is one reason why baseball is such a great game.

I am friends with some people on Wall Street and in Real Estate. One common denominator I have learned from these people is to never fall in love with one stock. When looking for a house, never fall in love with one piece of real estate. What does this have to do with baseball or bunting? Well, I learned that even though I love teaching the skill of bunting and enjoy watching its success on the field, overdoing it can actually hurt you in a number of ways. When you bunt in exactly the same situations every time, you become too textbook and predictable. And if you happen to have a super bunter on your team, don't have him bunt at every at bat. Ten years into my coaching career, I had the best bunter I ever had on my team. His father loved it when he laid down a bunt and beat it out for a base hit, which he usually did. Looking at my scorebook, I realized that I was giving him the bunt sign almost every other at bat. This was not fair to him so I told his father that for the next five games, he has to swing away and I don't want him to bunt at all. If we are trying to develop well rounded baseball players, this is the fair thing to do.

I always found it odd some players refuse to bunt. Because they consider themselves power hitters or they do not have burning speed, they feel bunting does not have to become part of their hitting repertoire. This is the same thing as having a landscaper say I only cut grass in the front of a property and not the backyard. If we are teaching young kids to be complete baseball players, we are doing something wrong if we only have some of the team bunt during games. The best high school and college coaches put in bunting strategies whenever they get players on base. And on the big field, there is nothing like a perfectly performed squeeze play.

I always like to tell players and youth coaches at clinics that one of the best bunters I ever saw was one of the best power hitters to ever play baseball. Mickey Mantle, one of the great switch hitting power hitters, was also one of the best drag bunters when he batted lefty. I remember even seeing him drag bunt a number of times late in his career when his knees were shot from injuries when the opposition never expected him to do it. He would get into the bunting position at the last possible second, and just before making contact with the baseball, he was almost out of the batter's box on his way to first base. So upon contact, it looked like he was actually racing the baseball, which he strategically placed just past the pitcher's reach between the first and second baseman and beat it out for a hit. Everyone should practice bunting.

As a coach you want your team to develop into proficient bunters, but you want to use this strategy and technique in only certain situations. Coaches in all sports at all levels will have different plays and strategies they practice all season but never use. I've had seasons where we practiced bunting over and over and hardly used it in the course of the season. This is fine because we are still teaching our players the skill. As they get older and continue playing, whether it is bunting to sacrifice a player over or a squeeze play or bunting for a hit, the skill of bunting is a huge part of baseball that should be introduced to players at the youth level. When you teach the concept correctly, it will also help your team understand how to defend the bunt.

Pivot Bunt

There are two prominent methods of bunting that I teach on the youth level. The first technique, which also seems to be the most popular, is called the pivot bunt. The batter will pivot on the front of his feet, without lifting them, when the pitcher is about to release the ball to the plate. The bunter's knees should also be slightly bent. The non-dominant hand should be wrapped around the bottom of the bat, by the knob, while the dominant hand loosely clutches the bat, between the thumb, index finger, and middle finger above the grip and close to where the bat barrel begins to increase in size. It is very important that the top hand does not wrap all the way around the bat, exposing the player's fingers to an oncoming pitch. The bottom hand's knuckles should face the pitcher. A good way to test for this is to have the batter wave to the pitcher in the bunting position. I teach the top of the bat should also be higher than the bottom of the bat. Some coaches will teach the bat must be level. Pivot bunts are good for surprising the defense and catching them off guard. It is therefore best to get into the bunting position at the last possible second. Each player will have a comfort zone as to when they will get into the bunting position. Some players will be a natural at it.

Using the pivot technique allows the bunter to pivot back quickly to his regular stance if the pitch is not a strike or inside. Some young players have a hard time with the pivot concept. If your team practices indoors in the winter in a gym, have your players take off their sneakers. This will let the players feel their feet pivot with their socks against the gym floor. A good technique is for coaches to wrap black electric tape around a bat at about the location where the top hand should end up.

Square Bunt

The other popular bunting method is called the square bunt. In this technique, the player will show that he is bunting a little earlier in the pitcher's delivery than the pivot bunt. This method is more for sacrifices than trying to bunt for a hit. When performing the square bunt, the batter moves his back foot forward lifting it off the ground so that it is parallel to the opposite foot with the toes now facing the pitcher instead of home plate. A good way to check for this is to see if the batter's shoulders are square to the pitching mound. Again, the top of the barrel should be higher than the bottom of the bat, which will force the bunted ball to stay on the ground. The worst thing to do when bunting is to pop the ball up to the catcher. The player should also wave his bottom hand in practice to make sure that it is facing the pitcher. Coaches must emphasize to the players that if they bunt the ball and accidentally step on home plate, they will then be called out. Even though we recommend performing the pivot bunt at all times, coaches should allow players to choose which method makes them most comfortable at the plate. If the player is capable and confident doing the square bunt, then by all means do not discourage him from doing so. Coaches will see that some players will automatically go into the square bunting position. This is a matter of individual comfort and the coaches should let players make the choice. I like the barrel a little higher just because young players tend to straighten the bat on a bunt. If the the barrel starts higher there is a better chance of the bat staying at least level.

Some players will naturally like the square bunt. Let them do what is comfortable. The issue of the player having his foot on home plate upon contact is always worrisome. If he does make contact like the second row of pictures, the players will be called out. Preferably, players should move up in the batter's box when bunting. This is so on contact the ball will hit fair. Players that move up should do it discreetly.

Getting Into The Bunting Position

One of the most common questions that come up is at what point do the players actually square to or get into the bunting position. I have considered this a gray area and I'll explain why. There are some players that for whatever reason are able to grasp the skill of bunting naturally. And I have noticed that these players will get into position very late and still be able to produce an excellent bunt. You don't even really have to coach them as to how to do it. When you see this, leave that player alone. The majority of players though will need an indicator in the pitcher's motion telling them when they should get ready to bunt. I teach my players to get into the bunting position when the pitcher's front leg begins to come down from it's balanced position. This by no means is written in concrete and I recommend coaches do a little trial and error with their team. It is also a good idea to spread your team out, each player with a bat. The coach should be on the pitcher's mound and go through the wind-up and actually yell out "now" or "square" to get them into the bunting position. Do not confuse the term "square to bunt" with the square bunt technique. The term "square to bunt" means to get into the bunting position. Another issue is when the coach gives the bunt sign. The ideal situation is if your team is in the third base dugout and you are coaching the third base coaching box. I usually tell a player as he walks up to home plate to bunt on the first "buntable" ball. This is important, whether you tell him or give him the bunting sign. A lot of youth players think that when they get the sign to bunt that they have to bunt at the next pitch no matter what or where the pitch is. I see players bunting

120

at balls out of the strike zone either too high or too low. We must coach and practice that when given the bunt sign, this means that the player will attempt it at a ball only if it is a strike or a "buntable" ball. When I practice bunting with my team, I will purposely throw balls out of the strike zone so players can bring their bat back. This is extremely important with young players. They must also learn to bend their knees on low strikes and not point the bat down to reach for the ball.

Chapter 10
Drills

"Baseball is like a poker game. Nobody wants to quit when he's losing; nobody wants you to quit when you're ahead."

~Jackie Robinson

Drills, Repetition, & Fun Are The Key Ingredients For Youth Baseball

We've all seen or heard stories about people who have jobs where they get paid for 40 hours of work per week and maybe they actually do about half that, or in some cases even less. In sports, the same holds true for coaching. Coaches can have practices that run from two and a half to three hours, but not accomplishing much in that time span is counter productive. The best coaches in sports, at any level, are all proficient in practice organization. They work on precise time allotments for warm-ups, drills, scrimmages, running, cooling down, and any other category that they integrate in their practices. They have their assistant coaches prepped on how to go from one activity to another in an efficient manner as to not to waste any time. There are coaches at all levels who know the importance of efficient practices and that most can get more accomplished in two hours than some coaches can achieve in three hours.

Of course we want to make practice fun, but we also want to maximize the time to teach fundamentals. Even though recreational coaches have full time jobs, there are enough resources to research where the parent/coach can run effective practices that stress the important things in youth sports.

I became my son's youth baseball coach after observing his and other teams' practices that I thought were a waste of time. I knew baseball is a game you teach fundamentals at practice. I wanted to be the best coach I could. I first went to about 4 libraries in my county looking for videos on baseball instruction. All I found was one video, which was inaudible and unwatchable. By the way, this is the catalyst that made me start producing sports instructional videos. I tried reading up on baseball drills and going back deep into my memories of when I played youth baseball. At our first practice, I was probably the most disorganized youth coach ever. After 15 minutes of trying different things, I then did the same thing that I criticized other coaches for doing: have batting practice for the rest of the two hours of my allotted practice time. During the ride home I was somewhat humbled. I never really played baseball at any competitive level in my life, but with my Master's degree in Physical Education and being critical of my son's coach, I was sure I knew what I was doing. Well back to the drawing board.

I spent more time investigating the whole make-up of youth players. I read up a lot on psychology. I also referred to numerous elementary school physical education textbooks. I then went to observe and speak to coaches, not only in baseball, but in other sports as well. I spoke to coaches at all levels, from the youth level all the way to the college level. I went to observe numerous practices. During this "quasi" research I noticed a few common elements. The most successful coaches ran the most efficient practices. At these practices there was very little and in some cases no standing around. Everyone was involved almost all the time. The coaches I observed implemented drills that provided the most amount of repetitions in the shortest period of time. The assistant coaches worked like clockwork moving players in and out of the drills then rotating to the next drill. If the team was scrimmaging, there was always a secondary activity going on for the players who were not immediately involved in the scrimmage itself. If there was an important teaching point to be conveyed, the head coach made sure the whole team stopped what they were doing and gathered around him to listen to the explanation, which was always brief but to the point. This was a terrific education for someone like me who wanted to be the best coach for his own kids. Obviously I was in a fortunate position to devote this important time to observe and speak to these other coaches. Many parents who get involved in youth sports do not have the time or resources to do what I did, which is also a great reason why we need resources such as books and videos to educate the parent coach.

The next step was to take what I learned and try to see how to best utilize it at the youth sports level. I looked at numerous physical education activities and decided to see if I could integrate these into youth baseball drills. My original list of drills was comprised of about 45. It was a rough list and a lot of the drills were made up or variations of other drills.

At my next few practices, I used a lot of these drills. Some worked and some did not. I also made sure during batting practice I had a secondary activity for the on deck and double on deck hitter. The practice lasted about two hours and the kids, as well as myself, were exhausted from going from drill to drill. At the next few practices, I refined the drills a bit and cut practice down to one and a half hours. The kids seemed to love this practice. At the time I thought it was only the drills themselves that made the practice a success. In retrospect, it was a combination of the drills and the shortening of practice that made it more successful.

This was the basis for my practices. Keep them somewhat short and up beat. Instead of just one or two drills or activities, I used between 5-7 drills and activities at each practice. I also integrated fun games with skills games. I made sure almost all my fun games had a baseball theme to it, whether it was for the younger kids participating in a relay race, or 10, 11 and 12 year-olds playing a game I called Baseball-Football. What started out as some modest success the first year, it became a way of practicing in years to come. I refined my practices over and over and got them down to one hour during the season. My preseason practices would go for about one hour and fifteen minutes to an hour an a half but after the team learned the drills, especially the new players, an hour was sufficient. In some practice clinics that I run, I remember having a coach walk out claiming it was impossible to do what I was practicing. He never gave me the chance to explain the organization aspect of my practices and utilizing the parents as assistant coaches. When organized properly, my practices that last 60-90 minutes are more efficient, and my players get more out of them than many of the coaches who practice for over two hours and run the same boring activities over and over again. And probably the most important practices are those right after a game. It is here that I go over a short list of some of the mistakes that happened during the previous game. I am 100% certain you have a better chance teaching your players in practice by showing them than by telling them during a game.

People have said at these clinics it sounds like I am running a glorified gym class for 60 or 75 minutes. Yes and no. My practices are very skill-orientated but in a way young people will be able to grasp what I am trying to teach. We also work hard at techniques and try to perfect every aspect of what we do. No team in my league works more on first and third offensive and defensive situations. No team in my league gives their hitters more practice swings than I do. No team in my league practices baserunning at every practice like I do. And the youngest of players all love competition so I make sure I put in some competitive games in practice. There is nothing wrong with purposely putting players in a pressure situation in practice. This will only help them and the team succeed in games when these pressure situations occur. I guarantee if you devote just a little preparation from the ideas I give you and refine them to suit your team, league, and area of the country, your players will be better for it in the long run. They will come away feeling positive about baseball for years to come. As a coach, you actually have a choice. Are you there just to win the league championship or are you there to teach fundamentally sound baseball tips and techniques that your players can build on? I know when I first began to coach, I put championships ahead of everything else. No doubt I have changed over the years and now strive to teach the game of baseball the most complete way I know. The success of the way you teach and coach baseball is not in the number of players that play on the high school team or get college athletic scholarships. The success in the way you coach is giving your players an appreciation for the game so that even the weakest players you had come back or stay in the game as umpires or appear in the opposing dugout coaching their own team.

As we go into the drill and practice section of this book, I will point out some of the tricks I have learned over the years. I'll explain how practicing certain aspects of the game will give you a residual affect in a different part of the game. I understand some of you may have issues with field availability. I know some of you have more than one job but have a goal to have least one practice a week once the season starts. The drills will be comprised of pictures of the players actually doing the drills as well as an explanation. If you are the least bit confused, don't worry. When you get on the field a few times, things will be a lot clearer.

When I plan my practices, I still do them the same way I've been doing it for 21 years. At the beginning of the year I buy a stack of index cards. You should follow your own routine as long as you are organized. I usually plan each practice the morning of the day I'm going to practice. If the practice is a day following a game, I usually have some notes from the game we played and make sure I review some of the game situations and go over where we made mistakes. If there were some outstanding plays, like throwing a player out at home, it is always good to go over this to explain why things worked out the way they did. Set it up with the original players but also substitute some other players. Just note that in this digital age, some coaches will not use anything other than a hand held device. Everyone has their own comfort zone, and if a hand held device works well for you, then by all means go ahead and use it. My index card system does have some drawbacks. There were times when it is hot out, and if I wrote down my agenda in pencil, it would smudge after keeping them in my back pocket. It is also good for the kids on the team to see the coach being organized. Here are four practices I took randomly.

Weds. April 22

1. Warm-Up 3-5 min.
2. Line Throw Drill 8-10 min.
3. Cross Infield Drill 8-10 min.
4. Review From Game 10-15 min.
   A) Coverage on bunt 2nd inning
   B) Wild Pitch with under hand toss from C to P
   C) Bunting on balls outside strike zone
5. Relay Drill 8-10 min.
6. Batting Practice 10-15 min.

In the above practice, I don't remember the exact situation if we won or lost a game before this practice, but it looks like I am spending some extra time on the game situations.

Thurs. May 14

1. Warm-Up 3-5 min.
2. 3rd Base Drill 3-5 min.
3. Line Throw Drill 3-5 min.
4. Run Down Drill 5-10 min.
5. Review Game 5-10 min.
   A) Stealing - 1st inning
   B) Calling for a fly ball - 5 inning
6. Continuation Drill 8-12 min.
7. Batting Practice 10-15 min.

In this practice, I'm limiting the time spent on game situations. Again, I don't remember what the results of the game were, but my guess is that we played pretty well and were successful.

Tues, May 26
1. Warm-Up 3-5 min.
2. 3rd Base Drill 8-10 min.
3. Cross Infield Drill 8-10 min.
4. 1st & 3rd Defensive Situations 6-12 min.
5. Bounce & Run Drill 5-10 min.
6. Bunt Man on 3rd 5-10 min.
7. Batting Practice 10-15 min.

This practice was 100% percent drills. Looking at it, this is one of the harder practices I would run. Chances are I'd follow this practice with a practice of just batting. If you think you'll be coaching for a few years, try to save the index cards. You can mirror some practices one year to the next.

Thurs, May 28
1. Mini Batting Practice 5-10 min.
2. Warm Up 3-5 min.
3. Two Team Relay Drill 10-12 min.
4. Desperation Throw 5-10 min.
5. 1st & 3rd Offensive Situation 6-12 min.
6. Game Review 5-10
   A) Running Ground Ball out 2nd inning
   B) Ball Hit to 2nd - Coverage at 1st 5th inning
7. Batting Practice 10-15 min.

This practice is one of my typical practices combining some fun games with skills and a batting practice at the beginning and at the end of practice. The mini batting practice at the beginning is an excellent way to show players the importance of arriving on time.

Warming Up

When I first began coaching, I really did not spend anytime warming up the team, which was not the correct thing to do. It has been proven that even young players should warm-up, if just for 5-10 minutes. The old expression "warm up to throw, don't throw to warm up" holds true for players at all levels. Some organizations have spent a tremendous amount of money with some of the best orthopedic doctors in the world who have proven the benefits of warming up. A jog around the infield with arm rotations and some arm resistance is what I do with my team before every practice. If the weather is a bit on the cool side, I will spend more time warming up. Make warming-up interesting for young players. It can help them carry this crucial aspect to staying healthy well into their adult life.

Baseball Relay Race

1) **Use of drill & players needed**-As a fun game. Any even number of players.

2) **Equipment**-At least four baseballs and four cones.

3) **Goal**-Win a relay race with each player passing two baseballs to the next person in line.

Being on the Board of Directors one year in our local Little League® I was in charge of Tee-Ball. The highlight of the year was Tee-Ball Night, which I planned a lot of activities for the kids. When having over one hundred 5 and 6 year-olds on the field at the same time doing activities, safety is a challenge. Many times the older players would come down to help assist or observe their younger brothers and sisters. It always amazed me how these older players would ask to do some of the drills and games these younger kids were enjoying on Tee-Ball Night. I began putting a few in my practices. The "Baseball Relay Race," is like a typical old fashioned relay race. Two or more teams run around one cone to the next. I add a baseball theme where the players who are running must wear their baseball glove and must squeeze two baseballs in it. When they get to the next runner, they pass (not throw) the two baseballs. We are teaching the concept of holding onto the baseball and squeezing the glove while running. This drill will be beneficial when defending against rundowns.

Batting Tee With Plunger

1) **Use of drill & players:** A progression to teach young players to hit a ball off a batting tee. Any number of players.

2) **Equipment**: A batting tee, a bathroom plunger, and different size balls.

3) **Goal**: Have young players progress to hitting a baseball off a batting tee, starting with a big ball then moving to a baseball-sized ball.

I am a huge believer in what I call "progression teaching" when it comes to teaching youth players sports skills. It was always curious to me when I see 7 and 8 year-old kids practicing basketball in their driveway with a ten foot rim when they could barely even reach it. When adjustable baskets came around, I thought it was the greatest thing in the world to be able to set the basket at a height reachable for youth players and move it up as the players get older and taller. Translating this to baseball is an obvious practice technique parents and coaches should adopt but don't. It can be difficult for a 5 years-old to try to hit a baseball off a batting tee. A great progression is to take a bathroom plunger (new and clean of course), turn it upside down, placing it right into the batting tee. Then place a plastic kick ball right on top of the plunger. Have the players hit the kick ball off the tee. Remember, we want young players to achieve as much success as possible. Making contact with the ball is the goal. The larger the ball the better chance of succeeding. Most first year tee ball players will be able to hit the kick ball off the batting tee at their first practice. After the player achieves success with the kick ball, then progress to a smaller ball. Eventually have the batter hit a ball an actual baseball. It has always amazed me how on the first day of tee ball practice, youth players 5 and 6 years-old who never held a bat are expected to hit the ball cleanly off the tee. As coaches, I always felt we have a responsibility to create a positive experience for youth players. Having them succeed will pay dividends. Youth baseball coaches' main goal is always to make sure their players return the next season. Coaches can also use those big red plastic bats early in the season.

Velcro Fly Ball Drill

1) **Use of drill & players needed:** A progression drill for players learning to catch fly balls. Any number of players can be used on a field or in a backyard.

2) **Equipment:** A velcro ball and paddle and either a racquetball racquet or tennis racquet.

3) **Goal:** The goal is to get young players to feel comfortable without fear and to eventually catch a fly ball.

Most young players have a hard time trying to catch their first fly ball. Probably the worst thing a youth baseball coach or parent can do is put a seven or eight year-old on the field and start hitting fly balls with a hard ball and expect him to catch it. This isn't to say all young players cannot catch a fly ball, but for the most part this skill is something that has to be worked on and developed. When young players get hit on the head with a hard ball or get hit by a pitch the first time they are in the batter's box, this is a great formula to turn them off from the game of baseball. In this drill, we are introducing catching fly balls to the players in the most basic way. This drill can be done as part of a station or individually. Players love to do this drill once they experience it. The coach will stand at home plate with the velcro ball and any type of racquet. After he hits the ball, the player gets under it and tries to catch the velcro ball on the paddle. Many kids will have used the velcro ball in some form as a toy. You can also show your players that if this type of ball does hit someone in the head, there is no real pain or injury. It is imperative for the players to feel comfortable and not have any real fear. This is also a great drill to do in a backyard. The kids love this drill because they have success at it. Coaches and parents can progress from this to a tennis ball. Here is a concept coaches need to understand: catching either the velcro or tennis ball is not the ultimate goal. You have to explain to these youngsters that just making contact with the ball on the paddle is a success.

Third Base Drill

1) **Use of drill & players needed**: As a warm-up drill usually performed right after warm-up exercises. At least six or more kids are needed.

2) **Equipment:** At least 2 baseballs plus a bat for the coach.

3) **Goal:** The goal is to not only warm-up the team but also get players used to throwing the baseball from third base to first base, the longest throw in the infield.

This drill is used with two baseballs. Divide the team into three groups, one group is at third base, one at first base, and one at home. The coach will hit a ground ball to the first player in line at third base. As soon as he releases the ball to first base, the coach will get the second ball from the first catcher and hit a ground ball to the next player in line at third base. The first player who went will go to the end of the line at third. The player at first who catches the throw will throw the ball home. He will go to the end of the first base line. The only base that the players don't rotate to after each throw is at catcher. Have the players at home only rotate after 3 or 4 throws. This is for safety reasons because the coach is swinging a bat. After each player at third base has 2 or 3 turns, rotate each group moving clockwise. The group of four at third moves to first and the group at first moves home and the group at home moves to third. Coaches have to make sure they have extra baseballs should overthrows occur. Just have the backups at each base roll the overthrown balls home. On their last chance at third, have players drop the ball, pick it up and throw it to first. We call this the "bobble drill." We are teaching players not to give up on the play. They will have enough time to make the out and this is an important concept for fielders to learn. Always emphasize how important it is to stop the baseball and not necessarily make catching it clean the ultimate goal. Multiple baseballs create almost constant activity and movement amongst the players. Coaches should make sure that the back-ups know to space themselves a good 4-6 feet apart.

Cross Infield Drill

1) **Use of drill & players needed:** As a warm-up drill usually performed right after warm-up exercises. At least five or more players.

2) **Equipment:** Four baseballs (with extras available) and one bat for each coach hitting.

3) **Goal:** Give players a good number of repetitions fielding grounders and to always keep the players moving.

There are four lines of players in this drill and two coaches. If you have 12 players, there is a line of 3 players at third base, 2 players at shortstop, 3 players at second base, and 2 players off of first base. There is one player and one coach between home and third base and another player and coach between home and first base. The coach between home and third will hit ground balls to the two lines on the right side of the infield. Initially he hits to the line with three players on it. The fielder catches the grounder and throws it to the player next to the coach, who is simulating a first baseman. The coach works with two baseballs because as soon as he hits the first ball to the first player in line, the player next to him flips him another ball so he can hit it to the first player in the other line. Players will rotate to the end of the opposite line. Creating movement and keeping the players active is very important to keep them stimulated. The coach between home and first base will hit the balls to the lines on the left side of the infield. Coaches can do this for a defined period of time or repetitions then can flip flop both lines on the field. Keep the players moving and get them to all areas on the field. A very important safety issue is for coaches to make sure that if they miss or hit the ball too softly, the fielders should not charge the ball. If they do they are exposing themselves to being hit by baseballs from the other line. Just hit another ball. It is great to introduce this drill early in the season. If you are short coaches or players, then just use one side of the infield with the two lines.

Line Throw Drill

1) **Use of drill & players needed:** As a warm-up with at least six kids.

2) **Equipment**: Several baseballs. Soft covered or tennis balls can also be used depending on the age of the kids.

3) **Goal:** Practice throwing the baseball to first base from the third base and shortstop position.

The players will line up behind one another in two lines, one at 3rd base position and the other at shortstop. One row of baseballs is set up in front of each line, the number of balls matching the amount of players in the line. One or two players are at first base with an empty bucket to collect the baseballs thrown to them. The coach can situate himself between each line of baseballs. The first person in each line should be in the ready position with knees bent, leaning forward with their glove hand, and the throwing hand between their thighs but not resting on their thighs. The coach will give the "go" command. The first person in line at third base will come out of the ready position and pick up the first ball in his line with his bare hand and throw it to first base. As soon as the coach sees the player release the baseball, he points to the first person in the other line and gives the "go" command for him to do the same, running to pick up the baseball closest to him and throw it to first base. Now here is a very important key to this drill. The first person who went at third base then goes to the end of the line at shortstop. And the first person to go at shortstop will go to the end of the line at third base. The coach must reinforce to the players when switching lines not to cross over in front of the other line but go directly to the end of that line. Constant movement by players will help keep the players involved at all times. The player at first base will catch the baseball and just drop it in the bucket. He rotates with the backup player every four or five chances. The players at first must pay attention when rotating because the baseballs will keep coming. Utilize your assistant coaches or parents. Once the baseballs are used up, one of the players at first base will bring the bucket to the coach and the drill can start again. Shorten the distance for younger players. Coaches can also use one line and have a coach catching the baseball at first base. You can be creative with this drill. At your next practice, move the two lines around the infield to shortstop and second base. Challenge your players to get 6 perfect throws and catches in a row and reward each player with one extra batting practice swing. You will be amazed how well this technique works when the players are motivated to succeed as a team.

Double Line Throw Drill

1) **Use of drill & players needed**: As a warm-up with any number of kids. A variation of the regular line throw drill.

2) **Equipment:** Several baseballs. Soft covered or tennis balls can also be used depending on the age and skill level of the kids.

3) **Goal**: Practice throwing the baseball a long distance in the infield accurately.

This drill is very similar to the previous line throw drill. We are using a single line of players and a double line of baseballs. The baseballs should be lined up in a kind of staggered location. The first player on the coach's "go" command will run up to the baseball closest to him, pick it up, and throw it to first base. But instead of going to the end of the line, he continues to pick up the next baseball and throws it to first base as well. The coach can use a predetermined amount of baseballs that each player will pick up and throw. If the coach says each player will throw six baseballs, he will be moving back and forth from line to line setting up and trying to throw an accurate throw to first. I have done this drill with as little as 3 players at practice and it works well. The coach must emphasize in this drill that when players rush their throw, errors occur. We are trying to achieve a kind of muscle memory so that during a game, the throw to first base from any infield position will be second nature. Again, I am a big believer in having a lot of drills originate from third base because of the long distance throw to first. Good form throwing to a good target will translate to success. The younger smaller player does not have to reach first on a fly early in the season.

Goalie Drill

1) **Use of drill & players needed:** A warm-up or skill drill. Any number of kids.

2) **Equipment:** A lot of soft covered baseballs and some cones.

3) **Goal:** Teach player to move their feet and keep the ball in front of them.

In the goalie drill, we are trying to teach youth players to move their feet and block the ball like a hockey goalie and not necessarily catch it in order to keep the ball in front of them. Youth players have a tendency to not move their feet and to reach for the ball. As coaches, we want to get players in the habit of moving rather than reaching toward the baseball. A blocked ball can also be converted into an out. We try to teach youth players to field the ball in the center of their body. One of the main reasons for this is if the ground ball is misplayed or takes a bad hop, the body will act as a backboard. Many players are afraid of the ball, but this is part of the game. The coach will set up two cones about 8-12 feet apart, depending on age and skill level. The coach will be in front with a bucket of soft covered balls. The coach will begin tossing the ball trying to get them in between the cones past the participant. Like a hockey goalie, the player must try to stop each ball from getting behind him. The player is allowed to dive to stop the ball. The drill can be carried on for a set amount of balls or by time before the next player goes. Other players waiting their turn should be backups. This should be set up as one station while other stations work on other skills or you can have multiple stations if there are enough assistant coaches. This is an excellent drill that parents can do in their own backyard. Using larger balls and slowing down the pace for young kids will work well. Diving for the ball should not be discouraged as long as it is safe. Coaches need to reinforce moving their feet. A good variation of this drill is to do it with no glove.

King Arthur

1) **Use of drill & players needed:** As a warm-up with any number of kids.

2) **Equipment:** A few soft covered baseballs or pickle balls plus a broomstick or closet pole 1 3/8".

3) **Goal:** Make contact with the ball. Once the player hits the ball, he should quickly get set and ready to receive the next throw.

This is a fun drill that young players love, not only for team practices but at home as well. It is very easy to set up. You will need a pole about 5-6 feet long. It can be a broomstick or a closet pole, which measures 1 3/8" thick. The player stands in front of a fence or a wall. He holds onto the stick in the center of his body, like a knight in the olden days of King Arthur. The coach, about 6-10 feet from the hitter (depending on the age of the players) will throw soft covered or plastic balls in fast rapid fire succession, trying to get the balls by the player. The player tries to hit every ball on the outside of the pole or stick before the ball hits the fence behind him. The coach should alternate sides and/or throw to the same side twice in a row. He should make his throws as unpredictable as possible. The coach or parent should be holding more than one ball at a time. If the ball gets by the player and hits the fence, the next player goes. Two stations are great for this drill. This drill conditions the player's eye/hand coordination. Drills like this are a great change of pace from regular baseball fundamental drills. Parents can do this drill at home. This is one of those reciprocal drills where the kids can also take a turn throwing the ball to the parent. Drills, such as this, are good for a number of reasons besides the fun aspect. The fact that the drill can be done in a small confined area is quite advantageous. Also, drills that have a lot of repetitions in a short period of time seem to be the most popular with younger kids. This can also be set up as a competition, seeing who makes contact the most times in a row or in a predetermined amount of time. How many can a player hit in 30 seconds? You can then progress to see how many that same player can hit in 60 seconds. This drill will actually help players focus on the baseball.

Over The Fence

1) **Use of drill & players needed:** As a warm-up and reaction drill with any number of kids.

2) **Equipment:** A few soft covered baseballs and a few helmets.

3) **Goal:** A fielding reaction drill teaching the players to turn around and pick-up the baseball coming over the fence.

In this drill we are utilizing the facility around us. Coaches should always have their minds in a creative mode, whether it is on the field or in their backyard. You'll be amazed how many drills can be created in the oddest locations or with the oddest structures. In this case, there is a fence surrounding the field. One coach can do this drill with three or four players while another coach or coaches can do another drill(s). Just make sure the kids that are not involved with the Fence Drills are a safe distance away. There are three or four players inside the fence on the field. There is another three or four players outside the fence near the coach. One of the players on the field will move up toward the fence. He must be wearing a helmet. The player stands with his back toward the coach. The coach will then throw a ball over the fence in the vicinity of where the players is standing, but not necessarily right to him. The coach yells "throw" after the ball leaves his hand. The player on the field will turn around quickly and look up at the top of the fence to pick up the baseball then try to catch it. This can be a challenging drill. The kids may not get comfortable finding a ball in flight until after one or two turns. The progression method of just having the players touch the baseball with their glove, not necessarily catch it, is a great way to introduce this drill to your team. Once players become comfortable, coaches can challenge the players even more by yelling "throw" an instant after they release the baseball. There is a lot of flexibility with this drill. Coaches can move the players back or set up the drill as a competition between teams. If you are lucky enough to practice on a facility with a lot of space, you might be able to utilize two coaches using two separate sides of the field. The helmet is imperative for reasons that are obvious. What might happen if a player turns around too late or really misjudges the baseball? You can start with a soft covered ball.

Know The Fence Drill

1) **Use of drill & players needed:** One or more players can be used on a field or at home.

2) **Equipment:** A few baseballs or soft covered balls and an area where there are objects to overcome.

3) **Goal:** Teach players to have awareness when catching near any kind of obstruction.

One of the hardest challenges for all ballplayers is to catch a ball next to structures, like fences. It always amazed me when watching professional baseball players how they can focus on a foul ball near the dugout and catch it right before they fall in. This is one of those drills that is extremely important for a number of reasons, but the actual situation may never come up during a game or even a season. Typically this happens with a foul ball or a long ball where the fence is the object the player has to locate before proceeding to catch the ball comfortably. Many times youth baseball players will give up on a ball that is hit near obstructions out of fear of getting hurt. Line up your team near a fence, One by one throw a fly ball near the fence. The player must stick out his closest hand toward the fence to locate the proximity of the man-made object. He then must focus on the fly ball, keeping his hand on the fence as long as possible, but always moving in the direction to where the baseball is coming down. It is important to have players do this drill with both hands, their free hand and their glove hand, by moving the coach to the other side. Coaches can use soft covered balls the first time through the drill, encouraging their players just to make contact with the baseball and not necessarily catch it.

Rapid Throw Drill

1) **Use of drill & players needed:** As a throwing competition with an even number of kids.

2) **Equipment:** Two baseballs for every pair of players in this drill.

3) **Goal:** Teach the concept of accurate quick throws in the form of a competitive game.

This game combines a number of catching and throwing concepts into a fun game that will combine technique with competition. Give each player on the team a partner. They will face each other approximately 20 feet apart. Each pair will have one baseball that they will throw back and forth to each other. Each pair will also get a second baseball that will be stationed at one of the player's feet. On the "go" command, the players will throw the baseball to their partner back and forth for a predetermined amount of time. They must throw quickly yet control their throws and catches. Usually I do this for about 15 seconds the first time through the drill. I time it and ask up and down the line how many throws and catches each pair had. Players are on the honor system. After the first turn, the coach can move the players further apart from each other or increase the amount of time. The extra baseball at the foot of one of the players is there in case of an overthrow. I tell my players we are giving every pair an extra chance. A few teaching points with this drill: reinforce to the players that if they hurry too much getting the baseball out of their gloves or hurry their throws, there is a better chance for an error. Players that do this drill correctly will get into a good rhythm and will automatically show good footwork. I usually have two talented players demonstrate the drill and point out the footwork and how they get the ball out of the glove quickly but not rushed. When dividing the players into pairs, make sure the teams are fair. Having the best athlete paired with the weakest athlete and so on is the most fair way to do this drill. It is important to space out the players. Soft covered baseballs or tennis balls can be used. You can do a ground ball variation, but do so only with hardballs. On ground balls,

147

it must bounce more than once. You can also alternate having one of the players throw ground balls and the other line drives, then switch. Remember, most players love competition. Any time you can teach a skill within a competitive fun game, do it.

First To Third Throw & Catch

1) **Use of drill & players needed:** As a warm-up with at least four kids.

2) **Equipment:** At least one baseball and two or more available for overthrows.

3) **Goal**: Make accurate throws and catches in the infield.

I love warm up drills that utilize practical game-like situations with challenging throws that cover long distances, in order to make the aforementioned throw routine. In this drill, we divide the team in half. One half goes to first base and lines up in a straight line and the other half does the same at third base. One player comes out from each line and is in fair territory at first base and at third base. The baseball can start at either line, but I like to start at third base. The player at third is handed a baseball. On the coach's "go" command, the player will throw the baseball to the player at first base. Once he throws the baseball, he will run by way of second base (he should touch it) to the end of the line at first base. When the player at first base catches the ball, he will then throw it back to third base where the second person in line has moved up. After he throws the baseball, he will run to the end of the line at third base by way of home plate (he touches it). The coach can have players straddle the base and lay down a tag before they come up with their throw. We have to make sure the players are warmed up fairly well before they do this drill. The fact that we are throwing from third to first and vise versa is a long distance. We are working on strengthening the players' arms while also practicing accuracy. The running the player does after he throws the baseball is creating constant movement. We are actually having the players do some conditioning in this drill along with their throws. Like all throwing drills, the coach should make sure the players are spaced properly so the overthrows do not hit anyone. Players do not have to reach on a fly especially early in the season. Besides the players needing to be warmed up, coaches have to make sure that players' arms are not hurting. Coaches should ask the players throughout the drill how their arms feel.

Turn Drill

1) **Use of drill & players needed:** As a warm-up and reaction drill with any number of kids.

2) **Equipment:** A few soft covered baseballs.

3) **Goal:** Players turn and react to the spot where the ball is thrown. Players should try to field the ball in the middle of their body.

The Turn Drill is a reflex or reaction drill that kids love. If a hardball is used and the receiver of the ball is not quick enough to react, there is a chance for injury. Because of this factor, coaches and parents should use soft covered baseballs or tennis balls. Two players will stand about 15-20 feet from the coach and about 10 feet from each other with their backs to the coach. The coach will designate one of the players to go first. The coach will toss a baseball underhand and yell "turn." When the player turns, he should expect to find the baseball in the air right in front of him. After the first player goes, the coach tosses another ball at the other player, and on the "turn" command, he turns around expecting the ball. Once the player catches the baseball he can just drop it or roll it away from him. The coach needs to have a bucket of baseballs. The coach or parent should use his judgement on the distance between him and the players and at what point he will yell "turn." All involved in this drill should make it fun and challenging. Once the players get the knack of how this works, you can start tossing the baseball and yelling "turn" later and later, thus making the player react quicker. Coaches can also add players using three or even four. Coaches can use their assistants and parents to have numerous stations with this drill. Getting numerous repetitions in a short period of time makes this drill popular. With very young kids, coaches can adjust by using plastic balls or even bean bags that are softer and travel slower. Coaches can have players just knock the ball away the first round of this drill before becoming comfortable with catching the baseball. Make sure it is understood that reaction time can vary amongst players. Coaches should try to pair two similar athletes with each other. This is an excellent drill to do at home with your own kids.

Face Off Drill

1) **Use of drill & players needed:** As a warm-up with four or more kids. Works best with a whole team.

2) **Equipment:** One baseball with others available in case of overthrows.

3) **Goal**: Have players throw and catch a ball while creating movement.

Many times coaches are faced with situations with limited space when they need to warm up their team right before a game. For instance, on Saturdays in May, the field associated with my league is used from morning to night. Once a game is over the next two teams will take the field. Warm-up time is limited. The space around the field is also limited. The parking lot is full of young kids playing all over the place. This is why coaches need to have a few drills that can be done in a limited amount of space on a small patch of field or even a surface like a parking lot. The Face Off Drill can be done in a limited amount of space and players get a good amount of repetitions in a short amount of time. The team is divided in two lines. Players will line up behind each other on each line. Each line will be facing each other about 20-30 feet apart. One baseball is used. A soft covered ball is preferred. On the coaches command, the first person in line will throw the ball to the first person in the other line. Right after he throws the ball, he runs to the side and goes to the end of the other line. The player who catches the ball will do the same throwing to the new first person in the line facing him. He will then run to the end of the other line. It is important for the coach to designate which side each line will run to. I like to always tell players in this drill to throw the baseball and run to the left. With each line facing each other, each left side is different for each team. You can have the players throw ground balls. Safety is very important in this drill because if a player misses a throw other players may be directly in the line of fire. Coaches must make sure there is some space behind the player who catches the baseball. This is the reason a soft covered baseball is preferred. Encourage player in this drill to give the thrower a target.

Circle Drill

1) **Use of drill & players needed:** As a warm-up or fun change of pace drill. Can use this drill as a competition. Will need at least six players.

2) **Equipment:** At least two baseballs and more for backups.

3) **Goal:** Have players focus on catching and throwing ground balls.

This drill is one of those drills that combines fun with skills. It is a great change of pace drill that can be done any time, but is especially good right after a skill session where you are teaching your players an important concept and want a change of pace. Put your players in a circle making sure the circle is fairly large. Start with one ball. The coach or a player can start this drill. On the "go" command from the coach, the player (or coach) will throw a ground ball to another player. The player will catch the ball and immediately throw it to another person. This continues, either for a time limit or until one player makes an error. The key rule to this drill is that the player can throw the baseball to anyone in the circle except for the person next to him on either side. Once the players get used to this drill with one baseball, try the drill with two baseballs. This is a real challenge for young players because it forces the players to pay attention and focus on the drill. The constant movement of the two baseballs in a confined area will create a kind of controlled chaos that is beneficial and will keep your players from wandering mentally. After they master doing this drill with two baseballs, divide the team in half, forming two circles, and do this drill as a competition. Have one assistant cover one circle while another coach covers the other circle. The coach can count out loud as the drill is in progress as to how many catches in a row their particular circle is up to. I will repeat this mantra a lot: "kids love competition." Longer and wet grass will slow down the baseball, so you need a good patch of grass. Soft covered baseballs are recommended for younger players. Coaches can and should participate in this drill every once in a while. This drill also works well with tennis balls in a parking lot or other hard surfaces.

Lead Drill

1) **Use of drill & players needed:** As a warm-up with at least four kids. Works best with a whole team.

2) **Equipment:** A bucket of baseballs or soft covered balls.

3) **Goal**: To get players used to catching fly balls on the move.

This is an excellent warm-up drill that also teaches players the correct way to turn and run after a fly ball. The players line up in single file. The coach is just off to the side of the front of the line with a bucket of baseballs. On the "go" command, the first player in line will begin running. The coach will lead him very much like a football quarterback leading a receiver. The player must track the ball in the air and catch it. He then returns, drops the ball in the bucket, and goes to the end of the line. A key point here is that the player's lead shoulder should be in the direction where the ball is headed. Reinforce for players when running to make sure to turn around and pick up the ball visually in flight every so often. This act of turning and seeing the baseball is a skill in itself that young players need to practice. In fact, early in the season when practicing this drill, coaches should emphasize that players should not be obsessed with catching the ball in their glove and just make contact with the ball with their glove. With two coaches, you can perform this drill facing each other with two lines staggered so the players are not running into each other. After the player goes in one line he should go to the end of the line with the other coach. This drill also works really well with tennis balls being hit with a racquet. I have had much success with this drill in our indoor practices. Kids love seeing and using props in drills. Just remember, a tennis ball is hard to catch in a baseball glove so the idea of just making contact is perfectly acceptable and encouraged. Having the players experience as much success as possible is the main goal. This is a great drill for parents to do at home. Try to do this drill in a grassy area. Players will really enjoy trying to make every catch. Some will dive for the balls.

Two Team Relay Drill

1) **Use of drill & players needed:** At least six players.

2) **Equipment:** A bucket of baseballs, a box (or boxes) and a cone.

3) **Goal** Knock down the cone. We want to teach players to get the ball from the outfield to the infield quickly and accurately. The infielder must turn to his glove side.

Out of all the drills I do with my team, this one seems to bring out some of the best in competition and the skills taught seem to stick with my players. The coach divides the team into two, about equal in talent. The coach and an assistant will each take a team into the outfield, one positioned in left centerfield and the other in right centerfield. The coach of each team will place one player in the infield, usually around the second base and shortstop position. The rest of each team in the outfield lines up in a straight line. The coach will call out the first person in line, who will step away from the line and face the infield. The coach throws a baseball behind him toward the fence or wall. On the "go" command, the fielder must turn, locate the baseball, run, and pick it up. He then throws the baseball to the infielder on his team. The infielder will turn and throw the baseball toward home where one or more boxes with a cone on top is set up as a target. The goal is for the cut-off man to knock down the cone with his throw. After one team goes, the other team takes a turn. As the other team is going, the team that went will rotate positions, the infielder going to the end of the outfield line and the outfielder then moving to the infield position where he will get a chance to knock down the cone. The outfielder must reach the infielder on a fly. The infielder must turn to his glove side when catching the ball because it will put him in the best position to throw home. A team is awarded one point for reaching the infielder on a fly, one point for the infielder turning to the glove side, and two points for knocking down the cone. Each team can get four points on a turn. Coaches can have a lot of fun with this drill by throwing the baseball further or closer to the outfielder or setting up the distances

159

appropriate to the age and skill level. Teach infielders to move out further for the cut-off, anticipating the longer throws. Also, players know who has the stronger or weaker arm, and should adjust their distance accordingly.

Three Man Relay Drill

1) **Use of drill & players needed:** A game using groups of three focusing on hitting the relay man from the outfield.

2) **Equipment:** One baseball for each group of three players.

3) **Goal:** Drill players on making accurate throws and turning to the glove side when receiving a relay throw.

This drill is similar to the Two-Team Relay Drill. The team is divided up into groups of three. If there is an extra player or players, just rotate them in and out after each round. Players are spaced out behind each other anywhere from 30-50 feet apart depending on the age, skill level, and the amount of space you have available. Place a baseball 5-10 feet in front of the first person in line. He turns his back to the ball. On the "go" command, the first player will turn around, run to the ball, pick it up, turn and throw it to the middle person in line. He catches the ball, turns, and throws it to the last person in line, who repeats this process of throwing the ball to the player in the middle and back to the first person. The team that completes one round of throws first gets a point. There are skills to teach here. The player in the middle who catches the ball should almost always turn to his glove side when throwing. When you teach this concept, don't just say "glove side." Show the players so they understand which side the glove side is. Teach players not to rush their throws and to try aiming for their teammate's chest when making the throw. In this drill, the players cannot skip or bypass a throw. After each round, the team will rotate positions, the first player in line moving to the end of the line and everyone else moving up. Players will improve in this drill over time.

Baseball-Football

1) **Use of drill & players needed:** 100% fun game with the whole team

2) **Equipment:** Two hard balls for each player and one tennis ball.

3) **Goal:** This fun game, with a baseball theme, is a great way to end a practice on a high note. Players should focus on squeezing the ball in their glove.

If there was ever a game that brings excitement to my players, then "Baseball-Football" is it. The game is such a hit that players out of the league for 15 years will always ask if we still play Baseball-Football. Players one year removed from my team have begged me to come back to play this game. The players are divided into two teams. One on offense and one on defense. It is a game of touch football using a tennis ball as the football. But the defensive team must hold two baseballs in their gloves, and this is how the player tags the player with the tennis ball. If one or both of the baseballs fall out of the glove then the play is still live until a teammate tags the offensive player. This is one of those fun games that is great to play at the end of practice. Any game is fine as long as you are creative and establish a baseball theme to it. We are teaching the players the concept of squeezing the baseball in their glove. I encourage coaches and parents to take any kids game and put a baseball theme into it. This game is good for the end of the season.

Stay Low Drill

1) **Use of drill & players needed:** A skill drill for catching ground balls with any number of players.

2) **Equipment:** A nylon rope and access to a fence. A few baseballs and batting gloves for the person holding the rope.

3) **Goal**: Teach players when fielding a ground ball to get down and stay low.

I remember when I played high school football my coach would explain to us the importance of staying low for power and leverage when we blocked our opponent. We would do a one-on-one drill with two players holding a rope over us while in our stance and we were forced to stay low going forward and making contact with each other. Using the same important concept of staying low to catch ground balls, I needed to come up with a drill that forces players to do this in youth baseball. Again, crossing over to other sports, I remembered my football days and transformed that football drill into a baseball one. In the "Stay Low Drill" you need to have access to a fence which is usually available on any youth baseball field or at any school you might practice by. Tie a rope about ten feet long to the fence. Have a player hold the other end. A coach will be standing directly behind the rope-holder. There is a line of players on one side of the rope. On the "go" command, the coach will roll a ground ball to the other side of the rope. The player must run underneath the rope, stay low, in order to field the ball. He should make the catch and roll the baseball back to the coach. This is one of those drills that only emphasizes one skill, which is catching the ground ball while staying low. We can combine catching with throwing by using another player located about 30-40 feet away to simulate a first baseman, but I like to break down the drill first to approach the different skills involved. I prefer to perfect one skill first before combining it with another. The player holding the rope is advised to wear batting gloves to prevent rope burn just in case the fielder does not stay low enough and makes contact with the rope.

No Glove Drill

1) **Use of drill & players needed**: As a warm-up or skill drill with an even number kids. A parent and child can also do this one-on-one.

2) **Equipment:** A few hardballs or soft covered baseballs.

3) **Goal:** Teach players to catch ground balls with two hands.

Players can become dependent on their baseball gloves too much. Sometimes they think all they have to do is put their glove down and it will do the work automatically for them. In this drill, we are forcing the players to catch the ground ball with two hands. When players do not have a glove on they have to use two hands. I want to emphasize right here that I always thought the concept of always catching the ball with two hands can be overused, especially on fly balls when the fielder is on the move. A player moving fast laterally might be better off catching the ball with one hand rather than two. A ball hit right to the player, where he has a chance to catch it in the middle of his body, should be executed with two hands. In this drill, we split the team in half, each player having a partner. On the "go" command, the player throws a ground ball to his partner. He must catch it with two hands. This drill covers a couple of concepts. Because the players are catching the ball bare-handed, they are most likely going to keep their head down properly and watch it go into their hands. Coaches can move the players further apart. This drill is great with really young players, however, it should not be restricted to only young players and

167

only early in the season. Soft covered baseball are recommended. Coaches should always review fundamentals, going back to basics all the time.

Shadow Drill

1) **Use of drill & players needed:** As a warm-up and skill drill simulating catching a ground ball.

2) **Equipment:** A few regular baseballs or soft covered baseballs.

3) **Goal:** Have one player catch a ground ball while the rest of the team simulates catching the same baseball.

Fielding drills don't always have to have everyone involved catching the ball. There is a lot to be said for players actually doing the correct motion without catching the ball. In this drill, called the "shadow drill," we combine both catching the ball along with going through the correct motion to throw the ball. The players all line up behind one another in a straight line. The coach will throw a ground ball to the left side or the right side. The first person in line is the only one who fields the ball. The rest of the line will follow the action like they are fielding the ball by bending down, watching the ball into the glove, and coming up to throw the ball to the coach. Once the first person completes the drill, he goes to the end of the line. The next player will be the live player and the rest of the line will continue to "shadow" the first person in line. The player who just had the turn as the live fielder must take a very wide turn as he goes to the end of the line. He will probably miss one turn until he gets back in line. Concentrating on techniques without worrying about catching the baseball is essential for the players. Skills, such as bending from the knees or keeping the head down on the ball, will translate into the correct technique for players in games. Developing the correct habits without the baseball will make it easier once the player is in a live situation. Coaches should learn to break down drills that have multiple skills and be able to drill each part separately. Drills like this where the action is only going to one player are effective but hard to do for a sustained period. I would not go through the line more than once or maybe twice.

Around The Horn

1) **Use of drill & players needed:** As a warm-up combining speed and accuracy with at least four players, but more are better.

2) **Equipment:** At least two baseballs with more available.

3) **Goal:** Quickly catch and throw without dropping the ball or throwing it wildly.

Just as players like competition against one another, they also love to be challenged even if they are racing at a task against the clock. The coach will divide the team into four groups of three. Each group will be at a base. For the first few rounds, a soft covered baseball is recommended. On the "go" command, the first person with the group at home plate will throw a ball to the first person in line at third base. The player catches the ball, puts down a "phantom" tag, and throws it to the first person in line at second base, who then throws the ball to first base. The first person in line at first base completes the drill by throwing home. As each player receives the ball, he should put down this phantom tag in front of the base. After the player throws the ball, he must move out of the way so the second player in line can move up to catch the ball. This drill moves fast and players have to be instructed to catch the ball, throw it, and get out of the way. Players at the bases should be straddling the base. An excellent challenge is also to try this drill with two baseballs, starting with one at second base. There will be two baseballs going around the diamond and players need to move in and out of their position even quicker. Using this drill with two baseballs should be saved for the middle of the season or when the coach feels the team has become proficient with one baseball. The coach should always have extra baseballs available for overthrows. This is one drill that the coach and the team will see improvement over the course of the season. The coach should use a stopwatch to time this drill at the beginning of the season then time it in the middle of the season and at the end of the season. This drill can also be set up as a competition, dividing the team into three teams of four and see which team has the best time.

Line Master Drill

1) **Use of drill & players needed:** As a warm-up drill that helps motor skills. At least six kids or more should be used.

2) **Equipment:** At least two soft covered baseballs with extras available.

3) **Goal:** Think ahead by being able to throw one baseball while simultaneously catch one.

The Line Master drill forces players to think ahead because there is more than one thing going on at the same time. We are also challenging the motor skills of each player. It is also one of those drills that is putting some subtle pressure on the younger players, who have not done this drill before. Line up the players in a straight line with ample space between them. One player faces the line in front of them with a baseball. A player at the the end of the line will also have a baseball. On the "go" command, the player facing the line will throw the ball to the second person in the line. At the same time the player with the ball in line will throw it to the player facing the line, who is the "line master." The line master will then throw the ball to the person next to the player who just had their turn throwing the ball. This continues all the way down the line. After each person in the line had a chance, a new line master is designated. He comes out front and begins the drill the same way. Young players will find this drill hard to do because of the multiple tasks. If one looks at the definition of a motor skill, it states that: it is a learned sequence of movements that combine a smooth, efficient action in order to master a particular task. This drill might be the perfect example of players trying to master the skills of throwing the baseball while simultaneously catching one that had just been thrown. Coaches should first use soft covered baseballs in this drill.

Shuttle Drill

1) **Use of drill & players needed:** As a warm-up or conditioning drill with three players.

2) **Equipment:** About 8-10 covered baseballs or hard balls.

3) **Goal:** Have the players moving back and forth picking up stationary baseballs and tossing them underhand accurately to a target.

Drills in small confined areas can pose a challenge to youth players. The Shuttle Drill can be used for players of all ages and can even be a conditioning drill for older or school players. We take a number of baseballs or soft covered balls and line them up. If we have eight baseballs, we line four balls on each side of a player. There are two players at each end of the baseballs. On the "go" command, the player will run toward the baseball closest to him on one side, pick it up, and toss it underhand to the nearest player, who just lays the ball down or puts it in a bucket. He will then quickly turn and move to the ball closest to him on the other side, once again tossing it underhand. He continues this until he is done with both lines of baseballs. This drill works on a number of things, including eye hand coordination. Coaches need to recognize that the player will be tossing the baseball a further distance the deeper he goes into the drill as the baseballs get further apart, by means of elimination. This drill can be timed individually or two stations can be set up for a competition between two players to see who can finish first. Coaches should reinforce that players tossing the baseball stay fairly low, making sure not to stand straight up when performing the task. It is a good idea when introducing this drill to use less baseballs and work up to more during the season. Coaches can be creative in this drill. Have the receiver of the ball move back and forth after each throw. This is forcing the player to focus on his target.

Catching A Ball In The Sun Or Lights

1) **Use of drill & players needed:** Expose players to catching a ball in the sun or lights. Any number of players.

2) **Equipment:** A few soft covered baseballs.

3) **Goal:** Have players feeling comfortable catching a baseball that is in the sun or in the lights.

Catching a regular hit fly ball is hard enough for youth baseball players to do. Putting an added handicap, like facing the sun or lights, makes it even more difficult. Most fields are built with the direction of the sun in mind. However, with the scarcity of land, many times leagues have to make due with the best they can and build a field in any spot regardless of sun. The different times games are played, including night games, almost makes it a certainty that one or more fly balls or pop ups will have the potential of being lost in the sun or lights during the season. It's hard for young players to make a catch facing the sun or light without practicing it. On the pop up, teach your players to follow the baseball while blocking out the sun or lights with their glove. While doing this, the players should keep sight of the ball, looking over the glove. Keeping the glove up, follow the baseball as it is going up. As the ball comes down, the player gets ready to open up the glove just before the baseball reaches the same height as the glove. This should be practiced in both the sun and lights. This is a good reason why most teams should have at least one night practice before the season starts. Seeing this for the first time in a game is tough. Initially soft covered baseballs or tennis balls should be used to practice.

Ground Ball Trio

1) **Use of drill & players needed:** Ground ball catching skill. Three players are needed.

2) **Equipment:** A few soft covered baseballs or hard balls.

3) **Goal:** Have players focus on technique catching ground balls.

I am a huge believer in breaking down fundamentals and instituting drills stressing these fundamentals. In the Ground Ball Trio, three players line up next to one another in the infield. Pictured above, they line up at the shortstop position. A coach rolls a ball to one of the players, who fields the ball. All three players transition from the ready position to the fielding position, even though only one of the players is fielding the ground ball. This drill reinforces to anticipate the ball and be ready to field at all times. The players not fielding the ball will focus on technique only, not concerned with making a play at the same time. This drill trains proper muscle memory so that when a ball is hit to any of the infielders, they will be conditioned into the proper technique. When fielding a ground ball, fielders should field the ball in the center and in front of their body then bring the ball up to their chest to protect from a bobble as well as for easy transition to the throwing hand. Fielders should always try to avoid catching a ground ball on a short hop. Coaches can call out whom they are going to roll the ball to or they can make the throws random. Coaches should also switch the positions for each of the players by putting a different player in the middle of the three. This is an excellent drill to be used as a station when you are able to use your assistant coaches or parents and can have more than one station to practice different skills. The concepts in this drill are similar to the "Shadow Drill" whereby we have players simulate the skill.

Colored-Coded Ground Balls

1) **Use of drill & players needed:** Teach players to keep their heads down on ground balls. One or more players.

2) **Equipment:** A bucket of color-coded baseballs prepared ahead of time.

3) **Goal:** Have players focus on keeping their head down on ground balls and following them into their gloves by identifying color-coded baseballs.

Keeping with the theory of using different techniques and challenges to work on a skill while keeping the players stimulated, the Color-Coded Ground Balls Drill will help ensure the players catch the baseball while keeping their heads down. It always drives me crazy when players misplay the easiest ground ball hit right to them. Most of the time an error is made because fielders will pick up their heads a moment too soon rather than following the baseball into their gloves. Not only on the youth level, but at all skill levels, whether it is professional baseball or amateur, lifting the head too soon seems to be the common theme nine out of ten times on a catchable ground ball turned into an error. In this drill, the coach must prepare baseballs with some color-codes on them. The quickest and easiest way is to take twenty baseballs and color code ten of them with a piece of blue masking tape. Begin to hit ground balls to the first person in line. As soon as he is able to identify the color of the baseball, which in this case will be white or blue, he will yell out the color. This drill forces the player to keep his head down. Young players also love the challenge. Coaches or parents can also use a third colored baseball with yellow masking tape. This will make this drill more of a challenge because the players have three options (white, blue, or yellow) to differentiate. When doing the color-coding, attach a large piece of the masking tape to the ball. Over the course of a season, you can make the tape smaller in size. Separate skills in this drill by not having the player throw to first but just roll the baseball aside after catching the grounder. This will keep the player focused on the one single skill of catching the ground ball. The act of keeping the players' heads down is a habitual skill that needs to be constantly reinforced in practice. I am always telling players in many of my drills to "watch the ball into the glove." This is especially true when an infielder tries to make a double play on a ground ball. The fielders need to hurry to get the lead out quickly, which can inadvertently cause them to look up too quickly and not even get a single out instead of one or even two. This even happens to the best fielders.

Two Fly Ball Drill

1) **Use of drill & players needed:** As a challenge for players to think ahead. Any number of players.

2) **Equipment**: A bucket of soft covered baseballs or tennis balls.

3) **Goal:** Challenge players to catch one fly ball right after another.

My players usually range in age from 10-12 years-old. I approach the start of every season the same way by telling them and their parents I will treat them as 13 and 14 year-olds. By this I mean I challenge them at almost every practice and expect them to give an effort beyond their years. Even the least talented players are expected to give the effort as if they were a year or two older. Some of the drills will put the players in front of their teammates with the chance of failure. I teach all my players never to be afraid of failing. I believe this is good for youth baseball players, which will not only benefit them on the field, but will also carry over into other aspects of their lives. This drill was actually introduced to me by my big brother in our backyard. In the Two Fly Ball Drill, I have a bucket of soft covered or tennis balls. The fielder is placed in a spot where he has to field a fly ball. I put two balls in my glove. I toss a high fly with the first ball. After a short moment, I throw a second fly ball to the same player. He has to catch the first ball and roll it out of his glove then quickly get ready to locate the flight of the second ball and catch it. This is a great challenge for youth players. The nature of the drill makes it obvious why we use soft covered baseballs. Determine the skill and comfort zone of your players so you can recommend they wear helmets in this drill. I have found that once you challenge players with a hard drill like this, presenting them with another hard drill will give them confidence so they will not be afraid to fail. You can adjust this drill according to skill level and age. Really young players do not have to catch the ball. They can just make contact with their glove or swat it away with the glove.

First Base Scoop

1) **Use of drill & players needed**: As a skill drill for first baseman. One or more players.

2) **Equipment**: Either a bucket of soft covered or regular baseballs.

3) **Goal**: Scoop up the ball in the dirt or keep it in front of you.

One of the most important concepts I try to teach youth players is to block the ball or keep it in front of them. Nowhere is that concept more relevant than at first base and in the scoop drill. Youth players have a natural tendency to turn their heads when playing first base or even the catching position on a ball that bounces in the dirt. With the scoop drill, we take a bucket of baseballs or soft covered baseballs, which are recommended for younger players. The coach will stand anywhere from 10-20 feet away from the first baseman and continuously throw balls in the dirt. The coach should make sure that he is not bouncing the ball in the same spot on every throw. He should also make sure the baseball sometimes reaches the first baseman on multiple bounces. Tennis balls can also be used with this drill. With some players who really have a fear of the baseball, I have them put on a catcher's mask with this drill. This gives them confidence to watch the baseball coming to them all the way. The coach can and should move back further away from the first baseman on every throw. The coach should stand around third base, generally because more short throws will occur from this position than any other. Bad throws are such a big part of youth baseball that it is important for first baseman to practice with both good and bad throws. Make sure all players on the team practice this drill. At first you can have the first baseman stay right on the base. But you should also have him play off the base so he has to get into position on the base. This is a bit harder and requires more work but is more realistic.

Outfield Still Ball Drill

1) **Use of drill & players needed:** As a skill drill for fielding balls that are not moving. One or more players.

2) **Equipment:** A bucket of hard balls.

3) **Goal:** Get outfielders used to charging a stationary baseball while it comes to a complete stop and to come up throwing the ball to a target.

The "Outfield Still Ball" drill is almost the exact same as the line throw drill we do in the infield. The only difference is that we move the line of baseballs to the outfield and the players have to run in, pick up the baseball and throw it to a target. Too many times youth players are expecting the baseball to come to them. We have to teach players in the outfield to expect to pick up the baseball in any number of ways. You can also challenge the players by simulating game like conditions, such as not letting them know where they are going to throw the ball until they pick it up. At the last second, the coach will yell out second, third, or home. This is teaching and conditioning the players to get used to making quick decisions or adjustments. Also, in a drill like this, players must get used to throwing long distances.

Charge Moving Ball

1) **Use of drill & players needed:** As a skill drill for outfielders. One or more players.

2) **Equipment:** A bucket of baseballs and access to a grassy field.

3) **Goal:** Teach young players to charge moving ground balls hit to the outfield.

The Charge Moving Ball Drill is similar to the Still Ball Charge Drill but here the ball is moving. In this drill, we set up a one or two lines in the outfield. The coach will throw or hit ground balls from between first and second base. Simply put, the players must charge the baseball and catch it in their glove. If the player is confident enough to pick up the moving ball bare handed, he should. Like infielders at all levels of play, the main reason for a misplay or error is because the fielder will lift his head before the ball gets into the glove. You have to teach the players to watch the ball go into their glove. This is not an easy task for youth outfielders so it must be practiced. This is one of those progression drills. At first, just have the players catch the ball without throwing the ball to a cutoff man or infielder. They should just roll the ball to the side. On the second turn, you can then add coming up to throw to a coach at second base. It is also good to have them throw it home. Coaches must teach players that a baseball hit hard will get slower and slower as it gets closer to them, and many times they must increase their speed going forward. Tall or wet grass can also influence the speed of the baseball on the ground. It is always a good idea for the coach to determine the field conditions at the beginning of the game.

Convey to the players if the grass looks like it hasn't been cut in a week that the ball will move slowly. Again, the key is watching the baseball into the glove.

Catcher Pop Ups

1) **Use of drill & players needed:** As a position-specific fielding skill for catchers. One player at a time.

2) **Equipment:** A bucket of tennis balls and a racquet.

3) **Goal:** Teach players who play the catching position to learn how to locate a pop up behind or near home plate.

Catching is my favorite defensive position on the baseball field. I love the toughness and the challenge for players at all levels. Many times on the youth baseball level, the players who gravitate toward catching remain in that position for their playing career if they go on to play school baseball. This position is full of responsibilities, even on the youth level. As the player gets older, the catcher becomes even more important. In this drill I take a bucket of tennis balls. The catcher will start in the catching position and I will simultaneously yell "go" while at the same time hitting a tennis ball around the home plate area. The catcher will stand up while at the same time take his mask off. Once he locates the ball, he should throw the mask away from where the ball is coming. The further away the better so there is no chance of tripping on it. He then gets under the ball, watches it into his glove, and squeezes it tight. In youth baseball, a high pop up around home plate is a rare occasion but it does happen. Players will at first keep their mask on. The skill of removing the mask is important to teach. Many times young players will not react quick enough. Each baseball field is different and sometimes the catcher is faced with different obstacles. To really challenge the players I set this up using our own obstacles. In this case I am using two empty garbage cans located near home plate. Just like catching a foul ball and feeling for the fence, the catcher should feel for the garbage can. Some school coaches will lay out two or three bats in this drill for their catchers to avoid. Young players love the use of props. When they see a racquet come out of my trunk, it is amazing how excited players get. Remember, when using tennis balls, they will tend to bounce out of baseball gloves, especially when using catcher's gloves. Tell your young players doing this drill that the success is just making contact with the glove to the tennis ball. You will see that other players who never thought about playing the catcher position will witness this drill and insist on participating in it. You may end up recruiting another catcher.

Rag Ball Creation

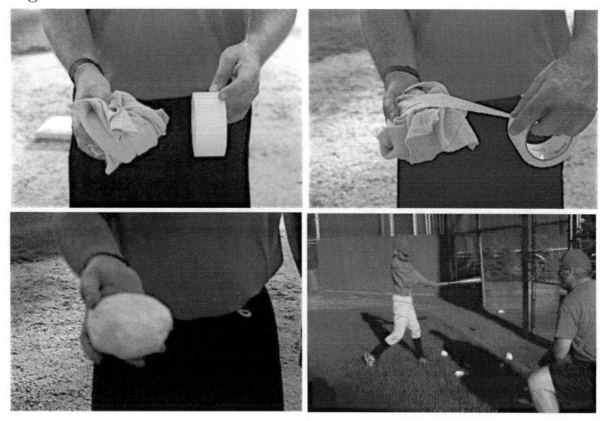

I learned the benefits of the soft toss drill when my oldest son was about eleven years-old. The fact that you can do a lot of repetitions in a short period of time within a confined space appealed to me. And not needing a full team to do this makes it extra special. I went down to the field one day with my son and his friend with a bucket of hardballs and began taking turns. On one of my son's friend turn, the baseball hit the bar that runs in the middle of the fence, bounced back, and hit him squarely in the eye. It was one of those unfortunate accidents. We spent four hours in the hospital. Luckily, he was okay. This put a bit of a shock into me so I went seeking alternatives. From this bad experience, and in the course of trying to discover baseball drills that are economically possible and safe for almost everyone to do, I came up with using a rag ball. All you need are some rags and two-inch masking tape. I take a rag and either roll it up into a ball or tie it into a knot. I then wrap this two inch masking tape completely around the rag. I would recommend you loosely wrap the masking tape so there is as little bounce back as possible when hitting them against the wall. If you are not the type to cut old clothes into rags, any hardware store or home center sells boxes of rags. For the past 15 years I have used these rag balls in toss drills. It is a great warm-up before a game. All you need is space and some supervision because of the swinging of bats with people around. I usually begin making my rag balls around the New Year. You will continually have to rewrap them throughout the course of the season, but I find it very worthwhile and economical. You can also create games with the rag balls. To this day I still see teams warming up hitting hardballs against the fence. I used to try warning them, but I learned long ago that you cannot change the world. Leagues should also recognize that hitting the hardball against the fence is not really healthy for the fence. Coaches should always stick to these rag balls or plastic type balls when hitting them against the fence. The rag ball toss drills are also excellent for doing at home.

Soft Toss Drill

1) **Use of drill & players needed:** As a hitting skill drill.

2) **Equipment:** Rag balls, which are made up of rags covered with loosely attached masking tape.

3) **Goal:** Hit the rag ball against a fence or wall the same height as the batter's eye level or lower.

The Soft Toss Drill has many variations. The basic concept is a coach, parent, or teammate are positioned about 6-10 feet from a hitter with a bat. At about a 45 degree angle, the coach, while kneeling, will toss balls underhanded to the hitter, who hits the baseball against a screen, fence, or wall. The goal is not to hit the rag ball too high on the screen. I like to reinforce for players to have a target eye-level or lower to aim for. A challenging variation is to toss two rag balls. When they are almost at their maximum height, the coach yells out "high" or "low." The player must quickly react and hit either the higher ball or lower ball, depending on the one yelled out. The same thing can be done wrapping a few with blue masking tape and yelling out "white" or "blue." Again, the player must react and hit the color called out between the two balls thrown. Young players love doing this. Another challenge after tossing two rag balls is to yell "middle." The player tries to swing his bat in-between the two rag balls without hitting either of them. This one is for the more advanced athlete. Using a concrete or brick wall at a schoolyard is also just as effective. You can also create a game with the rag balls like putting chalk targets on the wall. You can use a small square inside a large square. The goal is to hit the rag ball inside the small square for a run. This fun game is played like a regular 9 inning game where a hit outside of the inner square is an out. No one says you can't hit these rag balls straight into the field as well.

Multiple Hitting Stations

1) **Use of drill & players needed:** Utilizing multiple practice hitting drills. An even number of player, any amount.

2) **Equipment:** At least one batting tee and three buckets of rag balls or pickle balls, or a mixture of both.

3) **Goal:** Give players a lot of repetitions hitting in a short period of time.

When my team becomes familiar with some drills, I can then organize them in such a way that the players can actually run them by themselves. Of course, at least one coach has to oversee the drills for safety, plus kids will be kids and they have to constantly be motivated. In Multiple Hitting Stations, three different hitting stations are set up in a small confined area in such a way that the players doing them can get a lot repetitions. Using three buckets comprised of pickle balls and/or rag balls or even tennis balls, we are able to do three hitting skills. The first is hitting off the tee. The second is the soft toss drill with the batter taking a full swing. The third is a bunting station where the hitter is in the bunting position and the goal is to just make contact with the ball. The coach must be aware of bats swinging and balls rolling from one station to the other. Safety is the number one concern. All the players at the three stations will not end at the same time. The players will rotate but must pick up the balls near them before moving to the next station. The other half of the team can be doing fielding drills with another coach. Coaches don't have to limit this to three drills if they have the space and enough assistant coaches and parents available to oversee these drills.

Long Toss Drill

1) **Use of drill & players needed:** As a warm-up or skill drill.

2) **Equipment:** One baseball per pair of players.

3) **Goal:** Increase arm strength and accuracy over the course of a season.

The "Long Toss Drill" is thought to be one of the more effective drills to increase arm strength. Pitching coaches from the school level to the pros will make this drill a big part of a pitcher's regimen. In many clinics I have attended, pitching coaches speak about this drill for also enabling players to develop a better sense of rhythm and balance. Once you know the players' arms are warm, divide them into pairs. I start out about 30-40 feet apart and increase the distance every two or three throws. The players should have their throwing arm ready. The footwork is important as we combine a "crow hop" with the throw. When performing a crow hop, the player will lift his back leg (non-glove-side) after maintaining complete control of the ball in the glove. He will then put that foot down in front of the other leg, pointing toward the target, and lift the other leg up (glove-side), using the momentum to hop and throw to the target. I find the crow hop difficult to teach young players. If you try to teach this technique, do it separately from the throwing skill. The long toss drill itself will start with the coach yelling "Ready" then "Throw." The players must throw the ball to their partner accurately so they do not really have to move out of position to get the ball. After two or three throws, move one line back 10-15 feet. Continue this and make sure to ask during the drill if anyone has a tired arm. With the distance increasing, some players will find it hard to reach their partner on a fly, which is fine. In fact, I

195

always challenge my players to hit their partner on one hop then on two hops. This is a great technique to teach players to control their throw. An important factor to reinforce is that throwing, like hitting, encompasses the use of the whole body.

Sliding Drill

1) **Use of drill & players needed**: A team drill to teach the skill of sliding. One or more players.

2) **Equipment**: One or more loose bases.

3) **Goal**: Teach players the correct way to slide; not to start their slide too early or too late.

In youth baseball I have found that the first time players ever slide is in a game. Speak to a college coach who is big on baserunning and he will tell you about different sliding techniques and when to use them. On the youth level, I like to keep it really simple with two things to remember. First, I explain to players that sliding is done more on one's butt than legs. And second, keep your hands up while sliding to avoid injury. There are dozens of more things you can feed into your players' head about sliding, but I caution you that it is better to simplify it and practice it. I take my players into the outfield grass and have them take off their cleats. Some coaches even wet down the outfield grass a little bit to get a better sliding effect. This will exaggerate the slide itself to give the players a better feel for it. I'll put out 3-4 loose bases with as many lines of players and have them run and slide into the base. Tell them the base moving is no concern in this drill and in fact has to move upon contact. You can have one of your best ball players demonstrate their slide so your team can see at what point he begins his slide. My main goal in having the players practice sliding is so they know when to start their slide. You don't want them to start the slide too soon or too late. The coordination of players raising their hands on the slide must be also done correctly.

Infield Relay Race

1) **Use of drill & players needed:** As a fun drill. The more players the better.

2) **Equipment:** Just the players.

3) **Goal:** Have two teams compete against each other in a relay race.

Drills that are strictly fun have a place in any youth sports team practice. Coaches have to make sure both the team and themselves loosen up a bit at every practice. The basic relay race is a fun time for the whole team. Using the baseball diamond makes it baseball appropriate. Remember, coaches in youth baseball should be as creative as possible. Whether it is a small kids game or one that is created on the spot, putting a baseball theme into it makes it all the more accepted. Coaches have to constantly intertwine fun games with skill drills to stimulate practices. In the Infield Relay Race, the coach will divide the team into two equal teams as with regard to speed. So in a perfect situation you'll have six players lined up at home plate and six players lined up at second base. Both teams will run the bases the correct direction. To help the coach distinguish the players, have one team take off their hats. On the "go" command, the team will begin to run the bases starting at home and going to first, second, third then back home to touch the next player, who does the same thing. The other team of players will do the same starting at second base. They will run to third, home, first, and back to second to tag his relay teammate. Try it once, but generally the losing team will always want a rematch. This fun drill works great! Reinforce to players to try hitting the inside half of the base with their foot.

Bounce And Run Drill

1) **Use of drill & players needed:** As a coach's strategy and skill drill. Six or more players.

2) **Equipment:** A bucket of baseballs and a bat for the coach or player to bunt.

3) **Goal:** Teach players on second or third to advance safely to the next base on a ball hit to the left side of the infield.

I have said it before, if you practice baserunning at every practice, you can get 1-2 extra runs every game. And most if not all of the other coaches in your league will not practice baserunning. For the Bounce and Run Drill, I take two players for fielders at shortstop and third base. I use an assistant coach as a first baseman. The rest of the team will line up at second base in a single line with the first person as a baserunner on second. They should wear their helmets. The coach will be located right in front of home plate and will either hit or throw a grounder to either the shortstop or third baseman. The baserunner at second will bounce off the base. The fielder will catch the grounder, and on the release of the ball, and only the release, the baserunner will put his head down and run to the next base, which in this case is third. The next player in line at second will go. Now there is also a player on third. Both will bounce on the next grounder and again, only on the release of the baseball will they sprint to the next base. The player who went home from third will go back to the end of the line at second. I put a twist in this drill where I have a signal for my fielders, maybe scratching my face. On the signal, they fake their throw and try to tag the baserunner closest to him. I always catch one or two baserunners out in this drill, which is what you want as a coach. It will reinforce to the players how important it is to see the ball release from the fielder's hand. It is also important to tell the baserunners on third that they need to slide when going home in a game.

Bunt Man On Third

1) **Use of drill & players needed:** As a base running skill and coach's strategy. Six or more players.

2) **Equipment:** A couple of fielders and players to be base runners.

3) **Goal:** Combine the skill of bunting with baserunning.

One of the most rewarding things about coaching is when your players combine a couple of skills together with a team strategy that succeeds. The Bunt Man On Third is one of those strategies that if done correctly is almost a sure thing. When there is a player on third base with less than two outs, the player at bat will bunt toward the third baseman. The baserunner will bounce off the base with his shoulders squared toward the infield. He will be moving down the line as the third baseman goes deeper toward home to field the baseball. Once the fielder picks the ball up, the baserunner will hold his position. When the fielder releases the ball, the baserunner will turn his head toward home (a la "Bounce & Run" drill) and sprint home. When the player runs home he must slide. Sliding will sometimes be the deciding factor if the player is safe or out. When setting this up as a drill, all the players line up at third base. A third baseman and first baseman will be the only fielders. The coach will pitch. It is best to have another coach bunt just to move the drill along at a good pace. While practicing this drill, you do not need to have the players slide. The baserunner must slide during the game. With this strategy, as long as the bunt goes toward third base, even if the pitcher fields it, the play should work. If the bunt goes straight toward the pitcher's mound, this could be problematic. The third base coach must decide if he should send him home. All in all, this is almost a slam dunk with most baserunners.

Sometimes a good defensive team with a smart coach might have the shortstop sneak to third and have a signal for the third baseman to turn and throw back to the base. The coach has to watch for this.

Run Down Drill

1) **Use of drill & players needed:** As a skill drill with at least six kids.

2) **Equipment:** Soft covered baseballs and helmets.

3) **Goal:** Get the baserunner out in a rundown with the minimum number of throws.

Rundowns in youth baseball are one of those situations that can drive a coach crazy whether he is on the offensive or defensive side. I try preaching to my team that once they get a baserunner in a rundown the two most important things to do is to limit the number of throws and to get the baserunner in a sprint mode. Once the runner is in this sprint mode, it is hard for him to stop and change directions. If a throw is necessary, ideally I only want the baseball thrown once. In the Rundown Drill I use opposite base paths so there is no collision. I usually set this up where two teams of three are participating at the same time. Remember, you want to limit the down-time and have as many players involved as possible. One team of three will work this drill between first and second base. The other team of three will work this drill between home and third base. You can also mix it up and have a team of two between second and third. The objective of the baserunner is to get to either base. The baserunners will wear helmets. In this drill it is a good idea to use soft covered baseballs. On the "go" command, the two rundowns start. You can make it a competition with the baserunners competing against the fielders. Remember to reinforce to the fielders about getting the baserunner into a sprint mode. Tell them not to pump their hands and limit their throws. Some coaches encourage their team to just run the baserunner back to the base they came from. I don't agree with this. I want my fielders to be aggressive and get the out. And think about it. The team has a chance to almost get a free out. Coaches should not settle for just running the player back to the original base.

Reaction Drill

1) **Use of drill & players needed:** As a challenging fielding drill with any number of kids.

2) **Equipment:** Four cones or markers and a bucket of soft covered baseballs or tennis balls.

3) **Goal:** Run, turn, react to a ball thrown, and catch it.

I love crossing over into different sports and converting the drill to a baseball drill. A few years ago I attended a football training camp for a professional team. They did a drill with receivers running around a square, turning at each corner, and catching a football. This drill was testing their reaction to a thrown football. I thought this was a great drill. I simplified it to make a good quick baseball drill. In the Reaction Drill, four cones are set up about 10-15 feet apart in a square. The coach will be in the center with a bucket of balls. Soft covered baseballs or tennis balls are highly recommended. On the "go" command, the first player will start at one cone and sprint to the next one and turn around as they get to the cone. The coach will throw the baseball in such a way that it is thrown before the player even turns around. The player catches the ball, rolls it back into the square and proceeds to the next cone and does the same thing. As the player moves from cone to cone, the coach will have to move himself while inside the square. Coaches must use the progression technique, giving the players a chance to succeed at this drill. For first timers, the throw should be done when the player has already turned around. As the team gets more experienced with this drill, hc should challenge them more, anticipating when the players will reach the coach and turn and have the ball there. Coaches must also know each player's talent level. An alternative for young players is to do this drill with plastic balls and the goal is to

206

just make contact with the ball. You can then work your way up to tennis balls then soft covered hard balls. This is another good drill for at home.

Overthrow At First Base Drill

1) Use of drill & players needed: As an infield team skill drill. A full team is needed.

2) Equipment: A few soft covered baseballs and helmets for the base runners.

3) Goal: Have your team comfortable making a play on an overthrow.

Practicing plays the correct way is something all coaches do. We sometimes neglect to practice plays from the negative side where the team must think, react, and cover up their mistakes. Remember, in youth baseball, mistakes are made in every game. It is the team that is schooled at reacting and recovering from these mistakes that will put them in the position to be successful. Overthrows happen almost all the time in youth baseball games. In the Overthrow At First Base Drill we address what happens if an overthrow occurs with a player running to first base after hitting the baseball. The drill works like this. The coach will place a baseball behind the first baseman without the first baseman knowing where the ball is placed. To simulate a batter, we place a runner at first base. This is set up so the drill will have about the correct timing on a overthrow. On the "go" command, the first baseman will turn, locate the baseball, and react by running and picking it up. He should then turn and make the throw to second base trying to get the baserunner out. This can present a problem because the baserunner running to second will "screen" the view of the first baseman while he is trying to make an accurate throw. By practicing this drill, the first baseman will learn to adjust his throw or even move to a different angle like a step one way or another so he can have access to a clean throw to second. The fielder receiving the ball should give a good target for the thrower. Make sure the left fielder gets involved in the drill and knows how far to come in and at what angle to back up the throw. Give the whole team a chance at this drill. Use soft covered baseballs. Helmets are a must for base runners.

Wild Pitch Drill

1) Use of drill & players needed: As an infield team skill drill. A full infield is needed.

2) Equipment: A few soft covered baseballs and helmets for the base runners.

3) Goal: Have your pitcher and catcher get used to making a play on a wild pitch or passed ball when the baserunner from third runs home.

The number of youth baseball games I've seen in twenty-one years without a wild pitch or passed ball can be counted on one hand. The pitcher along with every infielder must be aware of what their responsibility is should the ball get by the catcher, for whatever reason. When I am coaching third base, I almost will always take a chance sending the runner once I see the ball get away from the catcher. I do this because, with all things being equal, a lot of things have to happen for the defensive team to get the baserunner out at home. On the other side, when I am on the defensive team, I make sure we practice the Wild Pitch Drill with each and every pitcher just to get them used to the situation. When the ball does get away from the catcher and he fields it then tosses it to the pitcher covering home, we try to break down every aspect of the play to give the defensive team a chance to get the out. Often the catcher will get to the ball in time and toss it accurately but the pitcher will be looking back and forth at the catcher and baserunner to see when both the ball and the runner will converge. What happens many times is that the pitcher will quickly look away once the ball is tossed his way and he will drop the ball because he was preoccupied with the runner. In the Wild Pitch Drill the coach places the ball behind the catcher in a spot unbeknownst to the catcher. There is a runner at third base. On the "go" command, the catcher quickly turns to locate the baseball while the pitcher runs home to cover with the baserunner running home. The catcher runs to the ball and tosses it to the pitcher covering home. The catcher is always trying to lead the pitcher with the baseball. The pitcher will secure the ball in his glove and swoop down to tag the baserunner. When running home, the pitcher usually instinctively puts up his glove as a target as he gets closer, which is good. When practicing this drill, we don't have the runner slide, but should do so in a game.

Outfielder Ball Cut Off

1) Use of drill & players needed: As a skill drill.

2) Equipment: A bucket of hard balls.

3) Goal: Take the correct angle on a ball hit into the outfield, such as one in the gap.

Youth sports coaches sometimes take too much for granted while working with kids. I learned that you have to explain and practice as much as you can. And even then, players will do it wrong. But you have to keep remembering that they are kids. When a ball is hit into the outfield between two players, they are slow to react because they are not sure whose ball it is. I not only encourage my team to be aggressive hitters but I want them all to be aggressive fielders. The skill that youth coaches must work on is to make sure all outfielders react to a ball hit in the gap. It used to drive me crazy when a player hit a ball into the outfield that went into the gap and the player did not cut it off. In fact I've seen players look like they are actually escorting the baseball deep into the outfield, almost running parallel to the ball. We have to teach these young baseball players to cut off the ball and learn how to anticipate where a moving ball is going. In the Outfield Ball Cutoff Drill, I move the whole team to the outfield. I have the first player come out. I then throw the baseball to either side of the fielder. He has to sprint to the baseball and not let it pass him. I start at a short distance and increase it as the players start their second turn. You can hit the baseball or just throw it. This sounds like an easy drill, and even might have some coaches saying, "why bother?" But you must do this drill at least one time during the year just to show players the fine art of pursuing the moving baseball and cutting it off at the appropriate angle. You should also address the fact that uncut and wet grass will affect the speed of a rolling baseball. If the ball is between two players, make sure they both go for it while communicating with each other about who has the ball and who backs up. A simple loud, "I got it" will work.

What To Do

1) Use of drill & players needed: As a skill drill with a full infield and two base runners.

2) Equipment: A few soft covered baseballs and helmets for the runners.

3) Goal: Have fielders learn to think quickly in odd situations.

Like chess matches, no two baseball games are exactly the same. And some of the oddest occurrences happen in games. In What To Do, we have a full infield with two baserunners. I will put the baserunners in different odd situations and instruct them where to run. I then give a player standing by the pitcher's mound a baseball with his back to the baserunners. On the "go" command, the fielder with the baseball will quickly turn around and assess the situation. The baserunners will break in the same or different directions or just stay still. The fielder must think quickly and decide what he has to do. Run at the lead runner or throw the ball to another infielder. This drill is invaluable for young players because it provides odd game situations. After the play, discuss with the whole team what the correct choice was or should be and why.

In Front Of The Line

1) Use of drill & players needed: As a skill drill working on the correct technique for catching ground balls. Any even number of players.

2) Equipment: A baseball for each pair of players.

3) Goal: Teach players to catch ground balls in front of them rather then between their legs.

The first few years I coached youth baseball I did not utilize the facilities around me as best as I could. If you look around a typical baseball field there are an endless amount of drills to do by using such things as the fence, the white lines, the foul pole, and light poles in the outfield, to name a few. In the In Front of The Line Drill, we want to teach and reinforce to the players to catch a ground ball in front of them. In this drill we do that by lining half the players on the team by an area where the dirt meets the grass. In this case we are using the third base line. You can also use the white lines on the field. All we are doing in this drill is pairing the players up. One side is throwing ground balls. The other side must field the balls in front of them. I tell the players that their glove should be over the grass, not the dirt, which forces them to have their hands in front of their body when they catch the ground ball. That imaginary triangle formed with the player's feet and where the ball is fielded should be pointed out. The fielders should throw the ball back. This should be repeated for a few repetitions before switching lines.

Ground Balls To Right Side

1) Use of drill & players needed: As a team defensive skill drill. A Complete infield, outfield, and baserunner.

2) Equipment: A few baseballs and hemet for the base runner.

3) Goal: Get players used to covering first on a ball hit to the right side of the infield.

If there is one play that can frustrate a coach, it is a ball hit between two players and they both just look at it as the ball rolls between them. The other is a ball hit to the right side of the infield and the players not fielding the ball are basically like a deer in the headlights, watching and waiting not sure how to react. I practice the Ground Ball To The Right Side Drill throughout the season. It is one of those drills that you can practice forever, and when it happens in a game, some youth players still do not seem to get it right. Nevertheless, we practice this situation because it is fundamentally sound baseball. And when we do get it right in a game, the kids, as well as the coach, love the accomplishment. I set up this drill by standing in an area in front of home plate. I will simultaneously yell, "go," and throw a grounder either to the first baseman or somewhere between the first and second baseman. I have a baserunner running so it is timed that he arrives almost at the same time as the pitcher. The pitcher must break for first base but not at a direct angle toward the base. He should run at a direct angle toward the foul line about 4-6 feet from the base then turn up toward the base, running parallel to the line. This can help avoid a collision. Remember that pitchers sometimes forget they are fielders and are only concerned about throwing the baseball. You can run this drill with different scenarios, but the key is to get the pitcher off the mound and running to first. In all infield plays where the fielder has options, I like him running to the base and touching it if he doesn't have to throw it. Notice in the picture that we have the right fielder coming in to back up an errant throw. Always reinforce the importance of backing each other up.

Team Baseball Swing

1) Use of drill & players needed: A relaxation technique for hitting. Any number of players.

2) Equipment: A bat for each player.

3) Goal: Teach players to relax while in the batter's box.

One of my pet peeves with hitters on the youth level is that they do not put themselves in the most relaxed situation. I addressed this in the hitting section. Time and again I see players in the hitting position when the pitcher, or even the umpire, is not anywhere close to beginning the play. The Team Baseball Swing Drill is a very short drill, but meaningful. I try to emphasize to players it is in their best interest to be relaxed as long as possible before the pitcher throws the baseball. It works like this. I have my whole team with their bats spread out around the infield with me on the pitcher's mound. I tell the players to relax until I am in the wind-up. Whether they relax by swinging the bat like an elephant trunk back and forth or just resting the bat on their shoulder, you want to give your hitters the best chance to be successful when it is their turn to hit. Too many times I see players standing like a statue very tense ready for the pitch and the umpire has his back turned to home plate. He is over at the fence behind him gathering new baseballs. The hitter has no idea what is going on. Another scenario is the pitcher will be tying his shoe and again the hitter is in his stance ready to hit. I teach the players to relax until they see the pitcher begin his wind-up. From the beginning of the wind-up until he let's go of the baseball, the batter will have 1-2 seconds to get ready, which is plenty of time. One of the best hitting instructors I ever met, Bobby Woods, taught me long ago "a relaxed hitter is a dangerous hitter." This should be done early in the season. Players that hit well don't change a thing.

Basketball Throw

1) Use of drill & players needed: A fundamental drill for catching and throwing. Two or more players.

2) Equipment: Two basketballs.

3) Goal: Have players focus on keeping their eye on the ball and bringing their arm back to throw.

I have mentioned numerous times already that crossing into other sports is popular with youth players. Attending a professional football practice years ago, I saw the running backs coach change the football to a basketball on a simple hand off drill, in which the quarterback is taking the snap and turning around to the running back and giving the basketball to him. The goal here is to make sure the player holds the basketball tight, and going from a basketball to a football will make it feel like a peanut to the football player. In the Basketball Throw Drill we are using a different prop the whole team is familiar with. When you first bring the basketball out, the kids get excited and then kind of scoff or laugh at the drill, however, there are actually a couple of fundamental concepts that can be accomplished in this drill. The team lines up around second base in a single line. The coach will throw the basketball as a ground ball to the first player in line. He fields the basketball as if it were a baseball and tries to catch it lined up in the center of his body. With the basketball, he is forced to field it with two hands plus he has to keep his head down. He then comes up with the basketball and throws it overhand to first base. You can adjust the distance of the line from first base depending on the age and ability of the players. This is a drill that should be done at least once during the season. With younger kids, it should be done a few times. A kick ball works almost as well but I prefer the weight and sturdiness of the basketball. Coaches should always be looking for other creative ways to work fundamentals.

Last Chance Throw

1) Use of drill & players needed: Teach players to throw a runner out from the outfield when that is the only option. One or more players.

2) Equipment: A bucket of baseballs and boxes and/or cones to use as knock down props.

3) Goal: Run to the baseball, pick it up, and knock done a box with a long throw.

Prepare your whole team in case they are ever in a position that a last chance desperation throw may be the only way to save the game. In the Last Chance Throw Drill, two lines of baseballs are set up in the outfield. On the "go" command, the first person in line will run to the first baseball, pick it up, and try to knock down the box with the cone or get close to it. Once a player goes, he then returns to the end of the other line. The ball can reach the boxes on a fly or one bounce. You have to make sure the players' arms are warm. Coaches should also simulate a fly ball-tag up situation the same way.

Miss The Cutoff

1) Use of drill & players needed: Learn how to cover up mistakes. A full team is needed.

2) Equipment: A bucket of baseballs.

3) Goal: Have the outfield miss the cutoff or relay man and continue the play.

It is amazing how many extra bases are taken because of overthrows and the fielders not reacting fast enough on the errant throw. Most coaches who practice a lot will spend a tremendous amount of time working on hitting the relay man, or in some cases, the cut off man. In Miss The Cutoff, I usually have a signal with the outfielders, such as rubbing my face, telling them to either hit or miss the cut off. In youth baseball, all teams will make mistakes at every game. It is the team that covers up for each other that stands the best chance to be successful. In Miss The Cutoff, I use a couple of baserunners. I either hit or throw the ball to the outfielders with players on base. The outfielder then overthrows the ball, over the head of the relay man, if the signal given prior to running the drill was for an overthrow. For instance, if the ball is hit to right field, and the second baseman comes out to get the relay throw, the right fielder will throw the baseball over the second baseman's head. We then see how the team reacts and covers for each other. Afterwards, I go through the steps of the play and we determine who should do what. We also hit the cutoff, but I find it very useful to practice both. Coaches should move players around while doing this drill. Another mistake to look for is outfielders standing still, holding the baseball and not knowing what to do. Simply, I tell my team if you are in the outfield and are confused as to who to throw the ball to, just throw it to the closest infielder with the same color uniform as you. At least we are moving the ball closer to the play.

Outfield Communication Drill

1) Use of drill & players needed: As a specific skill to communicate in the outfield on a fly ball. Six or more players.

2) Equipment: A bucket of hard balls.

3) Goal: Get players used to calling for the baseball when it is hit between two or more players.

Many times in youth baseball we see a pop fly hit in the infield or the outfield between two or more players. The players, as well as the coaches and parents, will watch the ball go up, then go down, dropping between two or more players. We have to teach players how to call for a fly ball or pop up and how to communicate with each other. I strongly believe in being aggressive fielders. We have to teach players not to be spectators any time during the game. In the Outfield Communication Drill, we set up two lines in the outfield about twenty feet apart. The coach will be in-between each line and will hit or throw a fly ball right in the middle of the two lines. The players at first are not given instructions to determine whose ball it is. Go through the line once this way just to see how they handle the situation themselves. You'll be surprised at how many kids will automatically communicate with each other. The second time around, instruct the players that the first person to call for the ball is the one who will catch the ball. If the other player thinks he has a better chance at it, he will call for the ball louder repeating the words, "I got it." My rule is if the first person is called off the ball, he has to yield to the second person. I do this drill first in the outfield then bring it into the infield where there can be more confusion because of the amount of fielders in a small area. Once in a while you will get a player who will

224

call for everything. I had a third baseman once that called for every infield fly. The coach must school this player that running too far for the ball will be more difficult than letting a teammate closer catch it. All this takes is some drilling and players will get it!

Hit The Target

1) Use of drill & players needed: As a skill drill for throwing accuracy. Any number of even players.

2) Equipment: A bucket of baseballs, hula hoops (or pieces of rope), and extra bases for each line.

3) Goal: Have players throw to their teammate, challenging the player catching the ball to keep one foot in the circle.

It is amazing how in almost any drill if the players are making sloppy throws or catches, you can put in motivating factors for them to achieve success. Here is a perfect example. Sometimes when I run the Third Base Drill, the players can be sloppy with their throws and catches. I'll stop the drill and tell the players that I only intended to give each player four swings in batting practice that day, but if they field the next six balls cleanly and make accurate throws, I'll give each player five swings instead of four. Almost 100% of the time they do come through with six quality throws and catches and they earn the extra swing. Notice that I tell the team they won't lose a swing on failure, only gain a swing on success. This is part of my coaching/teaching philosophy with young players. In baseball we teach players always to move to the baseball. A first baseman should come off the base on an errant throw to save extra bases. In the Hit The Target Drill, we are making it harder for the players to catch the baseball by the amount of room we are giving them to come off the base. The players throwing the baseball really have to focus on the target. I have three lines in the outfield. Three other players are in the infield opposite them with bases. I also set up a hula hoop near the base. A cut piece of rope shaped into a circle is fine also. The player catching the ball must keep one foot in the hoop. The ball does not have

226

to reach the other player on a fly. Each line will go one at a time. Giving them this challenge will produce more accurate throws. This works well as a competition. Rotate the infielders as you wish, say every 3 throws.

Wrong Tag, Right Tag

The wrong tagging technique on a slide, when the fielder tags the baserunner too high on his leg, happens many times in youth baseball.

The correct tag has the fielder getting low and tagging the first part of the baserunner's body to arrive at the base.

1) Use of drill & players needed: As a tagging technique drill. At least four players.

2) Equipment: A few soft covered baseballs and a kick ball.

3) Goal: Teach players to tag the first part of a baserunner's body coming into the base by keeping the glove low on the ground.

Here is another one of those things that can drive a youth baseball coach crazy. Suppose a ball is hit into the outfield. Your team does a great job getting the ball back to the infield. There is going to be a close play at a base with the ball getting to the fielder in plenty of time before the runner. But for some reason, the fielder will tag the baserunner on the thigh instead of the ankle or the first body part coming into the base. This allows the player to get into the base safely because his ankle hits the bag before the fielder tags his thigh. The correct play is to keep the glove low, preferably on the ground. The fielder tags the first part of the body that arrives at the base. One year, I finally figured out a drill that forces the players to tag the first body part he sees. In the Wrong Tag, Right Tag Drill, I cut off most of the body. By this I mean I put a fielder at third base. With two coaches, one will toss a baseball to the fielder and the other will roll a kick ball. The drill is to catch the baseball and tag the kick ball that is rolling into the base. The player has no choice but to get his glove down low to target the moving kickball. This drill reinforces for the fielder to get his glove low and tag the only item coming towards the base. Players will understand the concept after only a few times through this drill.

Carousel Drill

1) Use of drill & players needed: As a skill drill for underhand tosses. At least 8 players.

2) Equipment: A few soft covered baseballs and a few cones.

3) Goal: Get players used to tossing the baseball underhand at a short distance.

Coaching for over twenty years, I develop my own pet peeves with certain skills. Having youth players knowing when and how to toss the baseball underhand is one of them. Sometimes, when a fielder is very close to the base, instead of tossing the ball underhand so it is more manageable for the other fielder to catch, he throws the ball overhand, and the ball is then mishandled. Many coaches do not even go over the skill of tossing the baseball underhand. I think this is a mistake. In the Carousel Drill, I am setting up in a confined area. The players must toss the baseball underhand. I'm adding a lot of movement so there is very little standing around and a lot of repetitions. I use the area of the pitcher's mound, but any small area can be used. I set up cones opposite each other so there are four sets of two. The drill has four lines so we use two baseballs. The object is to toss the ball underhand to the person opposite you. On the "go" command, the two players with the baseball will toss the ball to the first person in line opposite them, who should stand between two cones. Once the player tosses the baseball, he quickly moves to his left. He waits for his turn to catch the baseball, and then tosses it underhand to the next person moving between the two cones. What this drill is doing is giving players the chance to toss the ball underhand. Hopefully this will translate to an underhand toss in the appropriate game situation. In game situations, players sometimes are unsure which way to throw or toss the ball. This drill will help, but sometimes only game experiences will condition the players to make the right decisions. Make sure soft covered baseballs are used.

Baserunning, First Base

These pictures shows how many youth players run to first base. They run to the base and stop short. The concept of running through the base is hard to convey, but is a basic baserunning fundamental.

1) Use of drill & players needed: As a warm-up with any number of kids.

2) Equipment: First base and a cone.

3) Goal: Teach players to run through first base and not just to the base.

As simple as it may seem, no matter how many times you reinforce to players to run through the bag at first base, many young players will stop at first base as soon as they get to it using the base seemingly like a wall. This will cause the player to slow up, and in essence, sacrifice his speed. In this drill, the coach places a cone about 15 feet past first base. The players line up at home plate. One at a time, they run through the base toward the cone. This will get players in the habit of running everything out hard. Many coaches tell players how to hit the bag at first. This might be over-coaching because it gives players too much to think about. When they go past the base, I always have the player turn to foul territory. The rule actually is that he can turn into fair territory as long as he does not make an intent to go to second base. Our league has volunteer umpires as young as 13 years old. I've seen these young umpires not know the rule and think the player can be tagged out if he turns into fair territory. I try not to take any chances, leaving as little as possible in the hands of the umpire. I explain to my team the correct rule. On a ground ball, I also try to teach and reinforce not to look at the ball. I even show my players in practice how much speed they sacrifice by taking a quick look at the ball while running.

Baserunning Sign Drill

1) Use of drill & players needed: A way to reinforce signs from the coach. The whole team should do this drill.

2) Equipment: Three throw-down bases plus the regular bases on the field.

3) Goal: Have the team run the bases practicing the team signs.

I have mentioned how much of a premium I put on baserunning. Every practice I run, I make sure we drill baserunning. In the Baserunning Sign Drill, we are reinforcing all the team signs. This must be done throughout the season because kids will forget. Remember that Major League players miss signs, so it is going to happen to 10, 11, and 12 year-old kids. Coaches, including myself, will get confused with team signs, so it is good reinforcement for everyone. In this drill I use two sets of bases. I keep either a second set of loose bases in my car or the rubber throw-down bases, which are just as good. The players are getting twice as many repetitions as they would with only one set of bases. Either two coaches or two players will be the pitcher and catcher. I instruct the pitcher not to throw the ball unless I say "pitch," this way it gives me time to give the players my sign. I give the sign to the first two players in line, and say, "pitch." The baserunning options I have is: a steal, a fake steal, a delayed steal, and a sign just to take off and run. After I give the player the sign and the pitcher throws the ball, the players react to the sign I gave them. Once they reach second base, we now have four players reacting to the sign when the ball is thrown. We eventually will have six players reacting. With the use of extra bases, we are getting more players involved at one time. I also make sure that on the delayed steal, the coach or player at the catcher position should not throw the ball back until I say, "Throw." The players that finish from third to home will go back to the end of the line at first. I reinforce to players going home that we always slide except in practice.

Tagging Up From Third

When you have a player on third base with less than two outs, he must be schooled the right way to tag up. Most youth baseball players on third will come off the base as soon as the ball is hit. The coach must really be focused, anticipating if the baseball is going to be caught. As the above pictures show, this is the wrong way to approach a tag up from third base. The player should not leave the base. I've seen teams blow playoff games because they did not tag up from third correctly.

The above pictures are showing the correct way to tag up on a fly ball from third. The player should stay on the base. He should not tag up on his own but should wait for the coach to signal him verbally. Either, "Go," "Now," or I have found the best word is, "Catch." Upon hearing the coach say "catch," he then runs home. Like most baserunners going home, I teach my players they must slide. I have also begun to teach players to look at home and not the fielder making the play. This is tough to do, especially because human nature tells them to look where the ball is hit.

Coaches need to constantly remind the baserunner of the number of outs when tagging from third base and to slide on any close play. If there is a question whether to slide or not, then slide.

Running Home From Third

1) Use of drill & players needed: As a baserunning drill with any number of kids.

2) Equipment: A few soft covered baseballs and a visible white line on third base.

3) Goal: Teach players when on third base to always run home in foul territory to avoid getting hit in fair territory with a ground ball.

One of the most fundamental base running concepts when a player is on third base is for the base runner to bounce off the base in foul territory when the ball crosses home plate. In the Running From Third To Home Drill, we are giving each player the chance to run home correctly in foul territory. When some kids reach third base in a game, this may be the first time they have been there. Coaches should practice this at least one time at the beginning of the year. The third base coach should reinforce this every time a player is on third base. On the pictures on top we see a player running in fair territory and getting hit by the ball, which, according to the rules, is an out. In many fundamentals for youth baseball, there is nothing wrong with showing the players the wrong way of doing a skill and what the consequences might be. Running in foul territory and being hit by the ball is only a foul ball. The bottom pictures show the correct way to run home from third on the foul side of the line.

First To Third On A Bunt

1) Use of drill & players needed: As a strategy when bunting. A complete infield is needed with a batter and baserunner.

2) Equipment: Baseballs and helmets.

3) Goal: The goal is use the bunt as way of getting an extra base for a baserunner on first.

I have mentioned several times already how I'm a big believer in bunting, both for fundamentals and as a strategy. In this strategy, the coach has to pick and choose when he will attempt this with the personnel he has and at the appropriate situation. A baserunner is on first base. He should be a fast runner. Also a good bunter must be up at bat. The coach has the hitter bunt to third. The player at first will run to second but will not slide. He will round the base and continue to third. If the third baseman fields the bunt fairly close to home, he will have a hard time getting back to third base to cover the throw. This works well, and the beauty is if the shortstop covers third base, the coach has time to send the runner back to second. To defend this play when my team is in the field I always have my left fielder sprint in to cover third base as soon as he sees the batter square to bunt.

Rob The Homer

1) Use of drill & players needed: As a fun game with any number of kids.

2) Equipment: Soft covered baseballs or pickle balls and a few cones.

3) Goal: Try to keep the ball from going over the fence for a home run.

Whatever the sport, kids love to make the dramatic play. Whether it is a hail mary pass reception in football or a last second half court shot made in basketball, the bigger the play, the more exciting it is for youth players. In the Rob The Homer Drill, all we really need is any fence, but preferably you want to use the fence on the field where home runs are usually hit in your league. Against the fence, I set up two cones about ten to twelve feet apart. The player starts in the middle of the cones. The coach will then begin to throw balls that look like they are going for a home run. The player must either catch the ball or swat it away before the ball goes out of the ball park. I usually try to alternate throwing the ball from side to side. You can make it as easy or hard as you want. You can run this drill any number of ways. Start with a finite number of chances, say five for each player. You can also run a "stay till you miss," where the player will keep his turn as long as he continues to rob the home run. You can make it a competition. Divide the team into two teams and give each player one chance. You can keep score this way as to how many balls get over the fence for each team. This game gets to be a whole lot of fun when the kids put some extra exaggeration into their saves. This drill is excellent for players' reaction and they love the challenge and the competition. Coaches can widen the cones and make the drill more challenging. I've had kids take this drill home and do it with their father or their brothers. It really makes for a fun time and is a productive drill.

Hitting Games

Soft Toss Game

There are an infinite number of hitting games you can do with your team. In the Soft Toss Game, we set it up like any baseball game with two teams. This game is really good when you have a limited number of players. The batter will be up, and the coach, and only the coach, will be the person who tosses the baseball. The player only has one toss to hit so the game moves fairly quick. You can play with baserunning or set up predetermined distances on the field that determine what type of hit the player is awarded. There is nothing like having a variety of ways a batter sees the baseball. Also, don't overlook young players' creativity. I've put hitting games that players suggest into my practices. Some work and some don't, but be flexible.

Tee Ball Game

I am always encouraging my players to practice hitting off the batting tee. Some take to it but with others it is a challenge to get them motivated. In the Tee Ball Game, we are setting up a real game, dividing the team in half. Like the previous Soft Toss Game, the players will get only one chance to hit the ball. You want games to proceed at a good pace to promote a good number of repetitions. You can always limit the inning by decreasing the number of outs to two. This way the game is moving rapidly and the players are not getting bored being in the field for a long period of time. If you coach younger players, I encourage coaches to play with a larger ball. Another challenge in this game is to set up cones in such a way that the players must hit the ball within the cones. This shortens the field and forces the players to hit situational or practice going up the middle. It is also beneficial to shorten the field when the number of players are limited to only 3 or 4 on a team. Also at some point during the season, some players will always ask to bat their opposite way. This game is a great way to give those players a chance.

Directional Hitting

1) **Use of drill & players needed:** As a fun hitting game with any number of kids.

2) **Equipment:** A good amount of cones.

3) **Goal:** Hit the baseball in a defined area.

With Directional Hitting, I am challenging players to hit toward a predetermined area. I try to have the players achieve this by setting up cones as a border. When throwing batting practice, I instruct the players to try hitting the baseball between the two lines of cones. This is very tough for youth players, but coaches should not be afraid to challenge their team. With a runner on second base with less than two outs, we have to explain that a ground ball hit to the right side of the infield moves the runner up a base. Important concept.

Continuation Drill

1) Use of drill & players needed: As a hitting drill with the whole team.

2) Equipment: Same equipment used for regular batting practice.

3) Goal: Teach players with two strikes to cut down or adjust their swing and just try to make contact with the baseball.

Out of all the hitting drills that give results, The Continuation Drill is it! This has been one of the most popular hitting games over the years. Each player is given a number from 1-12 or you can divide into two teams of six. The coach pitches. The object is to teach players that when they have two strikes, just make contact with the ball, or as some people like to say, "shorten the swing." The player batting stays up for five swings as long as the ball he hits is a ground ball or fly that is not caught. The batter is out if he swings and misses, hits a foul ball, or hits a fly ball caught by one of the fielders. If he makes out, the coach yells, "next," and the on deck hitter will run into the batter's box and take his shot to potentially hit five pitches. Coaches have to make sure the hitters take full swings and not chop down on the ball. This is a fast paced drill with players going in and out of the batter's box. There should be two on deck hitters ready to bat with their batting helmets and batting glove on. The coach has to be aware of safety and will at times delay his next pitch while players are running in and out to the field. The beauty of this drill is that it carries over into games. When the hitter has two strikes, the coach in the coaching box can yell out, "Continuation Drill," and you'll be surprised how well this reinforcement works with the hitters for making contact with two strikes. I've seen many of my hitters extend their at bats and I attribute it to this drill. If there is any drill that I can almost guarantee you will see success if you practice, it is this drill. Players will get conditioned by practicing learning to just make contact with the baseball. It will work with most of your team!

Home Run Derby

1) Use of drill & players needed: As a fun drill to end practice. Any number of players.

2) Equipment: A bucket of hard balls and three loose bases.

3) Goal: Give all the players on the team a chance to hit a home run.

There are not many other fun games that the players like better than Home Run Derby. There are many ways we play it during the year, such as with plastic bats, tennis racquets, and hitting either tennis balls or plastic balls. The following variation is the closest to the real thing. We use regular hard balls. I usually wait until the end of the season when I keep one bucket of used baseballs separated from good practice baseballs that may be water logged or just heavy and scuffed from use. In youth baseball, most players will never experience the thrill of hitting a baseball over the fence for a home run. Why not give all players on your team this opportunity and make it as realistic as possible? I run this drill in a way to give players a chance to hit a home run or ball over the fence according to their age. Between the pitcher's mound and second base, two loose bases are set up and represent home plate. Second base will represent a third home plate. If a movable "L" screen is available, it is highly recommended for the coach to use when pitching. Each player will line up at one of the home plates according to age. The home plate closest to the outfield is for 10 year-olds. The home plate in the middle is for 11 year-olds and the other home plate furthest from the fence is for 12 year-olds. A great teaching point, even in this drill, is that when you try to go for home runs, usually it does not happen. You can divide the players into two teams and can have a competition or game. You can also have your best hitters try switch hitting.

Hole In The Infield Game

1) **Use of drill & players needed:** As a fun game with 8 or more players.

2) **Equipment:** A dozen tennis balls and a racquet.

3) **Goal:** Try to hit the tennis ball through the infield.

A simple change of pace game or one that is good to end a practice on a high note is the Hole In The Infield Drill. Set up this game with four infielders, two between first and second and two between second and third. A coach or player will hit a tennis ball with a racquet and try to get it through the infield by the four fielders without hitting the outfield grass on a fly. If the ball does reach the outfield on a fly, it is an out. Any other ball not reaching the outfield grass on the ground is also an out. If the players reach the grass on a hit, bouncing at least once in the infield, their team gets a run. The object is to reinforce to the fielders to stop the ball and not necessarily catch the ball to prevent it from going into the outfield.

Bunt Tennis

1) Use of drill & players needed: As a game utilizing bunting skills. Two or any number of even players.

2) Equipment: A few pickle balls and two bats.

3) Goal: Bunt the pickle ball back and forth between two players.

In the Bunt Tennis game, we are actually taking the skill of bunting to a new level. This game is definitely for the most skilled bunters, but even younger players love this when they are successful at it. Don't be hesitant to give all players a chance to try this game. You can have multiple games of this with enough adults supervising. We have two players each with a bat and ready in the bunting position. They stand about 6-8 feet from each other. The coach will take a pickle ball (or plastic type ball) and toss it to one of the players with a bat. He has to bunt the ball off the coach's throw into the direction of the other player. He then tries to bunt it back. The object is to see how many times the players can bunt the ball back and forth to each other. This game is more about bat control than it is about pure bunting technique, but you will see that the best bunters are also the best at this game. It is not really a competition. The bunters are working toward the same goal of keeping the ball alive.

Tennis Racquet Home Run Derby

1) Use of drill & players needed: As a fun game with any number of kids.

2) Equipment: A bucket of tennis balls and one tennis racquet.

3) Goal: Hit the tennis ball over the fence with a tennis racquet. Pure fun!

There are many different variations of home run derby. In Tennis Racquet Home Run Derby we are giving all players a chance to hit a tennis ball over the fence. Again, we want players to experience success that they may not ever experience in games. Most players will never hit a home run over the fence in a youth baseball game. In this game, players will hit from the appropriate home plate between the pitcher's mound and second base. Three bases are set up to simulate home plate. Players use the one according to their age, the youngest using the one closest to the fence. The coach will pitch a very hittable tennis ball to the batter. He tries to hit the ball over the fence. The coach can run this drill anyway he wants, having one team vs. another or an individual challenge with 5 pitches for each player. I have also played this game in a parking lot that backs up to a fence. Try to have it in a location so the tennis balls are retrievable after practice. I have found that this is almost the perfect game to end a practice. Once your team plays it, they will be constantly asking to play it again. I usually try to save this game for the second half of the year. It is also one of those game that coaches can partake in. Parents have also told me that their kids have dragged them outside to play this game in their backyard. So save any tennis ball you see.

Pickle Ball Home Run Derby

1) Use of drill & players needed: As a fun game with any number of kids

2) Equipment: A bucket of pickle balls plus a big red plastic bat.

3) Goal: The goal is hit the pickle ball over the fence.

There are many different types of games of home run derby coaches can do with their team. I've already said that if you have a full field available, there is nothing better than giving each player a chance to hit a home run over the fence. In this variation of home run derby, we use a big plastic bat with pickle balls. Using the big bat will usually open up this game to even younger kids. If you do this game with younger kids, move home plate closer to the fence to make the task achievable. The coach will take a base and move it into the outfield to use as home plate like all the other home run derbies. The coach should put the base at a spot where most if not all of the team will have a chance to hit the ball over the fence. This game is "one pitch," where the player has to swing at the pitched ball no matter where it is. I use the one pitch concept in a lot of games just to keep the game moving at a good pace. Each player gets one chance or swing. We go through the batting order once with each home run counting as a run. This is one of those games where we are creating an environment that most of the kids will have a chance to be successful. The one thing I can tell you after coaching baseball for over 20 years is that no matter what the level of play, hitting a home run is the best feeling in the world for the batter, which is why I implement a lot of home run derby games with different variations just to give kids a chance to have that great feeling of watching a ball they hit go over a fence. This is also a great game to get the coaches to participate, and even parents who may be watching practice.

Alternate Props

In this section I am going to share some ideas about props you can use to integrate into baseball drills and games. As you know, sporting goods is a multi-billion dollar industry that produces incredible products all the time. I have found many of them useful and know many people in the industry. Before I got involved in youth sports, my wife and I (with three kids) bought our first house and probably went a little overboard. Needless to say, we both worked and did extra things to make it possible. My wife would tutor kids and I had a second job. It was tough going, but nothing out of the ordinary that millions of families are faced with everyday. On top of this, I knew my passion for sports would be the driving force that would get me involved in coaching my own kids. My oldest son was first enrolled in tee ball and I got my first exposure to what great lengths parents would go to for their own kids; buying the best gloves, bats, cleats, etc., put me on the defensive when my own son wanted equipment. We had to be creative. When other parents bought a two hundred dollar hitting net, we put together a "hitting tarp" with one 10'x12' blue tarp, four bicycle hooks, four bungie cords, and two already standing trees in our backyard. We did everything the other parents did with their hitting net, plus more! We created games with targets on the tarp and spent hours practicing and having fun. I'm not saying you should not buy good equipment if you can. What I am saying is that don't let any financial situation inhibit you from making the best of the situation. There are an endless amount of props you can create to be productive with your kids and their love for sports. When you make the prop, do it with your son and daughter. The bonding will become memories that will last for a lifetime.

I remember when I was young I was desperate to have my dad put up a basketball rim in our driveway. I was an endless pain in the neck until he agreed to do it. He made it a joint venture with me. And to this day, some 45 years later, I remember every detail, probably because I did it with him. Instead of buying a new metal pole with a backboard, we made our own with a four by four piece of lumber and we used plywood as the backboard. My dad and I worked on it a couple of hours each night when he came home from work. And of course he made me dig the hole. We treated the lumber and plywood with weather resistant liquid. The day finally came when we put it all together and it was one of the best days a kid can have with a parent. Once the cement dried that held the wood up, nothing could get me off that court.

Many times, if you can do the same activity or skill with different props, the kids will be somewhat stimulated each time you do it differently. For example, I can make a batting tee many different ways. From a regular tee to caution cones to a plastic office water cooler put on two milk cartons, each technique is doing the same skill. What I am basically doing is cooking chicken in a variety of different ways. I have done the same thing with home run derby by playing it a number of different ways and knowing that the kids will like all versions.

Another example is hitting. Who says youth players have to learn how to hit with only a baseball? When my younger son was about seven or eight, we began practicing different hitting drills with the tarp off a tee (or make shift tee) or doing the toss drills. One day I decided to take my recycling bin in my garage. I was by his side, and instead of tossing baseball-like objects for him to hit into the tarp, I took out plastic (never glass) recyclables in the bin and tossed it up for him to hit. He hit milk containers, cookie trays, soda containers, plastic bleach gallons, and more. When we first started, he giggled to no end but then he got a little serious and it was amazing how much he enjoyed this little drill. The fact that each item was different from each other made it all the more challenging for him. You can use almost any item and be creative this way. How about crushing up newspapers and doing the toss drill or hitting them off the batting tee? Anything that is safe, consider it part of your sports equipment.

Sometimes the time you spend doing a project with your kids will overshadow any toy or expensive bat that you may buy them. Time is the one commodity we need to cherish and manage better. Challenge yourself to come up with a creative idea that you can use in a sports skill with your son or daughter. And don't be afraid to challenge your child to come up with an idea.

Paddle Catch

1) Use of drill & players needed: An individual skill drill with one or more players.

2) Equipment: A round piece of 1/2" plywood or a table tennis racquet with the handle cut off and a cotton glove with the tips of the fingers cut off.

3) Goal: Teach and reinforce to players to catch ground balls with two hands.

One of the biggest objections I receive doing my coach's clinic around the country is that I don't instruct or encourage my players to catch with two hands. On fly balls that players have to run and get to with their arms stretched out, it is almost impossible to catch the ball comfortably with two hands. Think about it. If the shortstop is running from his position to foul territory behind third base and stretching out his arms to catch the ball, it must be a one handed catch. This is why I drill my team to catch with both one hand and two hands. With ground balls that players do not have to move too much laterally, I insist that players catch the grounder with two hands. In the "Paddle Drill" I have taken a piece of plywood and shaped it into about a 9 or 10 inch diameter. I then take a cotton glove. I cut off the finger tips about halfway. It is best to use either really good scissors or a utility knife. I then attach the glove to the back of the paddle with a strong staple or anything else that will hold it securely. The player then fits the glove on his hand just the way he does his baseball glove. We hit ground balls, and because the face of the plywood or paddle is flat, the player is forced to catch or stop it with two hands. He will almost automatically bring up the ball just as he is supposed to so he can control it. This drill also forces the player to move his feet to the ball rather than reach out for it. Because of the limitations the player has, he is almost forced to field the ball in the middle of his body. He is also forced to get the paddle down, just as he is supposed to do, with his fielding glove. This is a great drill to do in your own backyard. When making this paddle, make sure you include your son or daughter in the process. You can also use a table tennis racquet with the handle cut off and do the same thing to the back of it with the glove and/or staple to secure it.

Bunting With Props

I have been surprised at the success I had with some past players who had trouble bunting with a bat, but once I gave them some opportunities for success with different equipment, they progressed to using the bat with very good results.

Here we are using one of those big red plastic bats to teach bunting. This is especially useful for the very young players. The younger the players, the less important exact technique is. Just let him succeed making contact.

The tennis racquet is another excellent prop, not only for bunting, but for numerous other drills. The large face of the racquet makes the possibility for greater success.

This is a cardboard tube. Coaches and parents can use tennis balls or plastic balls. You can use larger, softball-type balls to give the player a better chance of making contact. Don't put too much emphasis on the location of the bunt. As in any sport, perfecting a particular skill will take time.

Here is an older player practicing bunting with a broom stick. When the players are older, reinforce the correct technique. Even with this thin item, notice how the player is still using only three fingers to hold the top part. Even more challenging is to bunt smaller balls. Plastic golf balls are good to use.

A broom can also be used as a simple prop for bunting with a plastic or soft covered ball.

One of the biggest mistakes coaches make is to treat our youth baseball teams too regimented and not look into ways to give the players chances to succeed in drills that will translate into better baseball skills. The phrase "think outside the box" is overused. I have heard it used to describe myself and the techniques I implement in drills like "Bunting With Props." I am just using props that will give players a different look at a drill while at the same time making it fun! You know by now how important I feel about bunting being a part of baseball. I am always looking for ways to give players a chance to master or improve this skill. In this drill, we take any of the above pictured items and turn them into tools for bunting. The coach will pitch either soft covered baseballs or tennis balls and the player must make contact with the end of the prop. The basic techniques should be reinforced, but in this drill, the main goal is to make contact with the ball. Coaches and parents can think of other props, such as a lawn rake or anything that might be hanging around in their garage

A ball bunted right back to the pitcher, or an area where the pitcher can easily field the ball and make a play, is not where you want to teach young players to bunt the baseball. Bunting the baseball toward the third baseman soft enough where he has to come running in fast but hard enough to get it past the pitcher is the ideal bunt. When the third baseman has to field the ball on the run and feeling rushed, there are two or three things that can go wrong to give a batter with only average speed a better than 50% chance of reaching base safely. I set up cones on the field to practice what I call directional bunting, which is bunting the baseball in a certain direction. The cones are set up on either the first or third base line about six to ten feet in front of home plate. The player must square or get into the bunting position and try to lay the bunt down between the cones. Coaches can make this as easy or as hard as he wants by making the cones wider or narrower. Remember, if we teach correct bunting on the youth level, there are even more options coaches can use, such as the squeeze play, a pure sacrifice bunt, and even the drag bunt, when the players go on to play on the bigger fields. Just as it is important to introduce the bunting skill gradually and by progression, coaches and parents should also always be challenging their players to get better once they become familiar with the skills. Advanced bunting tips can be introduced, such as moving to the front of the batter's box and holding the bat head up and out in front of home plate so if the ball goes straight down it will still be fair. Try to catch the ball with the bat and not push the bat into the ball. Imagine there is a large pane of glass right in front of home and you do not want to break the glass. Also as a coach, before every game I go behind home plate and roll one ball down third base and one down first base just to see how the ball is rolling. The height of the grass, plus any moisture will affect how fast the ball is moving.

Target Bunting

1) Use of drill & players needed: Perfecting bunting technique. One or more players.

2) Equipment: A bucket of baseballs with any type of prop that can be used as a target.

3) Goal: Make contact with the ball while bunting and hitting the target.

Bunting techniques transformed into games or challenges is an excellent way to motivate players to become proficient at this skill while at the same time keeping the player stimulated. Target Bunting can be used in any number of ways. Here we see a rope made into a circle. The goal is to bunt a ball to land in the circle. This can be made into a competition with one or more players on teams or seeing who can bunt the highest number of baseballs out of ten into the circle. The size of the circle can be adjusted for the age and/or skill of the player. Using cones is another great challenge and something that I use at each and every batting practice. Separating the cones anywhere from 6-10 feet with the goal being to bunt between the cones is the challenge here. Once this is practiced, cones can also be set up on the first base side the same distance. When the coach pitches the baseballs, the batter must alternate bunting to third base then to first base on each pitch. Coaches can also challenge the batter by calling out which side the batter should bunt to, yelling out either, "first" or "third" just before pitching the ball. This is also excellent for the backyard.

Bunting For Peanuts

1) Use of drill & players needed: As a fun bunting drill for one or more players.

2) Equipment: A bucket of baseballs, three or more hula hoops, and a type of popular candy in a bag.

3) Goal: Bunt the baseball into the hula hoop.

With my passion for teaching fundamentals such as bunting, I am always looking for creative motivators to get players to try mastering this skill. In Bunting For Peanuts, we are not really rewarding players with peanuts but with any other popular candy in a bag. I divide the team into two. With a full team you will have two teams of six. I put three or more hula hoops right in front of home plate about where a bunt should end up. I will pitch to each team, giving each player one chance to get his bunt inside one of the hula hoops. I actually place a few of the candy bags inside the hoops. This really gets the players' enthusiastic. The players can choose any of the hula hoops as their target. Once each team has a chance, the team with the most baseballs inside the hoops will get the candy. Generally I am not a huge fan of rewarding the players monetarily or with material goods. This drill is one of the few exceptions. I probably only do this drill one time during the year at the end of the season. When you practice as often as I do, you can reach a point in the season of getting a little stale. My recommendation is for coaches to have a number of drills similar to this so that it will leave an impression. One of your goals is not only to improve or win a championship, but also to get the players back for another year of baseball. A drill such as this is 100% fun. The players remember these drills. Years later, many former players actually come up to me in town to ask me if I still do certain drills such as "Bunting For Peanuts."

Hitting off caution cones can be a nice alternative to the regular batting tee. Any spherical object will fit fine right on top of the cone. You just cannot adjust the height. If you hit against the cushion, as seen above, you can use a hard ball. Hitting against a wall you would have to use a rag ball, which is made with rags wrapped loosely with two inch masking tape. I have also been successful crunching up regular newspaper. Pickle balls or plastic balls work well also. The variety with kids will stimulate them.

You can purchase an endless amount of items that will add weight or resistance to a player's bat. The theory here is that swinging your own bat with this weight or resistance and then taking it off, the player will feel that the bat is lighter and he will have a stronger swing and be able to control the bat better. I found that taking a common household towel will add the same resistance as anything you can purchase at your local sporting goods store. Tie the towel into a knot. Make sure you tape the top so the towel doesn't fly off. for extra weight, you can also dampen the towel.

Parking Lot and Small Area Practices

A number of years ago, when I first began coaching and before our league had the organization it has today, everybody was on their own for practices as far as getting an unoccupied field is concerned. In our geographical location, like in many areas, there is a huge lack of fields available. One day I met my team at a field to practice and another team arrived 10 minutes earlier. I stood there with my team trying to decide how to handle the situation. My inexperience as coach came through. I sent my assistant to speak with the other coach to see if he was willing to share the field, which was my first mistake. My assistant came back, and with a smirk on his face, he told me the coach said, "under no circumstances are we giving up even an inch of this field. We were here first." So I stood there with egg on my face in front of 12 kids and a few parents who had the wherewithal to stay for practice. While I was deciding what to do, a parent suggested another field. I was against this because we would not be sure if that field was available and I was concerned about the parents who had already bailed out and left their kids at a field they expected to pick them up at around 75 minutes later. So I sheepishly decided to cancel practice. And I regret that to this day. We had to get rides for each player by either contacting the parents or giving the kids a ride. This was one of my darkest days as a youth baseball coach. I felt defeated. But I decided to turn a negative into a positive and began working on how to run practices when there is no field available or limited space. I was already developing a modest list of drills to run my practices and decided to keep a separate list of drills that would work in a parking lot or in an area of limited space. And I decided to intentionally call for a practice in a parking lot just to try out some of these drills while moving around on blacktop or concrete. As it turns out, the practice went relatively smooth. Of course the players love practicing on a field, but this became a great alternative, especially at the beginning of the season when most coaches are enthusiastic and practice fairly regularly. Unfortunately for the kids, many of these coaches cut down or even eliminate practicing during the season until the playoffs. And parking lots are not the only place to do these practices. I have run some creative practice on a sloping hill. In the last few years, our league installed a batting cage that is about 75 feet long and about 20 feet wide. This has been a godsend, not just for the extra batting practices you can give your team, but also for learning how to structure and complete a one hour practice utilizing both the batting cage itself and the surrounding area, such as the fence to hit against with soft covered baseballs. Because of the incident I mentioned above, I have since always accommodated any team that shows up to a field I am already at by sharing it. This goes for tee ball teams to teams in my own division that we would eventually play. There is very little downside in being diplomatic when sharing a field. It will help you as well as the other coach become creative with these practices. The other coach will also remember you.

I go into each season, and reiterate this during my coaches clinic, that there should be no or very little reason to cancel a practice except for inclement weather. There are certain things coaches must consider when working these types of practices. In a confined area you will have more kids close together so safety becomes even more of a factor to be concerned about. Coaches may want to make sure there are extra assistants or parents available to help out. I have always pulled parents from the stands or their cars to help out. I've never had anyone turn me down in any sport I've coached, and I never put parents in a position that might embarrass them. Most kids love it when they see their own parents involved.

With these practices, you will be in a smaller area with players swinging bats. We must take caution. Of course there are some common sense things to consider, such as what type of drills to do. For instance, obviously you can't do any drills that involve any type of sliding or diving. Hitting can be done, but you must use the correct type of ball. I actually think that the soft covered baseballs are not the best things to use on a hard concrete surface. I like using the pickle ball, which is made up of durable plastic. Make sure that if you use these type of balls, your players should treat them like regular hardballs, even though they are harmless. I've been hit in the face with one and it does sting. Just like working with your team on a field, there are endless drills and games you can do with your team. I usually keep three or four tennis balls, pickle balls, and a couple of plastic bats in my trunk at all times during the baseball season. Of the drills we've described in the previous pages, I am going to list 20 of them that are appropriate for parking lots and other tough terrain.

1. Third Base Drill-Tennis balls can be used here. Shorten the distance if you must.

2. King Arthur-This drill can be done anywhere.

3. Line Throw Drill-Tennis balls can be used, though they will sometimes roll and not stay still.

4. Rapid Throw Drill-Tennis balls or pickle balls can be used.

5. Three Man Relay Drill-Use tennis balls and shorten the distance if you must, but make sure you tell your players not to gun the ball if players are in close proximity to each other.

6. Face Off Drill-This is a perfect drill for any areas. Use tennis balls.

7. Circle Drill-Using tennis balls, this is another great drill for small or hard top areas.

8. Lead Drill-Using tennis balls, this can be done on hard flat surfaces.

9. No Glove Drill-Use tennis balls for this drill.

10. Shadow Drill-Use tennis balls for this drill.

11. Around The Horn-I've done this on hard surfaces with tennis balls.

12. Line Master Drill-Perfect anywhere. You can use soft covered baseballs with this drill.

13. Home Run Derby-Use Pickle Balls and back up to a fence or lay out cones. There isn't any place young baseball players don't love to play home run derby.

14. Relay Race-Keep the baseball theme by holding two hardballs in the glove while running. This is another drill to do anywhere.

15. Reaction Drill-Use tennis balls for this drill.

16. Multiple Hitting Stations-Utilizing a wall or fence, you can set up numerous soft toss drill stations, bunting, and hitting off the batting tee. Remember to spread out the stations and monitor the kids holding the bats. Pickle balls or rag balls should be used.

17. Batting Practice-Pickle balls are the key here. Just shorten the players in the field and you can run a regular batting practice in a parking lot. You can have the players bunt at the first pitch or two between two cones. Remember to remind the players the ball will not stop like it does on the grass.

18. Continuation Drill-It works all over. Use pickle balls.

19. Run Down Drill-Use tennis balls but still have the base runners wear helmets.

20. Goalie Drill-If you use tennis balls and remove the diving aspect, this drill works on hard services.

In addition to the above drills, coaches should consider a lot of kids games with a baseball theme to them. We touched upon this with the relay drill where the players hold two baseballs in their gloves when running. A game like "Red Light, Green Light" works well with the players if you have them hold two baseballs in their gloves while playing the game. Also a game like "Tag" works. Again put a baseball theme into this by having players hold either one or two baseballs in their glove. They must tag their teammate with their glove-hand without any of the balls falling out of the glove.

To sum up this section, in an ideal world, practicing on a beautiful manicured field is great, but many of us do not have access to this situation all the time. With just a minimum amount of work, you can keep a list of drills to use with either the parking lot practices or in a small area. Challenge yourself to add to the above list. I highly recommend you practice in a parking lot at least once just to teach your kids, parents, and assistant coaches to have flexibility.

Chapter 11

Batting Practice

"There are two theories on hitting the knuckleball. Unfortunately, neither of them work."

~Charlie Lau, 1982

I'd like to spend some extra time explaining my philosophy on batting practice. In all my years of coaching youth baseball, I am always looking for the most efficient practice methods for every aspect of baseball. It took me only a few years to realize that most youth baseball coaches, and myself, were running batting practice, not incorrectly, but not efficiently. From what I have seen with the typical batting practice, a coach will pitch a predetermined number of balls for each batter with the fielders fielding the hit balls and throwing them to first base. Usually the coach will yell something like, "Run the last one out," and the batter will do just that. If the ball is an infield hit, they try to throw the runner out at first. If it is hit into the outfield, the batter usually runs until thrown out. This is all well and good, but it is wasting valuable time when a coach wants to be efficient. The following is the most efficient way of running a batting practice that I've come up with. First of all, batting practice is just what it is, batting practice. While running batting practice, we are not really emphasizing fielding practice or baserunning practice. So all youth coaches and parents should really define what a youth batting practice is and what they want to get out of it. This is not to say that we should not make corrections in the field when we see them, but our main goal here is to get each player quality swings and move players in and out of the batter's box safely to maximize efficiency. In some of my descriptions of my practices, sometimes it sounds more of a regiment than it actually is. Believe me, we also have our fun and have moments that we stop and laugh at each other, which I think is just as important as teaching youth players how to hit and field. Most of my practices do not run more than one hour and fifteen minutes from beginning to end. Every minute of wasted time will affect all other aspects and time of any other drills or techniques I want to accomplish. When the players arrive at practice, they are assigned a number in the order they arrive. The first person to arrive is number one and the second player to arrive is number two, and so on. This is the order they will bat in batting practice. This technique is also a great way of getting players to practice on time. If you don't use this technique, start using it, and not just in baseball but all recreational youth sports. I use this number technique throughout practice and it is amazing how all of a sudden you have young kids 10, 11 and 12 pushing their parents to get them to arrive to practice on time. So now we have the team numbered from one to twelve. Coaches need to have an over abundance of baseballs. The league will provide baseballs, but I always make sure I purchase a few dozen extras. I try to work with three-dozen or more and keep an extra dozen in my trunk. And don't think I'm not frugal, accounting for every baseball at the end of practice. I try to make sure we find each and every one. After practice, I comb the field myself to make sure I get them all. Usually I find extras. I keep almost all of them including the most weathered, worn, decrepit baseballs. I'll find a use for them somewhere down the road. Many old baseballs just need a day or two in the sun to get them usable again. Here is the actual logistics and set up that I do about 95% of the time when I run batting practice. Being a big proponent of bunting, I set up two cones on the third base line, about six feet apart, approximately where the bunt is supposed to go. You can be creative here and set up a second set of cones inside the first set.

I set up two empty buckets, one about three feet behind second base and the other one at the far base of the pitcher's mound toward second. I have another bucket with the baseballs on the mound easily accessible for me. Putting one bucket on top of another gives us older coaches a chance to save our back from bending over. It also saves time. You can buy these five gallon buckets at any home center or you may have one or more in your garage left over from a painter or contractor. Now, this is a key. As a youth coach who wants a well-run practice and a lot of repetitions for the kids, I move up almost to the front of the mound to pitch. I do this mainly so I can throw strikes consistently. For safety purposes, I recommend an "L" screen if you are pitching from a short distance. If your league doesn't have any, make them purchase at least one. We coaches always think that as 40 or 50 year-olds our reflexes are the same as they were when we were 17 and 18. This is totally not true. I know finances are a big issue for many leagues, but an "L" screen is a good idea. I will describe the batting practice with the assumption there is no "L" screen, which is probably the norm for most leagues around the country. If you think there is already too many items to transport or keep track of, then take away one or both of the empty buckets for the baseballs.

I keep at least two or three baseballs in my glove at one time. Again, this is to save time, but be aware that this takes away your ability to catch a ball hit right back to you. Baseballs will come right back to you. You should keep as many baseballs in your glove depending on your own comfort zone. The safety of your team and yourself are the top priorities. If it seems I'm going through this batting practice too quickly, more concerned about quantity rather than quality of swings, this can't be further from the truth. I move along at a good pace but never do I sacrifice the chance to correct a player who I think is doing something incorrectly. Whether it is stepping toward third base with the front foot or stopping the swing, I will always reinforce the correct method. The corrections should be made in practice not in games when in the batter's box.

I have the first person up at bat with the 2nd (or on deck hitter) ready to go. This on deck hitter is usually in the dugout or behind a screen in a safe area. I have the 3rd hitter (or double on deck hitter) on the other side of the fence on the 3rd base line hitting balls on a batting tee using pickle balls (plastic) or wiffle balls with another parent feeding the balls on the tee. If there are enough assistant coaches or if your team is capable of doing it, I have the #4 hitter on the other side of the fence with a coach doing the toss drill with the pickle balls. Now remember that the number 2, or on deck hitter, must be ready to hit. This is extremely important to keep the batting practice moving at a good clip. Once the batter is in the batter's box, he will bunt the first two pitches. For each successful bunt that goes between the two cones that are set up, the player receives an extra swing. A player gets five swings besides his two bunts. So if a player lays one bunt between the cones, he get six regular swings. If he lays both bunts between the cones, he gets seven swings (the maximum per hitter). You can play with the number of swings anyway you want, rewarding more swings for good bunts. After the bunt attempts, I'll usually say, "Okay, now swing away." There are certain things that have to happen to make this work. Remember, there are two buckets strategically located. When the hitter swings away, wherever the ball is hit, the fielder tosses it toward the bucket closest to him. If it is hit to the outfield, he will throw the ball as close to the bucket behind second base as he can. If he hits it to the infield, the fielder will toss it to the bucket behind the pitcher's mound. The fielder will not, I repeat, will not throw the ball to first base. Omitting the throw to first base will save tons of time. Reinforce to the players they must toss the ball to the bucket on one or two bounces or they will tend to play basketball with the baseball by aiming to get the ball in the bucket. The fielders do not make a play to first and the hitter does not run the last one out. We get more repetitions in a shorter period of time. The players are always facing the hitter. One might ask, "Isn't this boring for most of the players in the field?" Well, not really. Because of the amount of balls hit in a short period of time, the ball is usually hit all over the place. The coach throwing batting practice has the extra balls in his glove and is ready to pitch the next one right away. Very rarely do I turn around to see where the hit baseball has landed. Maybe one out of four hits do I turn around to see where the hit baseball has landed. Because I have been doing the batting practice this way for so long, I tend to know by the sound upon contact and the initial flight of the baseball going past me where the ball will land. You'll be able to recognize this also as the season goes on. The coach must realize that he must wait an extra second or two before pitching when a high pop up is hit. When out of baseballs, have the players in the infield hustle to gather up the balls, combine buckets, and we're ready to go again. I know that these are the most ideal conditions with use of a field, number of players etc., but even when I run a parking lot practice, these are the parameters I try to follow, with adjustments of course. The players that are working off the tee or doing the soft toss should get around 15-20 swings before it is their turn to bat. And if for some reason the on deck is not ready like he should be, skip him. I guarantee this will only happen once.

Gathering the baseballs in either the infield or outfield and throwing them to the appropriate bucket will save time in the long run, which will translate to more swings for the players.

Keeping the players motivated to help gather the baseballs can always be an issue. Coaches should reward their players with extra swings when they put in the extra effort to help the coaches. I always offer to stay after practice to help any player that wants extra help. The fact that players are rewarded for bunting will always bring some players in for extra bunting practice. Many coaches will say you'd be better off having players pitch to each other because of the realistic flight of the baseball. I tried this and found it was not too successful. First of all, you cannot move players up on the mound, close to home plate, just for safety reasons. The whole procedure, including how I hold extra baseballs, pitch the next pitch based on the flight of the baseball etc., is not something we want to put into the hands of 10, 11 and 12 year-old kids. Try it if you want, but I've done trial and error with this.

Chapter 12

Playoffs, All Stars And The Season's End

"The strongest thing that baseball has going for it today are its yesterdays."

~Lawrence Ritter

Playoffs

Baseball playoffs can be exhilarating and frustrating. I've had my share of successes and failures. As much as the coaches may look forward to the playoffs, the kids especially love them. It's amazing how everyone loves competition. I've seen coaches wanting to institute playoffs for kids as young as 7 or 8, which I think is ridiculous, though the kids probably welcome them. I've seen playoffs for teams this young where the winning team is crowned champs basically because their pitchers walked less batters than the opposing pitchers. I understand the concept of giving players extra games, but with the young kids, I would prefer to not start playoffs in leagues until players are at least nine years-old. Usually each league decides when playoffs should begin. And now with the immense popularity of travel teams, I'm sure that the intense competition with playoffs and tournaments trickles down to a pretty young age. You can find organizations that sponsor special tournaments for almost any age.

Playoffs can bring out the best and worst in players, coaches, and especially parents. Everything is magnified. Make no mistake, there is enormous pressure sometimes on these young kids participating. I've seen situations where coaches will try to manipulate game schedules to benefit their pitching rotation. I've also seen coaches try to have games cancelled when it was only drizzling rain just to give their ace an extra start. These rules, thank god, have changed.

I'm a huge proponent that all teams are eligible for the playoffs. In my mind, as long as teams practice, the more games played is better for the kids in the long run. I've argued with people about this. We even had a team one year finish 0-20 and they made the playoffs. With this said, I am also a huge believer in rewarding the top teams. It is absolutely fine to give them an advantage going into the playoffs. This usually means a "bye" for the first and/or second place team, depending on the number of teams in the playoffs. When I was a board member one year in my local league, I argued at a meeting for everyone in the majors (10, 11 & 12 years-old) to make the playoffs. The playoffs were about a month away and this should have been decided before the season started, like it should every year. Needless to say, we had to decide midway through the season. There were seven teams, with the 6th and 7th place team being very weak. I said that including the 6th place team and not the 7th would be a crime when there is not that much of a difference in talent. It ended up where one team was 4-16 and the other was 3-17. The league wanted to give the top two teams a bye. The next four teams would play each other, with the winners playing the top two in the semi finals. So what happened was one of the board members at this meeting asked me to come up with a fair way to have all teams in the playoffs and still give the top two teams a bye. They wanted an immediate answer. Not being a quick thinker, I pressed and was lucky enough to think of a solution. I proposed that the day after the season ends, which was two days away from when the playoffs began, the bottom two teams would play a "Wild Card" game. The winner would be in the pool of six playoff teams and the top two teams could still get a bye. Whichever team played the winner of the Wild Card game would be at an advantage because it would have the number one pitcher going. The Wild Card winner probably would use their number one pitcher in the Wild Card game just to get into the playoffs. It was one of the few times the board liked my idea because it was a win-win situation. Everyone made the playoffs. The teams in the Wild Card game were happy to play this game with a chance to proceed further in the playoffs. I remember this particular Wild Card game was a great game. The winning team was celebrating like they won the whole playoffs. The other teams were happy because they still had their number one pitchers available. The team playing the Wild Card winner had a distinct advantage, which was the fair way to do this.

I believe the best way to run playoffs in a local recreational or Little League® is to include all teams and give the top two teams a bye. Remember that in playoffs, pitching is usually the key to moving to the next bracket. Some leagues will have single elimination games or the best out of three. Some will have both, with the single elimination games in the first round and the best out of three for every round thereafter. It doesn't matter if your league has 5, 6, 7, 8, 9, or 10 teams. There is plenty of information on the internet as far as setting up brackets for tournaments or playoffs. Again, unlike what happened in the scenario I mentioned, the playoffs formats should be decided before the season starts and even the dates should be established.

I really enjoy the playoffs and like the fact there is added pressure on all involved. Over the years, I've noticed how some parents get so uptight. It is incredible. Remembering back to when my kids were playing, I have had extra anxiety myself. I used to call an extra Parents Meeting just for the playoffs. While during the regular season I try to play all kids at least three innings per game, in the playoffs there is only one goal. The goal in the playoffs is to win. So unless you prep the parents about what to expect, there will be hurt feelings. I did away with the Parents Meeting for the playoffs, but I make sure I send an e-mail to them prior to the first playoff game.

Dear Blue Hen Parents!

It has been a fun regular season that went extremely fast. Our playoffs start this Saturday. Finishing in second place, we have the advantage of getting a "bye" in the first round. In the past, I have coached the playoffs differently than the regular season. During the season I have tried to play kids at least three innings per game. During playoffs there might be games that players only get in for two innings. This is not a knock on any individuals. I try to coach to our strength. The regular season is a good barometer, showing me which players were the most successful against certain teams and pitchers.

Playoffs can get a little intense, but for the most part, it is a positive and integral part of most youth leagues. I know that all the Blue Hen parents will cheer our team enthusiastically. And if there is any controversial call, I know we will all be good sports, as we were during the regular season. I'll see you all on Saturday. Go Blue Hens!

Marty

This is the e-mail I send out almost every year before the playoffs. You don't have to do anything, but I always like to have communication before, during, and after the season. If you communicate certain things minimally, you will cut down on anywhere from 40-60% of any complaints and problems you may incur from parents. I've seen it from all sides. In the playoffs games, I coach a little differently and have different strategies. I've had a full season, about 20 games, to see which players are the most successful hitters and pitchers. I especially want to know which of my players are the best contact hitters. I love to bat my best contact hitters second in the order. I used to have my best hitter bat 3rd or 4th, but there were times when we were behind and rallying and we never got to my best hitter. So I usually bat him 2nd and have batted my top hitter first. I also play a lot of small ball bunting, trying to scratch out the first run. Because I believe playoffs are almost all about pitching, I think it is a huge advantage getting the lead run. It puts the other coach on the defensive, having him thinking about if he should pull his starting pitcher or keep him in. Playoffs are all about winning, but if you've practiced with your team and purposely expose them to some duress and pressure in some drills, they should be ready to play.

All Stars

All Stars are what some leagues will call the "second season" or the "real season." It is interesting how during a three month period during the regular season, or even one or two days after a very intense playoff game, some coaches and parents who have developed tense relationships after episodes of arguing to the point where sometimes they have to be separated physically, now have a common goal. I have seen numerous encounters that are too ugly to even mention. It is amazing people can get away from their emotions and act irrational in front of their own kids. Feelings get hurt in youth sports all the time when kids are overlooked for All Stars or even elite travel teams and high school teams. I've never seen anything like what occurs in youth sports. Not just baseball either. I've seen issues during basketball, soccer, softball, and even at a high school golf tournament. Then when All Stars begin, the same parents who were at each other's throats are now on the same side standing next to each other watching practices and games. Maybe it is that old expression, "Enemies of my enemies must be my friends." I just find the thing incredibly interesting.

I've coached numerous All Star teams and have had some success. I prefer coaching teams and developing players over two and three years. I find it somewhat frustrating to practice with 11-14 players in a matter of two weeks and try to teach them what I think is the best way to succeed on the baseball field. But I know most coaches gravitate toward All Stars and love the intense competition. As much as problems and issues happen during the season and are magnified during playoffs, the intensity during All Stars is even more magnified. Many times after an All Star game, whether winning or losing, the coach is subject to harassing phone calls from parents who have issues regarding their own child. Second guessing the coach runs rampant with dozens of wannabe General Mangers watching the games talking amongst each other about how the coach is screwing things up. This stuff used to bother me, but it doesn't anymore. Winning will cut down on much of the complaints. And it's funny, whether you agree or disagree, and it might be a negative reflection on our culture, but winning at all levels is the best remedy for problems. On the professional level, very rarely are there locker room problems, and injuries tend to be less on winning teams as opposed to losing teams. You hear less sniping in the newspapers with teams that are winning. On losing teams, one hears all sorts of issues, be it the defense blaming the offense for a six game losing streak. Some players anonymously call for the backup quarterback to replace the starter. On the amateur level and in schools, there are always conflicts. I've seen a basketball coach being harassed by parents in the parking lot of the local high school after getting off the team bus. On the youth level, things are not much different. The good news is the problems can be cut down if the league and coach takes the appropriate action.

When I coached All Stars, I made sure I immediately sent out a letter or e-mail scheduling a parents meeting. As much as coaches need to have a parents meeting before the regular season, the All Star coach must have a Parents Meeting before the first practice. In fact, when I coached All Stars, I did not allow any player to practice unless both parents attended the parents meeting. I know there are people who will bypass this and will just deal with the problems as they come up. Just as we do preventative maintenance on our cars, why not do the same thing as coaches? We are all so hooked on winning and learning different tricks so our team gets an advantage that we tend to overlook how coaching really encompasses not only having players and teams improve and win championships, but also the socializing of the kids as well as the parents. Some of the biggest problems in our world happen because of a lack of communication. These short meetings with parents and a flow of e-mails during the season will only help the coach be a good coach. I do all this preparation because I just want to coach kids in baseball and don't want to be wasting my time explaining each and every thing I do. So again, and I know I might sound like a broken record, have the Parents Meeting before your regular season, and if you coach All Stars, you must have a meeting then as well. If you are uncomfortable speaking in front of a group, have one of your assistants do it. If you are the coach, you may want to select your biggest competition in the league as your assistant. Over the course of the season he should know the nuances of his All Stars better than anyone. After all the administrative duties are taken care of, then you can proceed with your All Star season. So the first thing you should do as All Star coach is get that e-mail out right away. The e-mail I send goes something like this:

Dear All Star Parents,

We will be having a mandatory Parent Meeting this Monday night June 23 at 8pm at the Colony Elementary School. We will be going over the schedule and expectations during the All Stars. The league understands that during the summer families go away, but we are expecting anyone who has been picked to represent our community to make a commitment to this team. The meeting will not last more than 10-15 minutes. And those of you who have kids who never played for me will give me a chance to explain my own philosophy and how I go about coaching All Stars. It is imperative that both parents attend and if there is a problem with the date and time, please call me as soon as possible.

Best Regards

Marty Schupak

555-555-5555 (cell)

Parents will understand the seriousness of how you are approaching All Stars and I can almost guarantee that both parents will show up. Very rarely did I have anyone miss the All Star Parents Meeting. What I find to be the two most important issues to go over are playing time and communicating to parents that as All Stars you expect each and every player to play all nine positions with enthusiasm. I cannot begin to tell you how many times I've heard parents complain during All Stars. "Why does he have my son playing left field, he never played there before?" At the Parents Meeting I give each set of parents an agenda of what we will go over.

Dear All Star Parents,

Congratulations on your son making the All Star team. As a member, he is one of twelve kids who represent the 12,000 people who live in our community. All Stars can be a very positive experience but can also have it's share of anxiety. I have alway found it useful to have this parents meeting and go over certain expectations we can expect from each other.

1. Practice schedule-We will practice every day for the next 12 days.

2. Playing Time-Minimum All Star playing time is one at bat and one inning in the field.

3. Player Positions -All players are required to play all 9 positions enthusiastically.

4. All Star Team Parent-I am asking for two volunteers to help with phone calls and e-mails.

5. Water Bottle-All players must bring their own water bottle.

6. Vacation Schedule-We expect a commitment for our community from you and your son.

If you are going away, I must know as soon as possible when and for how long.

Marty Schupak

555-555-5555 (cell)

This is a lot shorter than the agenda for my regular season meeting, but I go over each and every point in detail. On playing time, I am explicit, telling the parents that if they have a choice to go to Cape Cod on a trip and might not be able to swallow the fact that your son might get only one at bat per game, my suggestion is to go on the trip. I am adamant about this point, and even tell them, "I have one or two kids who would love to be on this All Star team and are not concerned about playing time." In the past I have heard parents say, "If I knew my kid would only be playing this little, I would not have had him play and gone away." We are being proactive with the playing time explanation. Also on positions, I tell them I expect all players to play all nine positions. If they cannot play every position, tell me now. It may seem that I come across a bit strong, but if you were ever involved with All Stars, you know what can happen. The commitment and vacation schedule is huge. Parents will not break plans for a cruise. Some parents will schedule things at the spur of the moment. As a coach, parents need to fill out a form or just let you know their vacation schedule. Even after explaining these things, issues will still come up.

Season Ending Gathering

Every player on your team will not make All Stars. And for most, the season ends with the last game of the season or playoff game. No matter how good or how disappointing your season was, you always want to end it on a good note. I always like to leave a positive impression on the team. If you are coaching 12 players, it is almost impossible to have all the players and parents like the coach the same. I do the best I can during the season with the Parents Meeting, but I am also realistic about how things are. The season-ending party really levels the field because everyone enjoys themselves.

Everyone's schedule begins to get busy when the season begins to come to a close in my area in the Northeast. School begins it's final lap and parents are quickly making summer plans, either for vacation or camp for their kids. Toward the season's end, usually some parents will begin to talk about a season ending barbecue or pool party. In all my years of coaching, I think there was only one year that we didn't have a season ending gathering. Maybe it was something I did or did not do. Nevertheless, this is an excellent opportunity to have the team together one more time for a positive fun time. The reason it is a great way to end the season is because even if your team lost their last playoff game 12-0, everyone has a good time at the team gathering and this will be the last thing they remember. I have a few goals going into the season, but my number one goal is to have each player come back the following year to play baseball. Remember that baseball is losing participation so we coaches are all ambassadors of the game. We must always be selling the game of baseball and all the positive things that it has to offer.

Usually the season ending party will be entirely organized by two or three of the moms on the team. There will be one designated house for the party, which more often than not has a swimming pool for the kids to swim in, and even sometimes to throw me in. The parents that organize the food will usually have each parent bring a different dish, soda, or paper goods. Securing a date is one of the more difficult things to do. When you are the coach, this is one time where the party is scheduled so everyone can make it, but that is very difficult for this time of year. Once school ends, everyone goes in totally different directions, and you'll never be able to schedule a convenient date for everyone. If, as the coach, you find no one is talking about a season ending get together, then suggest it around the second to the last week of the season.

At this gathering, I usually will help organize some of the games we played in the backyard. Wiffle Ball seems to be the game of choice. Having the parents involved is usually a good thing. In the past, I bought tee shirts for each player. I also try to have a ceremony where I call each player up, two at a time, and say something about everyone on the team. The kids and parents seem to enjoy this as long as I keep it short so the kids can get back to either the food or the pool. I make sure to thank all my assistant coaches as well as the team parent and anyone else who helped during the season. If you have had any major problem with any parents, you must take the high road. No matter how insulting or how much they have bad mouthed you during the season, be a positive leader and leave the politics and bickering outside the door for this last get together.

The party usually lasts three to four hours. One of the most satisfying things is to see how many new friendships were formed by the kids during the season. This confirms what I touched upon that parents should always be flexible having their kids play on teams with kids they don't know. Remember, some parents will fight for their kids to be on their friend's team or a coach will insist a player must be on his team at the beginning of the season. The new friendships that are formed among the kids, and even the parents, are proof that meeting new people is always a positive.

After this gathering, I make sure that I follow it up with a letter or e-mail to the whole team. I have probably been e-mailing the team the whole season as far as practices and rescheduling games are concerned. For this last correspondence of the season, I try to send a hard copy letter, which I think has more meaning than the e-mails sent during the year. Of course you want this letter to be a very positive, thanking everyone who helped make the last 3 or 4 months a success. You want to write it in such a way that your returning players will truly look forward to coming back.

Dear Blue Hens Families!

Wow! What a great season for the Blue Hens and a great season ending barbecue! First of all thanks to our great host, the Carolls! As host, they provided a perfect party, with a guarantee of no rain! As a coach, I loved watching the players playing and interacting. This is what youth sports is all about. Thanks to Joanne Boykin, who provided the flowers for our host.

I want to thank everyone for that great gift. The tickets you got me for the Yankees baseball game was quite thoughtful.

A special thanks to Mark Bass, who did a great job as coach. Mark will be back next year. I also want to thank the other coaches who helped out: Joe Newhouse, Nelson Caroll and Joe Martin. The cooperation we had as far as the snack bar and raking the field was the best in the league.

Another thanks goes out to Yvette Caroll, who was again a stand out team parent. Most of all, I want to thank the people who really made this year a success:

John, Phil, William, Bob, Ed, Richard, Mike, Andrew, Lloyd, John, Dave, and Robert.

Their spirit and effort made this season a joy to coach. I want to wish everyone a happy and safe summer!

Good luck to anyone who is playing All Stars and are in travel leagues.

Already, I am counting the days till next year! Thanks again!

Best Regards,

Marty Schupak

Chapter 13
Injuries

"Sandy's fastball was so fast, some batters would start to swing as he was on his way to the mound."

~Jim Murray, on Sandy Koufax

Injuries, Overuse and Too Much Baseball!

In baseball, like in all sports, there are injuries that are avoidable and unavoidable. I remember a number of year ago, I was coaching my middle son, Michael, in All Stars. During a practice, a freak accident happened when he bent down to pick up a baseball to give to my assistant coach, who was hitting fungos with me for fielding practice. As he was getting up, the back swing from my assistant's bat met my son's head in a kind of "perfect storm." Not a tremendous impact, but the blood began to gush and I was one panicky parent/coach. To make a long story short, he ended up with 27 stitches by a plastic surgeon and is fine today. This actually made me a much better coach. When I do drills with my teams, they are spaced out much better than I used to do for safety purposes. I am highly cognizant of any potential disaster waiting to happen. No matter what precautions are taken, accidents happen. I mentioned the story before how my other son and his friend were using hard balls doing the soft toss and the ricochet hit him directly in the eye. I also mentioned that a number of years ago we had a player slide into third base and break an ankle. A couple of years ago during opening day, the opposing shortstop got hit by the ball square in his face because of a bad bounce. The result was eerily similar to that of my son's accident. These things will occur and it is no one's fault. Just as kids playing in their backyard can fall down and get a scrape, or something more serious, injuries are a part of all sports. Coaches and leagues must be prepared. The invention of the cell phone is great for these kind of emergencies, and when coaching, I always have 911 and my local ambulance on speed dial. Leagues should not just hand out First Aid kits, but should also instruct coaches what is in them and how to use them. Coaches may not need a complete first aid class, but there should be a yearly educational meeting on injuries. Leagues should also have defibrillator machines, and every member of the league board of directors should know how to use them.

Preparations is the key for on the field injuries. The injuries that are of big concern and preventable happen over a period of time. Overuse in baseball and being too sport-specific is running rampant. The overuse in baseball is especially harmful to players who throw too much. I am not a doctor. I have a lifelong friend, Ralph Sharaga, who follows sports with me and always told me, "Believe mostly what you see, not everything you hear." Ralph's reference was to pro players and how the media says one thing and we see something else. In youth baseball, I see most of the injuries occurring in a player's elbow and/or shoulder. There are many reasons for this. The number one is overuse of a specific body part, in this case the throwing arm over a long period of time.

I'll tell you what happened to me once. There are very few things I am good at around the house, which my wife will verify. I do have a wood burning stove at home that I love to manage during the winter. Preparing the fire and watching Sunday pro football is a tradition I hope to do for a long time. I enjoy the whole process of stacking the wood as well, not just making the fire. One year, instead of buying my regular three cords of split firewood for the winter, I had my neighbor, an excavator, drop off logs that I decided I would split by hand. I bought different types of axes, wedges, etc., and spent a good two hours doing this for about three weeks after I came home from work. Then it happened. I got a streaking pain in my arm that started at the elbow.

285

This became incredibly sensitive and I went to my doctor. He said it was obviously from overuse, and I stopped the splitting of the wood cold turkey and after 3 or 4 months it went away. A great lesson for the "coach" who should have known better. The same thing holds true with youngsters doing the same motion with the same body part over and over again. Wether it is the player's love of the game or the parents encouraging their child trying to reach a certain level of excellence, this has caught up in a negative way in our society. As young as high school, illegal drugs, such as steroids, have become more common to try gaining quicker recovery time from injuries. Some doctors have even seen parents getting their son, who pitches, unnecessary Tommy John surgery, in which a ligament in the elbow is replaced with a tendon from another part of the body. In some cases after this type of operation, the pitcher will throw the ball harder. Incredible where our minds are going.

A lot of this filters to the youth level with overzealous parents and/or coaches. And overuse has in the last few years began receiving it's just publicity. Earlier I mentioned how travel teams have taken baseball in a big way. Travel teams can work a number of ways. One or two parents that might be unhappy with the competition in the local Little League decide to form a team of All Stars. They will begin to investigate where there may be a U12 (under 12 years-olds) league that is looking for teams. It has become easier and easier for teams to find leagues to play in. So the two parents who will be the coaches contact 12-14 kids to gauge an interest. Upon finding a team, the two parents quickly figure costs such insurance, uniforms, umpire costs, and other incidentals. The coaches will get calls from some of the kids they called that they are not interested in playing on the team. They will get as many and more calls from parents who heard about the team and how come they weren't called about their own kids. Thus starts the dilemma for the coaches. They have in their minds who they want on this team to field the best team, but other parents disagree on the ability of their son. Right here some feelings get stung. The coaches go ahead and get the team they want. They also get into a league with a schedule. Really industrious coaches will quickly set up a web site for the team with the schedule and other information, which is a real good thing. The schedule can have anywhere from 20-50 games (I've seen more) over the course of a summer. Here in the Northeast, some of the most competitive travel leagues get into high gear the middle of June and go through the middle of August with their regular games sandwiched by tournaments in other parts of the country they have to travel to. Others go year round with indoor practices once or twice a week during the winter months. And most travel teams will end up playing a double header on one of the weekend days. I have nothing against these travel teams, but the problems occur when some players go into more than one of these leagues. Plus some will continue in their local recreation or Little League. And make no mistake, the kids I have asked personally love these travel teams.

But the overuse of kids as their bodies are growing is a huge problem. An organization was recently formed called STOP, to help make parents aware of what is happening to our young kids from all these leagues. The organization was started by some of the top Orthopedic doctors in sports medicine. Injuries to young athletes are growing. And according to the doctors in this organization, a big factor is the kids that specialize in one sport and play only that one sport year round can be vulnerable to injuries. According to an excellent article in the On Line Wall Street Journal on April 1, of 2010 by Robert A. Guth:

"Surgeons say the incidence of youth sports injuries is rising. Some of the increase

comes from the growing number of kids who participate in sports. Another factor is

the increasing number of kids who specialize in a single sport at young ages and who

play year-round." **2**

If you really look into the potential injuries kids may face, parents would think twice about putting them in more than one league. Incredibly, these experts in this field of study maintain that 50% of all sports injuries by middle school and high-school students are from overuse. As was stated by a doctor in the article:

"They're putting more stress on their growing skeletons," says Dr. Peter Millett,

a surgeon at the Steadman Clinic, Vail, Colo. "We're seeing injury patterns that

we haven't seen before at high levels."

Again, I have nothing against travel teams in any sport. It is playing on multiple teams at the same time that tend to do kids in. What maybe parents should do is determine a finite number of games to allow their son or daughter play in a year and monitor this. Say you or doctors determine 60 games in a year is the maximum number of games to allow your child. Then sign him up for one, two, or three leagues but do not deviate from playing more than 60 games. So the player can participate in Little League and play 25 games including playoffs. Then maybe 5 more All Star games. So he has 30 games to play on travel teams. He can divide this anyway he wants on one or two teams. But I can tell you, if I coached his travel team and his parents came to me explaining their son is on a "Game Count" and can only play 12 of our 20 games, I would have a hard time with this. There will eventually be a resolution to all this, but it will take time, and unfortunately when there is a barrage of injuries over a period of time, parents will pay more attention.

And don't get me wrong, I'm not blaming most baseball injuries on travel teams. Here are three stories about three different players. The first is one of my players. Let's say his name is Tommy. Now I drafted Tommy on my team when he was 10 years-old. I was told by one of my assistant coaches who saw him play in the minor division that he plays years beyond his age. I had gone to see him play and my assistant was right on the money. He was below average height for his age and has some quickness, but for someone his age, the anticipation he had on the field and the contact he made with the baseball was excellent. And if you have seen high school batting practices, when you have a talent, the ball just makes a different sound as it comes off the bat. Tommy had that sound. I had him three years on my team and he pitched and played every position, he hit the ball well, ran well and was the best pitcher in the league, even though he was not that tall. We won the league championship each of those three years. His best asset was making plays in the field. Backing other players up or just anticipating where the ball was going was out of this world. I knew then that the only thing that might keep him from becoming a really good high school player was maybe his height. Boy was I blind to what was just beginning to happen. He played for the Middle School and did well but I was told that he was getting hit more when he pitched than he did while he was on my team, which is very normal. Then the next year he only played first base. He ended up having some kind of diagnosis on his elbow, arm, and shoulder. Something was radically wrong. He had at least one and maybe two operations. We have all heard about people who are cut off from the thing they love most. Well this is what happened to Tommy. He lived for baseball, but could not play anymore. In fact, he had problems lifting his throwing arm above his shoulder. A really bad situation. I kept track on and off about how he was doing and he got into soccer, which was a great alternate and did not require him using his hands. He got into a great college and studied sports psychology. I spoke to him and he told me the frustrations of the whole situation and that he could not bear to watch a baseball game on television for 10 years. I had heard he hurt himself because of throwing too many curve balls. He said absolutely not. It was from overuse. Every waking moment he would throw a baseball. His father had set up a mat against a wall or screen. He would come home from school and just throw against the mat for hours. This is a tough story because as parents how can we convince our own kids when they are doing something they love in their own backyard that they have to limit this activity? This is hard to reconcile as parents. Taking a positive from this story, because Tommy is into sports psychology, he can help convince other parents about moderation is the best policy for one specific activity.

The second player, let's call him Ralph, was on another team in the league but the best player for his age. At ten years-old, Ralph was lights out as a pitcher and a hitter. He threw righty and batted lefty, which coaches love. He was tall and solidly built for his age. Besides our local league, Ralph was in one and possibly a second travel league. Because he was a stud as a pitcher, I know his travel coaches wanted him to be ready to pitch for their teams. Beyond this point I have no solid proof of what happened, but when he was 11, in his second year in the league, I noticed a vast drop off in his pitching velocity. He still hit but not as well as when he was 10. In fact, as a coach, and I saw it with some of my players, they really didn't fear him when he was pitching against us, and we hit him pretty well. When he was 12, he hardly pitched at all. I did not know his parents well enough to ask them what was going on, but I inquired with a few people on his team that I knew. My suspicions were correct. Pitching in multiple leagues over a two year period brought about some kind of injury that the people I spoke to weren't even sure of. Sadly, in the All Stars, Ralph played second base and had to make every throw almost underhand. Hopefully, his parents will do what is best in the long run for Ralph and not what is best for his baseball coaches. The doctors I read about all say that resting from the activity that caused the problem is the best immediate treatment. The problem here is at what point does the player complain about the discomfort and at what point does the parent just rest him? And I might have been as guilty as other parents if my own kids were involved in multiple leagues.

The last story is about a player on my team, we'll call Calvin. Like the previous two players mentioned, I picked Calvin when he was 10 years-old. He had an enthusiasm for baseball like nothing I ever saw before. Probably one of the five best kids I ever coached. Not because he was excellent as a ball player, but he was very coachable. He listened and soaked up everything you would try to teach the team. He never forgot anything the coach said. This kid was a true five tool player as a young player. He did everything for our team and played every position. During the season the high school coach approached me to ask what I thought would be his best position as he got older, and I told him centerfield. He lacked height, but had terrific lateral speed and would make great catches everywhere on the field. His first year was incredible. Probably Calvin and Tommy were the two best 10 year-old players I ever had on my team. He pitched and though he got hit a little, hardly walked a player. As a coach I was drooling with anticipation about him as a 12 year-old when he would grow a bit and be more polished on the mound. In my mind, when you have a young pitcher who throws strikes, this is the best quality a young pitcher can have. He was in a travel league and his parents were terrific and monitored every pitch he threw in each league. I cooperated as best I could trying not to over-pitch him. His first year ended up as a banner year. His hitting was uncanny for a 10 year-old. He struck out maybe twice and batted over .600. His baserunning and fielding was great.

The next year as an 11 year-old he was better in all aspects of his game but his pitching. I used him a few times while his parents and I monitored his pitches in both leagues. This year his pitching was suspect in that he gained little speed from the year before but was just as accurate. After a game that he was hit pretty hard for the second time in a row, I shut him down as a pitcher. He played outstanding baseball the rest of the season and never complained about not pitching. He batted around .700 and made maybe one error the whole season. Then at the end of the season he showed up in a sling the last game. When I saw him, my heart sunk. I asked him what happened and he told me he tore his growth plate. As mentioned before, the growth plate is the area at the end of the bone. I was of course concerned about his health first, but as a baseball coach my mind was going in a million directions running through different batting order and defensive scenarios. I then felt kind of embarrassed feeling this way and focused on him. He told me if we win the first round, he'll be ready to play, but I knew otherwise. As it turned out, the growth plate was only strained and not torn, which was great news. He was out of the playoffs, but in All Stars, he played centerfield and did a fantastic job. Every game I couldn't make to watch, I got a 3 or 4 text messages on my cell phone telling me about the game saving catch he made in centerfield. Even the coach called me up one night with accolades about his fielding prowess and his hitting. I believe this last story is actually kind of a blessing in disguise. The parents and myself got a real wake-up call just in time. No permanent damage was done and Calvin can still excel at a game he loves at a different position other than a pitcher. And his parents will monitor any overuse of his arm. Thankfully, Calvin also plays soccer, which is great. Remember concentrating on one sport is a big part of the issue.

Injuries in baseball can occur but it is not a guarantee that overuse will bring about problems to everyone. Nolan Ryan was somewhat of a freak of nature the way he pitched into his forties at such as high level of play. So kids are different from each other. Precaution through education is the best policy. And if you agree that this is a problem in baseball, I see it as more of a problem in contact sports as far as the concussion issue. Why anyone is anxious to get back on the athletic field quickly after a concussion is beyond me. I've had a concussion and it is not fun. The NFL has begun to raise the awareness of the concussion issue and putting a player back on the field too soon. A concussion is a temporarily loss of brain function that can cause a variety of symptoms. Injuries will never be reduced to zero, but parents, players, and coaches must continue to listen to the medical profession that specializes in these fields.

With everything going on, and with studies being done, parents should proceed cautiously, deciding how often and how much their kids should be involved.

Moderation seems to be the common sense approach when we are dealing with our own young kids. Maybe the Greek philosophers had it right as far as their feelings about moderation. It was Aristotle who said:

"The virtue of justice consists in moderation, as regulated by wisdom."

Chapter 14

Sample Practices

" Baseball is dull only to dull minds."

~Red Barber

In this section I will blueprint 60 practices. I will give a brief explanation of each. I usually try to run between 8-10 practices before we play our first game. Then, during the season, I try to practice two times for every game played. So in the course of a twenty game season, my goal is to practice about 40 times. Sometimes I end up practicing more, and sometimes I end up practicing less. Each of the practices is organized from the drills in the previous pages. Use the practices as they are or change them up to suit you or your team's needs. Remember to try to run the practices no longer than 75-90 minutes but try to be closer to 75 minutes. At the start of the season, my practices run longer than during the season. So I might run 90 minute practices early in the season and then cut them down from there. The reason being is I have to teach the new players what each drill is and how we set it up. In practices, a lot of time is wasted when you have to take extra time to explain every detail of the drill. I will also go right into a drill, putting team "veterans" in the front of the line, telling the new players at the end of the line to pay attention to the player in front of them. This works really well. On some drills, I will ask one of my veteran players to explain the drill. This is accomplishing a couple of things. First of all, it is getting young people used to speaking in front of their peers, which to me is extremely important. Also, sometimes teammates seem to listen to each other better than listening to the coach all the time. If you do let the player explain the drill, beware though that young people will tend to go on too long with their explanations. Don't be afraid to cut them off and help them with the drill description.

In all drills and practices the coach's goal should be to involve as many players as possible at all times. Sometimes this is not possible. Try to utilize your assistant coaches or parents, so if you have drills that do not involve everyone, you can have them supervise something like hitting off the batting tee. Remember, the more things you have going on at the same time, the greater potential for injuries. Safety is of the utmost importance. In most of the fielding drills, you can use soft covered balls.

The most important part about practices, which I spoke about earlier, is not to deny your players batting practice. Of all the drills covered in this book, players will enjoy most of them, but nothing like how they will enjoy batting practice. No matter how great any or all of the drills that you do are, most baseball players live for batting practice. One year I had gotten too smart for myself. After winning a league championship, I guess I thought I had invented the game of baseball. I decided to invent a new type of baseball practice technique. For whatever reason, I began running a practice one day where we almost exclusively did defense. And the next practice I would exclusively do offense. What a huge mistake. Instead of trying to be Vince Lombardi and run baseball practices like football practices are run, I should have listened to my players to find out what they liked best. Don't be afraid to reward them. So I shuffled the deck so to speak and realized the best practices I could run would always be highlighted by batting practice. Either the typical batting practice or a type of batting practice or hitting game.

Batting practice can accomplish other constructive things during the season. I will always reward players with extra swings. So if after a game I see two players working hard to put the equipment in the equipment bag, I will yell out so all can hear, "Daniel and Justin are putting the equipment away, they get an extra swing at our next practice." Here is a great teaching point. Don't just say, "Whoever puts the equipment away gets an extra swing." Always reward players on the action after it is done. This works great and you'll be amazed at how many kids get involved helping the coaches do extra things.

This rewarding of extra swings is always on the honor system. If Daniel gets into the batter's box, I always will ask, "How many swings do I owe you?" If he says 6, then I'll say we'll give you two today so I'll owe you four. Of course this is in addition to whatever swings I determined I'm giving each batter. This works so well I even carry players' swings over year to year. Make no mistake, if a player is owed swings after one season, I guarantee at the very first practice the following year, the player will say "Coach, you owe me 4 swings from last year."

I also will run mini batting practices as the first activity at a regular practice. With these mini batting practices, it is the only activity I'll do without a regular warm up. I do this for a couple of reasons. First of all, early in the season, if you have one of these mini batting practices and run it the way I described in the batting practice section with each player getting a number as they come, this is teaching the kids the importance of getting to practice on time. As soon as I have maybe 5 players, we begin this batting practice. Players strolling in afterwards first look a little bewildered and surprised and aren't sure what is going on or if they got the wrong time for the practice altogether. I also like to do this just for a change of pace and to show the players that the practices are unpredictable as to how they will be run.

When running practices, transitioning from one drill to another is extremely important. If the coach is enthusiastic going from one drill to the next, the players will also exhibit this enthusiasm. This is especially true if you go from a skill building dill to a fun drill. For instance, if you are going over first and third defensive situations, this is tough for young players to keep focused, but a must in youth baseball. After you are done with this drill, quickly tell the players we are going to play Tennis Racquet Home Run Derby. And then proceed to set it up quickly. Integrating a skill learning drill followed by a fun drill is the formula I have found most successful.

After about a third of the season is over, and I have my practices down to about 60-75 minutes, I will offer for players to come 10-15 minutes early to work on anything they want. I will do this with no more than two players so you can give each ample attention. Also, during practices, I make sure I give pitchers who have not pitched some throws. This is where you need to utilize assistant coaches taking the pitchers off the field and throwing on the side.

I supplement my regular practices with what I call "Opportunity Time" on Sundays. You have to watch it if you do offer practices on Sundays. This can be a sensitive issue being a religious day for many people so you have to emphasize the practice is totally optional. Usually during these practices I just do batting practice. I set it up like this. If I have two assistant coaches, we will alternate each week, always getting at least one parent to assist. Say the opportunity time is set up from 11:15-12 each Sunday. I will run it the first week with one parent. One assistant coach will run it the next with a parent and the other coach the following week with his volunteer parent. This works great so each coach only has to be there every three Sundays.

The actual Opportunity Time is set up with a very loose structure. I run it at our batting cage. One coach or parent will pitch while the other coach will supervise hitting activities on the outside of the cage. Hitting skills, such as hitting off the batting tee, doing the soft toss, or bunting pickle balls.

Even though Sunday is tough day to do this, you will have players come if you run it the way I describe. I tell the parents that coaches are there from 11:15 to noon. The players can come down anytime between that time and do any and all drills available. They can take their swings in the cage then leave as soon as they are done. They can go through each station more than once and stay there till the end. This sounds like it is set up just for batting practice, which it is, but you'll find that eventually more parents will want to volunteer. This Opportunity Time as it turns out is also an Opportunity Time for parents who could never give a commitment to coach full time for their kids. This works very well for both players and parents, but again, you must state that any practice scheduled for Sundays is always optional.

*The e-book version is interactive in this section with live links and makes a great supplement to this book.

Practice #1

Warm-up

Third Base Drill

Line Throw Drill

Bounce & Run Drill

Bunt Man On 3rd

Know The Fence

Rapid Throw Drill

Batting Practice

Practice #2

Warm-up

Third Base Drill

Two Team Relay Drill

1st & 3rd Defensive Situation

1st & 3rd Offensive Situation

Circle Drill

Game Situations

Batting Practice

Practice #3

Warm-up

Cross Infield Drill

Line Throw Drill

Overthrow At First

Tagging Up From 3rd

Baserunning Sign Drill

Two Team Relay

Batting Practice

Practice #4

Mini Batting Practice

Warm-up

Ground Ball To Right Side

Infield Relay Race

Run Down Drill

Basketball Throw

Tennis Racquet Home Run Derby

Batting Practice

Quick Tip

When speaking to your players and a bright sun is out, make sure you face the sun and do not have the players look into it. This will help give you the best chance they are paying attention to what you are saying.

Commentary

As part of practice #2 and practice #4, set up game situations with baserunners and then tell the fielding team how many outs there are and hit the ball somewhere in the field. You then must go over what was the right way and the correct person to throw the ball to. Be sure to move

295

players around to different positions. You can also throw the baseball instead of hitting it with a bat.

In practice #2, it is good to transition on 1st & 3rd situations from defense to offense, or vice versa. The players are already in the proper fielding location. Make sure on the defensive side, you use all your catchers. After only a few practices, you can designate captains and they can actually help set up the baseballs like in the Line Throw Drill. Utilize your assistant coaches to take pitchers aside to throw 15-25 pitches at about 75%. Accuracy, not speed, is important.

Practice #5

Warm-up

Game Situations

Third Base Drill

Line Throw Drill

Reaction Drill

Bounce & Run Drill

Wild Pitch Drill

Batting Practice

Practice #6

Warm-up

Cross Infield Drill

Line Throw Drill

Bounce & Run Drill

Bunt Man On 3rd

Outfielder Ball Cutoff

Last Chance Throw

Batting Practice

Practice #7

Warm-up

Third Base Drill

Line Throw Drill

Hit The Cutoff

Miss The Cutoff

Bunting For Peanuts

Rapid Throw Drill

Continuation Drill

Batting Practice

Practice #8

Warm-up

Third Base

Three Man Relay

Bounce & Run Drill

Bunt Man On 3rd

Game Situations

Home Run Derby

Batting Practice

Quick Tip

Players fall in love with their own bats or one of the team bats and do not want to use any others. At one batting practice, make players hit with any bat except the one they usually use. This teaches flexibility, and in case their favorite bat is lost or missing, they already used another.

Commentary

As you move into the second week of the season, put in game situations in just about every other practice. Recreate the actual game situations from the games your team played that happened and the mistakes made. Then go over the correct way. In Practice #6, we are following the Outfield Ball Cut Off with the Last Chance Throw because it is a natural fit as both drills take place in the outfield. In Practice #7, we do the Continuation Drill and transition right into batting practice. If you find that the kids are really into one drill, then extend it, as long as they are getting something out of it. You'll notice how often I use the Third Base Drill. The long throw from third combined with a good amount of repetitions reinforces muscle memory. Emphasize, especially early in the season, that it is more important that the throw from third is on target and does not have to reach on a fly. This helps the younger or weaker players. It will also help the players at first get used to balls in the dirt.

Practice #9

Warm-up

Cross Infield Drill

Long Toss Drill

Game Situations

Turn Drill

Ball In Sun or Lights

Line Master Drill

Batting Practice

Practice #10

Warm-up

Cross Infield Drill

Line Throw Drill

Bounce & Run Drill

Bunt Man On 3rd

Outfielder Ball Cutoff

Last Chance Throw

Two Man Relay Drill

Batting Practice

Practice #11

Warm-up

Third Base Drill

Line Throw Drill

Game Situations

Rapid Throw Drill

Target Bunting

Continuation Drill

Batting Practice

Practice #12

Warm-up

Third Base Drill

Reaction Drill

Bounce & Run Drill

Bunt Man On 3rd

Game Situations

Batting Practice

Quick Tip

If a player on your team made a spectacular play during a game, give him a chance to describe to the team the play, and if there were any thoughts going through his head at the time. Sometimes an 11 or 12 year-old can inspire his teammates with his own words.

Commentary

As you move into the third week of the season, keep introducing new drills. In practice #9, it may be a good idea to have a night practice to teach catching the ball in lights. In practice #10, I almost always follow the Bounce & Run Drills with the Bunt Man On Third Drill because they are similar in nature, and the transition from one drill to the next is easy. In practice #11, during the Bunting For Peanuts, try to run it so by the end of the drill all the participants will end up with a bag. Utilize your assistant coaches to take pitchers aside to throw 20-30 pitches at about 75%. Accuracy not speed is important.

Practice #13

Warm-up

Continuation Drill

King Arthur

6 vs 6 Scrimmage

Hole In The Infield

Batting Practice

Practice #14

Warm-up

Cross Infield Drill

Game Situations

Color Code Ground Balls

Two Fly Ball Drill

Run down Drill

Two Man Relay Drill

Batting Practice

Practice #15

Warm-up

Long Toss Drill

Line Throw Drill

Stay Low Drill

In Front Of The Line

Tagging Up From 3rd

Wild Pitch Drill

Batting Practice

Practice #16

Warm-up

Third Base Drill

Three Man Relay Dril

Bounce & Run Drill

Bunt Man On 3rd

Game Situations

Batting Practice

Quick Tip

As a coach, when running a prepared practice with drills, maintain flexibility. If one drill works really well, keep it going. If one drill doesn't work, skip it. And most important, if a game-like mistake occurs in a drill, use this as a teaching point by correcting it in front of the whole team.

Commentary

As you move into the fourth week of the season, you should have been introducing new drills. Players can get a little stale. In practice #13, it is basically a hitting practice. Kids will love this practice. When you run the 6 vs 6 scrimmage, make it a "one pitch" game. Players have to hit the first pitch thrown no matter where it is. In practice #14, in the Color Code Ground Ball Drill, set up at least two stations for this drill with assistant coaches. The balls should be prepared the day before with colored tape. In practice #15, it is a good transition going from Tagging Up From 3rd to the Wild Pitch Drill as the focus for both revolves around 3rd and home.

Practice #17

Warm-up

Third Base Drill

Carousel Drill

1st & 3rd Defensive Situation

1st & 3rd Offensive Situation

Rapid Throw Drill

Ball Hit To Right Side

Batting Practice

Practice #18

Warm-up

Cross Infield Drill

Line Throw Drill

Outfield Communication

Tagging Up From 3rd

Baserunning Sign Drill

Two Team Relay

Batting Practice

Practice #19

Warm-up

Long Toss Drill

Line Throw Drill

Game Situations

Outfield Ball Cut Off

Rob The Homer

Batting Practice

Practice #20

Warm-up)

Third Base Drill

Three Man Relay Drill

Bounce & Run Drill

Bunt Man On 3rd

Game Situations

Batting Practice

Quick Tip

When going over game situations by reviewing the previous game(s), always ask the players if there was anything that happened in the game that they did not understand. There may be a very basic play that confused a player that the coach did not pick up.

Commentary

As you move into the fifth week of the season, your new players should begin to become familiar with most of the drills that are being repeated. In practice #17, make sure you rotate new players into the 1st & 3rd offensive and defensive situations. In practice #18, with the Line

Throw Drill, it is a great opportunity to have a player organize the drill. Tell him not to touch any baseballs, but to supervise teammates to set up the baseballs and set up the lines. In practice #19, a good transition is going from the Outfield Ball Cut Off to Rob The Homer, figuring you'll be in the outfield for both. In practice #20, when you run batting practice, on the first at bat to each player after their bunts, start each player at a two ball two strike count. The coach pitching is also the umpire calling the next pitch.

Practice #21

Warm-up

Third Base Drill

Long Toss Drill

Rapid Throw Drill

Ball Hit To Right Side

Batting Practice

Baseball Football

Practice #22

Warm-up

Line Throw Drill

Lead Drill

Baserunning Sign Drill

Two Team Relay

Tennis Racquet HR Derby

Batting Practice

Practice #23

Warm-up

Cross Infield Drill

Line Throw Drill

Game Situations

Reaction Drill

Baserunning Sign Drill

Batting Practice

Practice #24

Warm-up

Third Base Drill

Three Man Relay Drill

Bounce & Run Drill

Bunt Man On 3rd

Baseball Relay Race

Batting Practice

Quick Tip

In batting practice, give everyone a chance to bat opposite once for an at bat or two. There will be players that want to switch hit. Giving the whole team this opportunity is a chance at something new.

Commentary

During the sixth week of the season, in practice #21, I am introducing the game Baseball-Football. This will be one of the most popular games for your team. Almost guaranteed! It is fine to use this as a reward at other practices during the season. In practice #22 and #23, when doing the Baserunning Sign Drill, have an assistant coach give the signs from the 3rd base coaching box. This is giving players the chance to see another coach. If he ends up doing it during the game, at least the players have seen it once. Utilize your assistant coaches to take pitchers aside to throw 20-30 pitches at about 80%. Accuracy, not speed, is important.

Practice #25

Warm-up

Third Base Drill

Game Situations

Two Fly Ball Drill

Bounce & Run Drill

Bunt Man On 3rd

Circle Drill

Ball Hit To Right Side

Batting Practice

Practice #26

Warm-up

Cross Infield Drill

Double Line Throw Drill

Long Toss Drill

Tagging Up From 3rd

Baserunning Sign Drill

Three Man Relay

Shadow Drill

Batting Practice

Practice #27

Warm-up

Long Toss Drill

Line Throw Drill

Game Situations

Around The Horn

1st & 3rd Defensive Play

Batting Practice

Practice #28

Warm-up

Third Base Drill

Three Man Relay Drill

Bounce & Run Drill

Bunt Man On 3rd

Game Situations

Batting Practice

Quick Tip

Take suggestions from your players about drills. I have received some excellent ideas for new drills as well as for revising one of my own from 10, 11 and 12 year-olds. Remember, they are at an age where their imagination knows no bounds. You will have players who are creative in devising new drills.

Commentary

As you move into the seventh week of the season, you can increase or decrease the time spent on each drill. By now, you can gauge the number of drills that are comfortable for your team. My experience has been in the middle of the season anywhere from 6-9 drills per practice is sufficient and can be done in the recommended 60-75 minutes. Notice in practices #25 and #26 I am squeezing in 9 drills. Remember that different teams will respond positively and negatively to certain drills. This can vary from one year to the next where one drill will be very popular with a team and the next year with the same drill the team might not like it. I mentioned with the Baserunning Sign Drill to have an assistant coach give the signs. After numerous practices, try to have a player give the signs.

Practice #29

Warm-up

Continuation Drill

6 vs 6 Scrimmage

Tennis Racquet HR Derby

Batting Practice

Practice #30

Mini Batting Practice

Warm-up

Ground Ball To Right Side

Rapid Throw Drill

Run Down Drill

Two Team Relay Drill

Batting Practice

Practice #31

Warm-up

Cross Infield Drill

Long Toss Drill

Game Situations

1st and 3rd Throw & Catch

Goalie Drill

Line Master Drill

Batting Practice

Practice #32

Warm-up

Third Base Drill

Two Team Relay Drill

1st & 3rd Defensive Situation

1st & 3rd Offensive Situation

Circle Drill

Batting Practice

Quick Tip

Feel confident always challenging your players. If your team is comprised of 10, 11, and 12 year-olds, try treating them like 13 and 14 year-olds. Most will respond, and one of the rewards is that your team will "play up" in age and can have more success on the field.

Commentary

As you go into the eighth week of practice you can begin to challenge the players more. For instance, when they are bunting for extra swings in batting practice, have the two cones closer together and give them two extra swings for each bunt that goes through the cones. You will be amazed by how players will focus for extra swings at the smaller target. In practice #28 you'll notice that this is again an almost exclusive hitting batting practice and one of the few practices where I have only 5 drills or activities. You can extend any of the hitting drills. In practice #30, we are starting with the mini batting practice, just to keep the players always guessing and motivating them to arrive on time. In practice #31, in the Goalie Drill, you can adjust the cones further apart to again challenge the players.

Practice #33

Warm-up

Third Base Drill

Line Throw Drill

Bounce & Run Drill

Bunt Man On 3rd

Shuttle Drill

Wild Throw Drill

Batting Practice

Practice #34

Warm-up

Double Line Throw Drill

Ground Ball To Right Side

Circle Drill

Run Down Drill

Two Team Relay Drill

Batting Practice

Practice #35

Warm-up

Cross Infield Drill

Long Toss Drill

First stop . . . the SOUTH.

Welcome to
the SOUTH!

Game Situations

Face Off Drill

Communication Drill

Batting Practice

Practice #36

Warm-up

Third Base Drill

Two Team Relay Drill

Bounce & Run Drill

Bunt Man On 3rd

Circle Drill

Continuation Drill

Batting Practice

Quick Tip

When practicing, if you see a couple of parents in their cars reading or on their cell phone, ask them to come out and help for a drill or two. It doesn't matter if they are a mom, dad, grandma or grandpa. Include them in a safe environment. Sometimes this becomes an unexpected thrill for the players that will end up being a strong positive memory.

Commentary

As you go into the ninth week of practice, there are still some drills that I haven't introduced yet. It is always a good idea to keep some drills for the second part of the season just to keep the practices new and fresh. In practice #33 we are introducing the Shuttle Drill for the first time. In practice #35 we are doing the same thing with the Face Off Drill. Also with batting practice, you can change things up a bit by pitching closer to home from the base of the mound as long as your league has an "L" screen. I call this type "Short Pitch" batting practice. The ball is coming in faster and the players' reactions have to be quicker also.

Practice #37

Warm-up

Game Situations

Third Base Drill

Bounce & Run Drill

Bunt Man On 3rd

Rapid Throw Drill

Continuation Drill

Batting Practice

Practice #38

Warm-up

Third Base Drill

Three Man Relay Drill

Bounce & Run Drill

Bunt Man On 3rd

Batting Practice

Baseball-Football

Practice #39

Warm-up

Cross Infield Drill

Line Throw Drill

Game Situations

Lead Drill

Bunt Man On 3rd

Rapid Throw Drill

Batting Practice

Practice #40

Warm-up

Third Base Drill

Reaction Drill

Bounce & Run Drill

Bunt Man On 3rd

Game Situations

Batting Practice

Quick Tip

As the season progresses it is a good idea to have practice no longer than 75 minutes. Your team will probably be playing 2-3 games per week, so when it comes to practice time, "less is more."

Commentary

As you go into the tenth week of practice, don't be afraid to put a little extra into hitting ground balls to your team. The players by now have fielded no less than a few hundred ground balls at practices alone. Also, their throws from third base should reach on a fly by this time in the season. Notice in all the practices I am going heavy on baserunning. As we go toward the playoffs, baserunning becomes an almost hidden advantage if practiced consistently. In Practice #38 we do the Baseball-Football game for the second time. I try to have my teams work a bit harder at this point in the season, but reward them with the games they ask for.

Practice #41

Warm-up

Third Base Drill

Line Throw Drill

Bounce & Run Drill

Bunt Man On 3rd

Rapid Throw Drill

1st & 3rd Defensive Situation

1st & 3rd Offensive Situation

Batting Practice

Practice #42

Warm-up

Third Base Drill

Line Throw Drill

1st & 3rd Defensive Situation

1st & 3rd Offensive Situation

Tennis Racquet HR Derby

Bounce & Run Drill

Bunt Man On 3rd

Batting Practice

Practice #43

Warm-up

Continuation Drill

6 vs 6 Scrimmage

Directional Hitting

Batting Practice

Baseball-Football

Practice #44

Warm-up

Third Base Drill

Game Situations

Long Toss Drill

Three Man Relay Drill

Bounce & Run Drill

Bunt Man On 3rd

Batting Practice

Quick Tip

With baserunning, always have one sign where the baserunner just takes off as soon as the signal is flashed. The defensive team can get caught sleeping as long as the runners pay attention to the coach. This has worked for me a lot right after a player walks and the defense is not ready, as they are getting set for the next batter. Also, coaches can call for a steal on a controversial play when the opposing manager comes out of his dugout in a hurry to argue a call and forgets to call time.

Commentary

As I move into the eleventh week of the season, I begin to think playoffs. I have in my mind who I want at certain positions and try to pay special attention during drills who is making the correct strong accurate throws to the right place. During games I also like to begin them with my best fielding team. I like having a strong defensive team up the middle at catcher, pitcher, shortstop, second base and centerfield. If we are playing a good bunting team, I may adjust putting my best infielder at third. Notice on practice # 41 and #42 they are almost exactly the same. I am picking up the intensity, but always have a fun drill between a couple of skill or strategy drills. In practice #43, I followed up two intense practices with a fun one comprised mostly of hitting drills. In practice #44 and all the practices for the rest of the season, when you go over game situations, make sure you reinforce one or two that happened earlier in the season.

Practice #45

Warm-up

Third Base Drill

Game Situations

Double Line Throw Drill

Bounce & Run Drill

Bunt Man On 3rd

3 Man Relay Drill

Continuation Drill

Batting Practice

Practice #46

Warm-up

Third Base Drill

Cross Infield Drill

Game Situations

1st & 3rd Defensive Situation

1st & 3rd Offensive Situation

Tennis Racquet HR Derby

Baserunning Sign Drill

Batting Practice

Practice #47

Warm-up

3rd Base Drill

No Glove Drill

Boom Bat HR Derby

Lead Drill

Run Down Drill

Continuation Drill

Batting Practice

Practice #48

Warm-up

Third Base Drill

Continuation Drill

Batting Practice

Coaches should think outside the box. I love to bunt when a player has two strikes. After he squared to bunt twice and missed, the opposing coach usually tells the 3rd baseman to back up because the batter won't bunt. This is a green light for me to have the batter attempt to bunt again. Of course it depends on who is at bat and the game situation, but many times the best coaching book you have is your gut.

Commentary

In week twelve of the season, whether you are practicing only one day a week or more, you must be even more efficient running the practices from the minute it starts until the last pitch of batting practice. Practices #45 and #46 have nine drills. This may run somewhere from 75-90 minutes. If you try to run these two practices in an hour, you may have to cut down the number of drills. In practice #47, notice I put in the No Glove Drill. This is a basic fundamental drill that on the surface sounds like it is a drill for the beginning of the season. This is true, but I always love to go back to the very basics and review fundamental techniques toward the end of the season. Practice #48 may look kind of bare, but it is basically a batting practice-only session. These work great. I like to leave them toward the end of the season and do them at the end of the week.

Practice #49 (at batting cage)

Warm-up

Use of two cages

Soft Toss

Soft Toss Bunting

Hit off the batting tee

Practice #50

Warm-up

Third Base Drill

Game Situations

Two Fly Ball Drill

Bounce & Run Drill

Bunt Man On 3rd

Circle Drill

Ball Hit To Right Side

Batting Practice

Practice #51

Warm-up

Third Base Drill

Line Throw Drill

Game Situations

Bounce & Run Drill

Bunt Man On 3rd

Tennis Racquet HR Derby

Batting Practice

Practice #52

Warm-up

Third Base Drill

6 vs.6 Scrimmage

Continuation Drill

Batting Practice

Quick Tip

When a player is in a slump, instead of dropping him down in the order, try putting him up first for one or two games. He may get an extra at bat or two. This may raise his confidence level. Bunting to get out of a batting slump can also work.

Commentary

In week thirteen of the season, in practice #49, it may seem a bit odd to call an indoor batting practice when the weather is probably at its best outdoors. I will do this some years as a change of pace if I find we are practicing a lot. If I had only one practice during the week, I would probably not have the indoor practice. In practice #50 and #51, I practice heavy with game situations and baserunning. By this time of the season, if you have played 16-18 games and your players have watched others, there are plenty of things you can go over that happened during games. In practice #52, I am again keeping it mainly for hitting. I pick up the pace on the 6 vs 6 scrimmage, throwing the ball harder to batters and changing speeds. I keep it a game of "one pitch."

Practice #53

Warm-up

Third Base Drill

Game Situations

Two Team Relay Drill

Rapid Throw Drill

Wild Throw Drill

Circle Drill

Infield Relay Drill

Batting Practice

Practice #54

Warm-up

Third Base Drill

Game Situations

3 Man Relay Drill

Bounce & Run Drill

Bunt Man On 3rd

Circle Drill

Baserunning Sign Drill

Batting Practice

Practice #55

Warm-up

Third Base Drill

Game Situations

1st & 3rd Defensive Situation

1st & 3rd Offensive Situation

Rapid Throw Drill

Overthrow Drill

Wild Pitch Drill

Batting Practice

Practice #56

Warm-up

Third Base Drill

6 vs.6 Scrimmage

Continuation Drill

Batting Practice

Quick Tip

Many parents work one or even two jobs and their time is limited. I have often gone into the stands and asked one parent to keep track of the pitch count for both teams. They are happy to do it. Make sure you let their son know that his parent helped out during the game.

Commentary

In practice #53 of week fourteen of the season, I do something a little different. Usually I follow a skill or teaching drill with a fun drill. Here, after the game situations, I am doing two fun drills in a row. I repeat this again. Toward the end of the season give the kids some extra fun with some practices. In practice #54, I go heavy on the baserunning drills again. In practice #55 I am focusing a lot on defense and fielding. In practice #56, I again am doing mainly batting as we end the week. If you can only practice one day, practice #54 is the most well rounded practice.

Practice #57

Warm-up

Game Situations

Tennis Racuet HR Derby

Football-Baseball

Batting practice

Practice #58 (Players' choice)

Warm-up

Game Situations

Home Run Derby

Football-Baseball

Batting practice

Practice #59 (Players' choice)

Warm-up

Game Situations

Two Team Relay

Football-Baseball

Home Run Derby

Batting practice

Practice #60 (Players' choice)

Warm-up

Game Situations

Tennis Racuet HR Derby

Rob The Home

Football-Baseball

Batting practice

Toward the very end of the season the long term goal is to have the players come back to play baseball next season. I like to give players a chance to make practice decisions. Pick any and all ideas that will help keep players coming back to play.

Commentary

In week fifteen, or whatever is the last week of your team's practices, do it a little different. Unless there is a huge difference in how the results will affect the playoffs, I will usually have two twelve year-olds decide what to do during practice. If you have a lot of twelve year-olds, I will pick the two or three that have been on the team the longest to be assisted by the other twelve year-olds. They will pick the drills. The only caveat I tell them is we have to have a warm-up. I also must have 10 minutes to go over game situations. Then it is their practice. Tell me what they want to do and I will help organize the practice accordingly. Inevitably, I have listed the most popular drills and games that the players will choose.

Practice Section Addendum

I know it will be impossible for most recreational teams to run 60 practices in a season. Four in a week is almost impossible in addition to playing games. I wanted to give coaches the options from these 60 practices to choose from. I have had seasons where, for whatever reason, be it a very rainy spring or my own scheduling, I was only able to run one practice a week. This is my ultimate goal; get every youth baseball coach to run at least one practice each week during the season. I promise this will help make your players better skilled as individuals and as a team. As I mentioned before, this is where the real teaching and coaching happens, not during a game explaining things from the third base coaching box.

If you do only practice one day a week, get away from the typical two hour batting practice I've been preaching against throughout the book. The one thing I can tell you if you do run these boring two hour practices comprised with no more than two activities is that you will find people that will love these practices. The people who will love the boring practice that turn young players off from baseball are the lacrosse and soccer coaches because they know the more bored the players are practicing baseball, the better chance they have to get many of these athletes in their sport. We all have to get away from this trap of typical practices. Baseball does not need to be labeled as slow and boring. The players that play for you will get as much out of the season as what you put into it.

I did not cover a lot on parking lot practices. Don't overlook the practicality of these practices. Like everything else you do, planning and preparation is the key and will make the actual practices easy.

How do you really organize yourself so you know what you have planned coming up next? If you are not experienced, you will be wondering what is the next drill? In this digital world where everyone is becoming dependent on these wonderful hand held devices, I still love the old fashioned index card. I will plan my practice and write down the ones I plan to do. I will also write down what to cover in game situations referring to something that happened in our last game. When you go over these game situations, make sure you include other games that people might have seen in your league as well as your local professional team or teams. One thing about baseball, like the game of chess, no two games are exactly alike. No matter how long you follow baseball, whether on the amateur level and up, something new always comes up.

I want to again emphasize how important safety is when you have 12 kids who almost all have bats that they love swinging and hard balls being hit or thrown all over the field during practices. The importance of the assistants cannot be overlooked. If your are short on help and see one or two parents sitting in their car on their cell phone, very politely go over and ask them if they can help you out. Having one or two other sets of eyes on the field can help prevent injuries. Utilize the soft covered hard balls in practice. Many coaches look down on this practice, but for ground ball fielding drills, these balls are just as good as the real baseballs.

Just as my main goal every season is to have the players come back to play baseball the following year, my goal in practices is to have them wanting more, and thus hopefully they cannot wait to come to the next practice. This is why it is important to end each and every practice on a high note. Batting practice will accomplish this, as well as some of the other games mentioned. Remember, kids love competition. We live in a competitive society. It always amazed me that even at the tee ball level kids want to win. Setting up competitive games in baseball practices is a good thing as long as coaches try to keep the sides fair. If you can recognize one or two kids are rarely on the winning side, try to put them in the position that they will be on the winning team.

Running my type of practices does take a certain energy level. We have a responsibility as youth coaches to show that we are active also. Being participants in some of the drills is really good providing you are in good enough shape with your doctor's okay. The concentration span of kids 7-12 are really putting us in a position as coaches to come up with numerous activities during practices. One of the most satisfying things is to see your team succeed in certain game situations during a game that you have practiced all season.

Chapter 15
Conclusion

"I see great things in baseball. It's our game-the American game."

Walt Whitman

Conclusion

The material in this book will hopefully help youth coaches at all levels of play, whether it is recreational or the most competitive travel teams. Coaches and parents can build upon or subtract whatever they want as far as the content. Approach the season with your own goals. If you want to focus on exact technique, then do so. If you want to be an expert on hitting or pitching, read as much as you can and attend as many baseball clinics as you can. If practices are your thing, like they are mine, then get yourself totally immersed learning all the drills you can. Many of you reading this book will coach just to do so with your own son or daughter, which is fine. Even if you only coach one or two years, you still leave an impression on the other kids, whether it is positive or negative. Encourage your players to attend live games. It doesn't have to be a major league professional game. You don't have to spend a lot of money. You can seek out a good high school or Division 1, 2, or 3 college team. A number of years back I found out about a Division 3 coach who was a stickler for baserunning. This is my type of coach. I made the effort to attend a couple of games, and it was an outstanding experience. Remember, when you attend live games, it is not like watching them on the television where you are at the mercy of the camera. You can point out to your kids different fielding and baserunning tendencies you would never see on a 42" flat screen TV.

The youth baseball season will vary depending upon what part of the world you are living in. In some parts of the country the season will run almost year round with games being played 12 months a year. Even in areas with a change of weather, the baseball season is running longer and longer. We tend to sometimes concentrate on one particular sport with our kids. We've all heard the theories in youth sports about how parents will relive their childhood through their children. Many people will frown on this, with good reason. But as long as we are not overly obsessed with one particular sport and give our kids some variety, I think it is a really good thing. Today's parents sometimes work more than one job, and in some broken homes, it is incredibly tough for a single parent to be involved. It is a great idea for youth coaches and leagues to give each parent a chance to volunteer. Parents need to take advantage of this. Make no mistake, when your kids see you involved, if only for one game, it leaves a huge impression on them.

For a local youth recreation league or Little League, I mentioned the benefits of parity and a level playing field for the league. I maintain this will produce better baseball players. Local leagues should strive for this. A number of years ago the National Football League made a concerted effort to bring parity to their league. The success of this league has been enormous, both for the league financially and the fans. Each and every year there is a team that goes from last place, or close to it, to the playoffs with a chance at the Superbowl. This gives hope to fans each season.

In youth baseball, having closer games with less teams with a chance of going 0-20 during the season will benefit individuals and team play. Youth coaches should not be afraid of putting their players under a little duress or pressure. As hard as it is, parents should not be afraid of seeing their kids handle this pressure. Coaches can condition players with some pressure during practice with some of the drills and techniques I described. I would hope that leagues would not just encourage, but make it a requirement for coaches to practice at least once a week. Not all parents/coaches have the time or the passion like I do, but if teams were able to go over their past game situations, players would learn a lot from this.

As far as myself, baseball has always been a game I was never very good at as a youngster. I thought my own coaches could have been better, but in truth, I was not the most motivated kid in the world. I try to give the kids I coach what I didn't have on the baseball field growing up; confidence and a chance to succeed. Each and every year there is a certain degree of politics that go on in leagues, which happen all over the country. Without being taken for a sucker, I have a made a concerted effort to stay away from this stuff and coach the best way I know. I still find it a thrill being outdoors in the spring after a long cold winter and being part of a kid's game. And when I run into one of my players years later, or they reach out to contact me from another part of the country asking about a few drills they did when playing and want a refresher as they are entering their first year coaching, nothing can be more satisfying. I hope to continue coaching as long as I can or until my league has had enough of me. I need to strive to become a better coach, whether it is going to more baseball clinics to learn more about pitching or traveling three hours each way to observe my good friend Bobby Woods give a few hitting lessons, we all cannot stay still. There is still a ton of things we all need to do with baseball, trying to make the game more interesting for kids to get involved in and stay involved in.

I have used many of my favorite baseball quotes on the chapter pages. In closing I can't help but think of one of my all time favorites quotes. It was from Jim Bouton, who wrote one of my all time favorite baseball books, Ball Four. It surely sums up how I feel about baseball:

"You spend a good piece of your life gripping a baseball and in the

end it turns out that it was the other way around all the time."

Marty Schupak's Coaching Resources

Baseball Videos

T-Ball Skills & Drills
The 59 Minute Baseball Practice
Backyard Baseball Drills
Pitching Drills & Techniques
Hitting Drills & Techniques
Baserunning & Bunting Drills
Drills & Techniques For The Catcher
Fielding Drills & Techniques
Infield Team Play & Strategies
44 Baseball Mistakes & Corrections
Advanced Toss & Batting Tee Drills

Baseball Books

Baseball Coaching: A Guide For The Youth
Coach & Parent ebook
Baseball Chronicles 1: Articles On Youth
Baseball
Baseball Chronicles 2: Articles On Youth
Baseball
Youth Baseball Drills
44 Baseball Mistakes & Corrections
T-Ball Skills & Drills

Other Sports Products By Marty Schupak

VIDEOS

48 Championship Basketball Drills
Driveway Basketball Drills
Offensive Basketball Moves
Basketball Fundamentals
Championship Soccer Drills
Backyard Soccer Drills
34 Soccer Goalie Drills
Soccer Shooting Drills
Soccer Fast Footwork Drills
Advanced Soccer Drills
Backyard Golf
Championship Hockey Drills
Backyard Lacrosse

BOOKS

Basketball Chronicles: Articles on Youth
Coaching
Soccer Chronicles: Articles on Youth Coaching
Sports Chronicles (Baseball, Basketball, &
Soccer): Articles on Youth Coaching

CLIFF VERMONT SERIES (Young Adult)

Playoff Fever & Split Pants
Shoot the Pill & Smashed Puzzle

I have tried to make all of my products available for free. All of my videos are free on Amazon Prime. Your library should, and will, carry the DVD format of every one of my videos. You have to ask them. If your library has "Hoopla" my videos are there. All my videos are also available as Apps at the Apple App store, Keyword: Schupak Sports. If your league or recreation department wants a T-Ball clinic, contact us at: www.tballamerica.com.

Baseball & Softball League Resources

T-Ball America
9 Florence Court
Valley Cottage, NY 10989
Phone: 845-536-4278
www.tballamerica.com

American Amateur Baseball Congress (AABC)
AABC National Headquarters
100 West Broadway, Farmington, NM 87401
Phone: 505-327-3120
Fax: 505-327-3132
Email: aabc@aabc.us
www.aabc.us

Babe Ruth Baseball
PO Box 5000, Trenton, NJ 08638
Phone: 609-695-1434
Fax: 609-695-2505
http://www.baberuthleague.org/

Continental Amateur Baseball Association (CABA)
82 University St, Westerville, OH 43081
Phone: 740-382-4620, 740-382-4620
www.cababaseball.com

Dixie Youth Baseball (DYB)
PO Box 1778, Marshall, TX 75671
Phone: 903-927-1845
Fax: 903-927-1846
Email: boys@dixie.org
www.dixie.org

Dizzy Dean Baseball, Inc.
2470 Hwy 51 S, Hernando MS 38632
Phone: 662-429-4365, 662-429-7790
Email: dizzydeanbaseball@yahoo.com
http://dizzydeanbbinc.org/

Hap Dumont Youth Baseball (National Baseball Congress)
PO Box 17455, Wichita, KS 67217
Phone: 316-721-1779, 316-838-1467
Fax 316-721-8054
Email: hapdumontbball@yahoo.com
www.hapdumontbaseball.com

Little League® International
539 U.S. 15
Williamsport, PA 17702
(570) 326-1921
www.littleleague.org/

National Amateur Baseball Federation (NABF)
PO Box 705, Bowie MD 20715
Phone: 301-464-5460, 301-352-0214,
Fax 301-352-0214
Email: nabf1914@aol.com
www.nabf.com

National Association of Police Athletic Leagues (NPAL)
658 West Indiantown Road, #201, Jupiter, FL 33458
Phone: 561-745-5535
Fax 561-745-3147
Email: copnkid1@aol.com
www.nationalpal.org

PONY Baseball, Inc.PONY Baseball, Inc.
PO Box 225, Washington, PA 15301
Phone: 724-225-1060
Fax: 724-225-9852
Email: pony@pulsenet.com
www.pony.org

USA Baseball
403 Blackwell St. Durham, NC 27701
Phone: 919-474-8721
Fax: 919-474-8822
Email: usabasebal@aol.com
www.usabaseball.com

Footnotes

1 Robert Pangrazi, Dynamic Physical Education For Elementary School Children (2004 Pearson Education).

2 Robert Guth "Red Flag on Kids, Sports and Injuries" On Line Wall Street Journal, April 1, 2010

Bibliography

There are an endless number of baseball resources. I have found the ones below the most useful.

Books

Baseball for Brain Surgeons and Other Fans By Tim McCarver, Villard Books 1998

Baseball Forgotten Basics, By Marc Shoenfelt, DEStech Publications, 2006

Dynamic Physical Education For Elemnetary School Children by Robert P. Pangrazi, Pearson Education, 2004

Lau's Laws on Hitting By Charlie Lau Jr., Jeffrey Flanigan, Taylor Trade Publishing, 2000

Men At Work By George Will, Macmillan, 1990

You Can Teach Hitting By Dusty Baker, Jeff Mercer, Marv Bittinger, Bittinger Books, 1993

Youth Baseball Coaching by John T. Reed, Pulished by John T. Reed, 2000

Youth Baseball Drills by Marty Schupak, Published By Human Kinetics Publishers, 2005

Videos & Software

Mom, Can You Teach Me How To Hit? Bobby Woods, Bobby Productions, 2003

Where's The play CD-Rom ® , John Fishback, P & P Studios, 2006

Videos & Software

About The Author

Marty Schupak has been coaching baseball for 25 years. He has coached over 1,400 kids in youth athletics in a variety of sports in addition to baseball. Many of his former players have gone on to play in high school and beyond. Many have received athletic college scholarships. In addition to coaching baseball, Schupak has coached children in basketball and soccer. He has served on many leagues' boards of directors and is a member of the American Baseball Coaches Association.

Thousands of youth baseball coaches have been trained at his clinic, How To Run A Youth Baseball Practice. He is the founder and president of Schupak Sports and The Youth Sports Club, a group dedicated to improving coaching and youth baseball practices. His Web site, www.SchupakSports.com, is one of the most popular resources for youth coaches and parents. He is also the founder and President of T-Ball America (www.TBallAmerica.com).

Schupak has written numerous articles on youth sports and developed the best-selling baseball video, The 59 Minute Baseball Practice, Backyard Baseball Drills, Winning Baseball Strategies, Hitting Drills & Techniques, and six others. He also authored the popular book Youth Baseball Drills. He received a bachelor's degree from Boston University in 1975 and a master's degree in physical education from Arizona State University in 1978. Schupak lives in Valley Cottage, New York.

Made in the USA
San Bernardino, CA
16 May 2018